GOD
IS STILL
SPEAKING

GOD IS STILL
SPEAKING

365 Daily Devotionals

THE STILLSPEAKING WRITERS' GROUP
Christina Villa,
Editor

THE PILGRIM PRESS
CLEVELAND

The Pilgrim Press, 700 Prospect Avenue, Cleveland, Ohio 44115
thepilgrimpress.com
© 2013 The Pilgrim Press

Scripture quotations, unless otherwise noted, are from the New Revised
Standard Version of the Bible, © 1989 by the Division of Christian Education
of the National Council of Churches of Christ in the United States of America
and are used by permission. Changes have been made for inclusivity.

Printed in the United States of America on acid free paper

17   16   15   14   13   5   4   3   2   1

ISBN 978-0-8298-1979-3

INTRODUCTION

Have you noticed that some of life's very best things seem to happen unexpectedly, even accidentally, and quite apart from our careful planning? It has been something like that with the Stillspeaking Daily Devotionals.

In 2005, a group of pastors and writers came together and began writing all sorts of things in support of the United Church of Christ's Stillspeaking ministry. "Stillspeaking" is the shorter version of "God is Still Speaking," a campaign by the United Church of Christ to simply remind people that God didn't stop speaking at the end of the Bible and still has a lot more to say.

In 2008, we got the idea of doing daily email devotionals for Lent. We had no idea if it would work. We were more than pleasantly surprised, thrilled really, to find thousands of people signing on and making the devotionals a part of their daily life.

Suddenly, it seemed the devotionals were popping up all over and being mentioned at denominational meetings, congregational events, and in personal contacts. People we writers had never met felt connected with us. The devotionals were being commented on and shared via email, text messages and phone conversations, and have since made their way to a healthy presence on Facebook and Twitter. Given the response, which we never anticipated, we felt led to continue the Stillspeaking Daily Devotionals beyond Lent, and have since made it a daily email devotional that now goes to over 20,000 people in the United States and abroad.

We try to write devotionals that are light-hearted, God-filled and provocative. In that spirit, we thought it would be fun to compile a collection of a year's worth of daily devotionals in book form—and this is it.

God is Still Speaking: 365 Daily Devotionals is a collection of devotionals for the person who thinks they don't like devotionals ("too religious"), for the person who wonders if God is still speaking in the world today, and if so, what difference does it make? For the person who wonders if God has anything to say about what they face each day when they get up in the morning, for the person who isn't interested in a lecture or simple-minded inspiration. These are devotionals for the person who isn't always sure that the Bible has much to tell them, but is curious and willing to find out.

If you are that person, this collection may surprise you and will certainly engage you. Here are short reflections for every day of the year, each one based on a Bible passage, that address a wide array of subjects, including many not usually considered "devotional" material. No matter the subject, they are always heartfelt, frequently humorous, and occasionally provocative.

These devotionals are written to help you see God in your daily life and not just on Sunday morning or in stereotypically spiritual settings. They will show you that there is nothing in human experience that is beyond God's presence or grace. And they will deepen your life while lightening your day as you find ordinary life opening with extraordinary and unexpected grace.

Anthony B. Robinson,
for the Stillspeaking Writers' Group

JANUARY

I Can't Forgive Myself

Martin B. Copenhaver

If you, O L ORD, should mark iniquities, L ORD, who could stand? But there is forgiveness with you, so that you may be revered. Psalm 130:3–4

I OFTEN HEAR PEOPLE say something along these lines: "I am finding it hard to forgive myself." Hard? How about impossible? As someone once put it, we can no more forgive ourselves than we can sit in our own laps. What we *can* do is receive the forgiveness of another. Forgiveness is not an achievement. It is always a gift. And that is part of what brings us to worship each week—to receive the gift of God's forgiveness.

Someone I know left the church early in his adolescence, but difficult circumstances in his life prompted him to go back to worship—just to check it out, mind you. He wasn't about to get carried away. He was will-ing to make a small tentative step, however. He sat in the back pew, so he could observe. But when they came to the prayer of confession and he heard everyone say together, "We have done those things which we ought not to have done and we have left undone those things which we ought to have done," he smiled and said to himself, "Sounds just like my kind of crowd. I came to the right place."

PRAYER: Dear God, forgive me, because, try as I might, I am not able to forgive myself. Help me to receive forgiveness as the gift it is. Amen.

An After-hours Invitation

Kenneth L. Samuel

Hear a just cause, O LORD; attend to my cry; give ear to my prayer from lips free of deceit. . . . If you try my heart, if you visit me by night, if you test me, you will find no wickedness in me. Psalm 17:1, 3

ACCORDING TO EPHESIANS 2:8, we are saved by grace, through faith, so we have nothing to boast of, regarding our own self-righteousness. But an exclusive emphasis on God's grace and mercy can sometimes give license for lack of integrity and moral accountability.

It is said that integrity is who you are when no one is looking at you. Integrity is who we are in the dark. It is our "after-hours" character. It is the values we live out through the night. The mercy and the grace of God should never allow us to renege on our responsibility for personal integrity.

There is something ethically reckless about crying out to God for justice while we compromise our moral values and live our lives in moral duplicity. The psalmist was not morally perfect, but he was also not morally irresponsible. He invites God to test the integrity in his heart by investigating his life after hours to see if his daytime persona was consistent with his nighttime behavior. This is not about being boastful; it is about being consistently faithful.

Public pleas for justice and righteousness are one thing, but how much scrutiny can our personal lives really stand? What inconsistencies in our own character do we continue to pamper and propagate? Aside from the religion that we practice in public, can anyone tell who we really are in private?

Mahatma Gandhi admonished us, "Be the change you want to see in the world." That change begins with our own commitment to practice what we preach—even after hours.

PRAYER: Dear God, please place us on the path toward greater honesty and integrity in our public and in our personal lives. Guide us in truth and sincerity as we commit ourselves to becoming all that we know we should be. Amen.

DISCIPLINE YOURSELVES, OR ELSE

Lillian Daniel

Therefore prepare your minds for action; discipline yourselves; set all your hope on the grace that Jesus Christ will bring you when he is revealed. 1 Peter 1:13

IF HOLINESS IS RELATED TO DISCIPLINE, I may be in trouble. I didn't join the UCC to be told to discipline myself. I associate that kind of talk with churches that I do not want to belong to. But here it is in the Bible. If the early Christians needed to be told this, maybe I do too.

Many of us associate discipline with cruelty at the hands of another; therefore it is not something we want to do to ourselves. Who wants to give themselves a punishment? But this scripture is about self-discipline, not discipline from someone else. We are told that this kind of discipline will "prepare our minds for action."

How many times have you wanted to do something good for God, but, somehow, it never happened? Maybe we need to focus less on the action and more on being a disciple. Our discipline is not the result of a cruel and more powerful person threatening us. We are disciples of Jesus, who offers love as the discipline. What is it that Jesus wants you to focus on?

PRAYER: Gracious God, what action should I prepare my mind for? In what area do I need to discipline myself? Jesus, help me to pay attention, so that I may be holy by doing your work in the world. Amen.

BRICKS WITHOUT STRAW

Anthony B. Robinson

That same day Pharaoh commanded the taskmasters of the people, as well as their supervisors, "You shall no longer give the people straw to make bricks." Exodus 5:6–7a

LATELY, I'VE BEEN RUNNING INTO GAY AND LESBIAN COUPLES who have adopted children with special needs. Often the children they have welcomed into their lives are the kids no one else wants, children with problems associated with the addictions of their birth mothers.

Somehow this strikes me as similar to the Exodus story of the Egyptian taskmasters making the already hard life of their Hebrew slaves harder by telling them to make bricks without straw or to find their own straw, and yet still produce the same quantity of bricks.

Society says to gay and lesbian people, "We're not sure you belong. We doubt you should be married. We're not at all sure you should be parents." And yet I keep bumping into these couples who are doing parenting I can hardly imagine.

One such couple, two gay men, were in court not long ago to finalize an adoption of two children with fetal alcohol syndrome. Someone showed up and objected, saying that they were not fit parents, though they have been successfully fostering the children for several years. The judge, an older man, looked with disbelief at the person who protested and said, "These boys (the gay couple) are heroes."

As a society we've pretty much said to people who are gay and lesbian, "Make bricks without straw." Make a sane life without any of the usual supports. It's time to leave Egypt behind.

PRAYER: God, I pray today for the kids who are born with tough challenges and for the parents who love them and raise them. Let the children and parents know they are precious to you. Amen.

DISTRACT US

Christina Villa

By the sweat of your face you shall eat bread until you return to the ground.
Genesis 3:19

I WAS WALKING MY DOG around the local pond when I saw a
father with his two small daughters riding along the bike path toward me.
The dad was steering his bike one-handed while talking on his cell phone,
using the tone of voice I think of as "business-pompous." The two girls
pedaled behind him silently.

Just after they passed me, I spotted a mother duck and baby ducks
swimming around in circles and squawking at the water's edge. Exactly
the kind of thing you take young children to a pond to see. What other
spontaneous, kid-appropriate, free-of-charge nature sights would they miss
before they went home? The big ugly carp circling under the footbridge?
The flock of geese coming in for a water landing?

Maybe that father regularly takes his children on hikes and bike rides
and walks, pointing things out to them, or just talking, and that day on
the cell phone was not how it usually was. When my kids were young, I
was certainly too distracted much of the time to notice plenty of great
sights I could have pointed out to them. Everyone survived.

And I know every profession has its version of "business-pompous"
that people are required to speak if they want to get ahead. There's nothing
wrong with working hard and doing what it takes to support yourself and
your family.

But the Sunday bike-riding Dad on the cell phone reminded me of a
term coined by Viktor Frankl, a psychiatrist and Holocaust survivor. "Sunday neurosis," he said, is "that kind of depression which afflicts people
who become aware of the lack of content in their lives when the rush of
the busy week is over and the void within themselves becomes manifest."

Frankl wrote in the 1940s; today, technology means we need never be
freed from the work week. People complain about this, often with an un-

dercurrent of self-congratulation: see how important I am? But sometimes there's a less obvious undercurrent—one of relief. How much of our checking our various devices for the latest from work is really necessary, and how much is instead a rush to fill some emptiness?

PRAYER: Distract us from work, help us change the subject, show us that we are more than our jobs. Show us some ducks by the edge of a pond. Amen.

JANUARY 6

TRUSTING DOUBT

William C. Green

Thomas answered Jesus, "My Lord and my God." From John 20:19–31

THOMAS IS NO MORE OF A DOUBTER than the other disciples—or most of us. But he has to find out. The risen Jesus shows his hands and side to the gathered disciples. They were assured. Thomas wasn't there and wanted proof. When Jesus appears again he doesn't rebuke Thomas but offers to let him touch the wounds of his body. Thomas then exclaims, "My Lord and my God!"

"There lies more faith in honest doubt, believe me, than in half the creeds," wrote Alfred Lord Tennyson. Unless it's simply acquiescence or blind trust, faith involves caring enough to want to see the truth for one-self. The doctor may tell you a close loved one is doing well after emergency surgery. But her words aren't enough. You would want to see with your own eyes.

It's hard to think about Thomas because he dares to bring doubt into our lives of faith. But did he doubt—do we—just because we're ornery or don't care? Or could it be the opposite?

How many of us struggle alone with deep questions because we're afraid of how others might react to our doubts? Maybe we can make sure doubt gets expressed and doesn't remain suppressed in church and spiritual life. Learning from Thomas, maybe we can claim doubt as an expression of faith and even love.

PRAYER: Inspire me to trust my doubts and not hide them, O God, trusting in the spirit of the risen Jesus. Amen.

JANUARY 7

NOT ONCE-UPON-A-TIME, BUT ONCE-AND-FOR-ALL

Martin B. Copenhaver

If for this life only we have hoped in Christ, we are of all people most to be pitied. But in fact Christ has been raised from the dead, the first fruits of those who have died. From 1 Corinthians 15:19–28

AS THE APOSTLE PAUL REFLECTED on the death and resurrection of Jesus, it became clear that this was not a once-upon-a-time story. Rather, he recognized that this was a once-and-for-all reality with implications that stretch farther than the eye can see and are larger than the mind can grasp fully. Jesus' resurrection is such a transformative event that it is as if the world now rotates on a different axis.

Paul understood from the start that the resurrection was not simply about what happened to Jesus; it is about what happens to all who trust in Jesus, and about what can happen to all who claim his story as their own. The resurrection is not simply the assurance that Jesus was victorious over death; it is also a promise that we can share in that victory with him. The resurrection does not mean only that Jesus was triumphant over evil; it also assures us that evil will not be ultimately triumphant in our own lives.

Jesus is the "first fruits," the initial harvest, of God's grace. But that is not the end of it. Not by a long shot. The resurrection of Jesus ushers in and reveals a promise offered to all. Saint Jean Vianney said of Easter: "Today one grave is open, and from it has risen a sun which will never be obscured, which will never set, a sun which bestows new life."

PRAYER: God, we thank you that the resurrection of Jesus is not merely a story to be heard, but also a reality in which we can share. Amen.

JANUARY 8

HOLLOWED OR HALLOWED LIVES?

Donna Schaper

What shall I return to the LORD for all his bounty to me? . . . I will offer . . . a thanksgiving sacrifice. From Psalm 116

WHAT SHALL WE RETURN TO GOD for all the bounty we know? Anxiety? Lethargy? Numbness? Hollowed or hallowed lives? We could return vitality, energy, joy, and engagement: that would please God and constitute a bountiful return.

The way to move from one posture to another has to do with which future we claim. According to Gallup, one half of the American people think something "terrible" is going to happen. There is another version of apocalypse, one that understands its biblical meaning, as what God is going to finally do, with humanity, "when all is said and done." It moves us from hollow to hallowed lives. It allows us to return to God what God offers, which is promise and future and hope.

The first step in the movement out of the tomb of the negative into the resurrection of bounty is to change your language. Whenever anyone does the hand wringing, whining "Oh, my God" routine, your job is to return bounty. Or at least comfort. "Oh, my God" can be said with reverence or with fear. Say it with reverence. That will change your language from tragic to comic, positive to negative. It will return to God the bounty God has given and spread it around among ourselves.

Odd that the psalmist calls such an action "a thanksgiving sacrifice." Apparently, we sacrifice our fear and turn it into thanksgiving.

PRAYER: Change me and my language and my picture of the future, O God, so that I may offer bounty as my sacrifice to you. Amen.

JANUARY 9

THE PEACE OF GOD

Kenneth L. Samuel

I am leaving you with a gift—peace of mind and heart. And the peace I give isn't like the peace the world gives. So don't be troubled or afraid. Remember what I told you: I am going away, but I will come back to you again. If you really love me, you will be very happy for me, for now I can go to the Father, who is greater than I am. I have told you these things before they happen so that you will believe when they do happen. John 14:27–29 NLT

THERE IS ALWAYS A CERTAIN PEACE to be found in the presence of those we love and cherish. There is a warmth and a satisfaction in a loved one's presence that words cannot adequately express. We love people so much that we determine to keep them with us always, and we assume that if they love us they would never want to depart from us.

We are not comfortable with the love of someone who has to leave us temporally in order to come back to us eternally. Still, perhaps the greatest expression of our love for someone is our willingness to let the person go.

PRAYER: God, give us the faith to let go of our temporal securities as we reach toward eternal assurance. In the transitions of those who are dearly departed, help us to find abiding love. Amen.

THE RESPONSIBLE LEADER

Ron Buford

Gideon said to God, "If this is right, if you are using me to save Israel as you've said, then look: I'm placing a fleece of wool on the threshing floor. If dew is on the fleece only, but the floor is dry, then I know that you will use me to save Israel, as you said." From Judges 6:36–40 TM

COLIN POWELL ONCE SAID he was proud of being called a "reluctant warrior." Powell is typical among warriors who actually risked their own lives to save others and who can also never erase the brain-searing memories of horrific death and human carnage—of friends and enemies, comrades and combatants, all believing they were "right." Such warriors are rarely eager to go to war—stereotypes notwithstanding. So it is with Gideon: if he is going to battle, he wants to be absolutely certain his cause is just, that it is God's will.

Each day we face battles. Some days we take on battles that satisfy our egos but that leave behind human and spiritual carnage. Is it worth it?

Look at what it costs you to be right. Is it at the center of God's divine purpose for you, your family, those for whom you are responsible? Slow down; take time to be mindful today.

PRAYER: Gracious God, thank you for the gift of divine choice. May my choices and actions today maximize your divine presence, power, and creativity in the world and in my home, for good in the world. Amen.

AFTER THE END

Quinn G. Caldwell

On this mountain the LORD of hosts will make for all peoples a feast of rich food, a feast of well-aged wines, of rich food filled with marrow, of well-aged wines strained clear. And he will destroy on this mountain the shroud that is cast over all peoples, the sheet that is spread over all nations; he will swallow up death forever. Then the LORD God will wipe away the tears from all faces, and the disgrace of his people he will take away from all the earth, for the LORD has spoken. It will be said on that day, Lo, this is our God; we have waited for him, so that he might save us. This is the LORD for whom we have waited; let us be glad and rejoice in his salvation. Isaiah 25:6–9

WHAT COMES AFTER THE END of everything? What is there left after it all falls apart, after circumstance whirls and storms its way through the world, leaving nothing behind but the wreckage of what was? In this passage, Isaiah has just finished describing the doom of the nations, the destruction of all that stands on the face of the earth. The end of the world.

OK. So then what? What does God have planned for after the end, after all hope has gone underground and all chance of salvation has been buried in the rubble?

A feast. The God that made the earth the first time will make it again, and this time, it will taste like a party. This time, there will be no shrouds, no tears, no disgrace. This time, there will only be a feast, big enough, wide enough, full enough for everyone. Big enough for you, and me, and everyone we've ever known.

With our God, says Isaiah, no end is final. There is no end without a beginning. No destruction without rebuilding. No death without resurrection. No end of the world without a party to announce its rebirth.

PRAYER: God, when my world has fallen apart, when all around me is in shambles, remind me of the greater things you have yet in store, and give me a foretaste of the feast you have laid for us all. Amen.

JANUARY 12

JUST BELIEVE

Christina Villa

Then one said, "I will surely return to you in due season, and your wife Sarah shall have a son." And Sarah was listening at the tent entrance behind him. Now Abraham and Sarah were old, advanced in age; it had ceased to be with Sarah after the manner of women. So Sarah laughed to herself, saying, "After I have grown old, and my husband is old, shall I have pleasure?" The LORD said to Abraham, "Why did Sarah laugh, and say, 'Shall I indeed bear a child, now that I am old?' Is anything too wonderful for the LORD? At the set time I will return to you, in due season, and Sarah shall have a son." From Genesis 18:1–14

SARAH LAUGHS WHEN SHE HEARS that she's supposedly going to have a baby. She's an old lady—you can practically hear her muttering behind the door, "Yeah, right."

So this makes me wonder: how often have you been told that you just have to have faith in order for things to work out? How many motivational speakers and inspirational books boil down to this: just believe fiercely enough that something will happen, and . . . it will happen. You make it happen: just believe.

But not in this story. Sarah doesn't believe. And it happens anyway. It is, apparently, a miracle. It's hard to believe in miracles, which are examples of the power of God. It's easier to believe in the power of me. Certainly there are plenty of books and speakers telling me to. But this story says that, sometimes, what I believe or don't believe just doesn't matter. This story says that something good can happen even if I don't believe it will. Something great can happen even if I'm convinced it won't. And when it does, I can say in all truthfulness, "Thank God."

PRAYER: Here are my hopes and dreams. Please watch over them. Amen.

JANUARY 13

ACTION COMMAND

Donna Schaper

Therefore prepare your minds for action; discipline yourselves; set all your hope on the grace that Jesus Christ will bring you when he is revealed. From 1 Peter 1:13–16

ACTION HAS A GREAT PUBLIC RELATIONS AGENCY. People want to be active, not passive; engaged, not distant; they remember the folk wisdom that "actions speak louder than words." But action without a prepared mind is dangerous.

Don't just stand there, we say, do something. Most of what we do when we are just "doing something" is pointless. Actions without intentions—and action without humility—can fake us into thinking we are "doing something." Such action is a short-term solution to life's long term.

Unprepared or unmindful action has become tyrannical. It is divorced from reflection, and the children, after the divorce, are suffering. Whether it is speeding up at work; e-mails at home, at work, on the subway, or even while riding a bike; or the way "we have become the tools of our tools," as Thoreau said, action is overblown. It has become something that puffs us up, while exhausting us.

The old-fashioned way of talking about this dilemma is to contrast works and grace, the way our doing of even good things can conflict with our way of being grace-filled people. If you think it is all up to you and you work hard to do good, you are in danger of thinking your works have saved you and not your faith. *Sola fide,* only faith, say the old timers. And they had no public relations agency at all.

PRAYER: O God, when action threatens to get in the way of grace, permit us conscientious objection to joining its military. Amen.

GOD'S HOLY FOOLS

Martin B. Copenhaver

Do you have eyes, and fail to see? Do you have ears, and fail to hear? From Mark 8:14–21

I HAVE ALWAYS IDENTIFIED WITH THE DISCIPLES as they are depicted in Mark's gospel. Far from holy and wholly together, they are the original "Gang That Couldn't Shoot Straight," fumbling and fickle, often missing the point. In fact, the first sermon I preached after I was ordained was on this passage, Mark 8:14–21, and I picked up on these themes. The sermon was entitled "God's Holy Fool," which was my description of the original disciples. Unfortunately, I didn't think about how that title would look on the board outside the church: "God's Holy Fool, Martin B. Copenhaver, preaching."

In this passage, Jesus is speaking to his disciples after the multiplication of loaves and fishes. They were present when the crowds were fed. They had picked up the baskets of scraps that were left over after all had their fill. But when Jesus asks them to recall what happened, they simply report the facts: five loaves for five thousand people and twelve baskets of scraps. Jesus had given them a stunning glimpse of God's power and all they could see or remember was a picnic in the sun.

I wouldn't be so dim-witted. I wouldn't miss a miracle like that. But then I remember that the word miracle literally means, "sign that points to God." So, yes, I am still one of God's holy fools, because I am quite sure that I miss miracles—signs that point to God—every day.

PRAYER: Jesus, thank you that you love me and claim me as your own, even when I am being a dim-witted fool. Amen.

PERFECT

Quinn G. Caldwell

If you wish to be perfect, go, sell your possessions, and give the money to the poor, and you will have treasure in heaven; then come, follow me. From Matthew 19:16–22

I READ THIS ONE BOOK IN ELEMENTARY SCHOOL about a hapless kid who's always making a mess of things. One day, he finds a guide that promises to make him perfect. Hilarity ensues. In the end, he discovers that perfect people spend all day sitting around drinking weak tea with the window shades drawn.

Which is just about what happens when people try to make themselves perfect.

A young man asks Jesus what he should do to inherit eternal life. Jesus tells him to follow the commandments; he says he has been. Jesus tells him it's time to let God do the rest. Sell your possessions, get rid of all your stuff and all your power and all your ability to believe you can do this on your own, he says. Trust God to do the rest. Which doesn't sound any better to the young man than it does for most of us.

Most of us want to make ourselves perfect—which usually ends up meaning boring, tightly controlled, and disengaged. Weak-tea perfect. But Jesus isn't offering weak-tea perfect; he's offering new-wine perfect. Burst-old-wineskins-and-run-all-over-the-place-staining-everything-with-holiness perfect. Delicious, strong, brave, loud, outside, un-window-shaded perfect.

Following rules will only get you so far; after that, you're going to have to let God do the rest. Which is hard, but worth it; you don't want to be the kind of perfect you could manage to achieve on your own, anyway.

PRAYER: God, help me go as far as I can, and then help me let go and let you. Amen.

WHEN YOU FEEL LIKE QUITTING

Ron Buford

Do you love me more than these? From John 21:1–25

THE DISCIPLES' HIGH HOPES INSPIRED THEM to drop their fishing nets and follow an odd new teacher named Jesus, who would show them a world beyond their wildest dreams. Their hopes had then been dashed. Jesus had been executed. "Now what? They asked, "After Jesus, whom could we love?"

Here, it is as though Peter says, "Hell, I'm going back to my old love . . . fishing." The others join him. Fishing all night, they catch nothing . . . until the resurrected Jesus mysteriously appears. And then the old magic is back. They are inundated with fish. They have breakfast with Jesus—like old times.

Jesus then teaches them one more lesson. He asks Peter, "Do you love me more than you love these fish? Don't you remember? I called you away from the safety of fishing for fish to fishing for God's dangerous dreams and dreamers on the earth. Though you feel like quitting, don't quit. Though you will surely suffer for it, don't quit. Others will get rich financially and you won't, but don't quit. Keep loving through the mystery of uncertainty to experience a sustaining abundance of divine joy . . . just don't quit."

PRAYER: Gracious God, I want to be the person you have called me to be for today. Please help my love for you overcome doubt, discouragement, and fear. I love you more than these. Amen.

THE EVER-PRESENT GOD

Martin B. Copenhaver

Even though I walk through the darkest valley, I fear no evil; for you are with me; your rod and your staff—they comfort me. From Psalm 23

THESE ARE THE FIRST VERSES OF SCRIPTURE many of us commit to memory. In a way it is odd that we would teach this psalm to children because it speaks of realities that most children have yet to confront. So when we teach children this psalm, we are giving them a gift that may take them a lifetime to appreciate fully. Memorize this, we say, bury it deep in your consciousness, and mark well where you left it, because someday, you will need it.

I once heard about a species of bird that migrates over huge expanses of water carrying a twig in its beak. When the storms come, the bird can float atop the water, kept from drowning by the twig. And so this psalm has been for many people, when the storms come, as they inevitably do, on our long journeys. The words of Psalm 23 also are the last words many people hear. I have recited them at countless bedsides and seen people who had seemingly lost all consciousness moved their lips to silently form the familiar words and taste them one more time. It is fitting that these words accompany us from the beginning of our lives until the end, because the words speak of God's everlasting presence with us. The everlasting psalm is an audible reminder of the ever-present God.

PRAYER: God, I praise you that you accompany me throughout my days and even as I walk through the darkest valley. Amen.

Today We'd Put Them on Reality TV

Lillian Daniel

All who believed were together and had all things in common; they would sell their possessions and goods and distribute the proceeds to all, as any had need. From Acts 2:42–47

I LOVE MY CHURCH but I find it difficult to imagine all of us emptying our savings accounts and dumping them into a common pot. I can't picture us all selling our cars, so that everyone gets the same vehicle, be it a bike, a Chevy, or a skateboard. I'm in awe of the early church in the book of Acts, where they shared it all in common. Today, we would talk these people into doing a reality TV show. We'd film them squabbling over who brought the most bread or wine to this giant ecclesiastical yard sale. In other words, I don't believe this was actually easy for them.

I see this scripture as a goal. And at church, we come closer to living it out than we do at work, or school, or the sports arena. At least every week in church, we do share some of what's in our pockets. For this reason, I am in favor of always putting something in the offering plate when it is passed. You may pay most of your pledge by check through the mail, but that weekly act of taking something out of the wallet that is "mine" and putting it in the plate that is "ours" is a spiritual discipline. It reminds us that none of what we have is really ours.

PRAYER: Generous God, whether I need to share my money, my time, my feelings, or my thoughts, help me to imagine a more generous way of life. Amen.

SIBS

Quinn G. Caldwell

So his brothers were jealous of him . . . . From Genesis 37:1–28

THE STORY OF JOSEPH AND HIS BROTHERS reads like a textbook on birth order dynamics. There's Joseph, he of the famous coat, who's effectively though not literally the youngest. He spends all day coming up with ways to annoy his older brothers, from tattling on them to having dreams in which he finally becomes the boss of them all.

There are the middle brothers, always misbehaving and beating up on the youngest one—or selling him into slavery.

There's Reuben, the oldest and the responsible one, who calms the middle-child hellions down, tries to protect the baby, and is forever freaking out about what Dad's going to say.

It will take a prison, a famine, a scheming minx, dreams, psychic powers, a Pharaoh, and God to get this family back together. And you thought your family was screwed up.

God cares as much about your family as Joseph's. Got a sibling rivalry that's gone on long enough? A wound that's not going to heal till somebody says something important, like "I'm sorry" or "I forgive you"? Does somebody need to break out of his or her birth order? Perhaps today is the day to pray for God to intervene.

PRAYER: God, thank you for promising not to let separation and discord be the end for the families you love. And thank you that the youngest children always grow up to be more awesome than their two mean older sisters, which just serves them right for always calling their little brother names and never letting him play with their Barbies. Amen.

S T U C K   I N   T H E   K I T C H E N

Christina Villa

Whoever wishes to be great among you must be your servant. From Matthew 20:17–28

BEFORE I HAD MY OWN FAMILY—before I had a house, a dining room table—I was always a guest at someone else's house for the holidays. Somebody else made all the invisible preparations, whatever they were, and all I had to do was show up, have a seat, and eat. I would sometimes feel a little sorry for whoever was stuck in the kitchen, but the feeling passed.

Then, one day, it started to be me who was stuck in the kitchen. I hated this. It made me feel like a servant. I could hear people talking and laughing in the other room—probably spilling things I'd have to clean up later—and I felt excluded and taken for granted: a martyr to everyone else's good time.

But somehow, over the years, I gradually stopped feeling like a servant, even though I was still doing all the same things. No sermon would have worked this magic. It was only doing it, over and over again, year after year, that turned being a "servant" into something I didn't mind being.

I think of this as an everyday, nondivine example of what Jesus meant by "Whoever wishes to be great among you must be your servant." How can you be "great" and a "servant" at the same time? I don't know, but as usual, Jesus is right.

PRAYER: Make me question all my resentments, because no one loves a martyr. Amen.

MONEY AND VALUE

Kenneth L. Samuel

Now a man named Ananias, together with his wife Sapphira, also sold a piece of property. With his wife's full knowledge he kept back part of the money for himself, but brought the rest and put it at the apostle's feet. Then Peter said, "Ananias, how is it that Satan has so filled your heart that you lied to the Holy Spirit and have kept for yourself some of the money you received for the land? . . . You have not lied to human beings but to God." When Ananias heard this, he fell down and died. From Acts 5:1–10 NIV

WE DON'T OFTEN ADMIT IT, but how we spend our money says a lot about what we value in life. Cash transactions and credit card accounts do say something about character. Jesus puts it even more directly when he says that wherever our treasures are, our hearts are there also.

The first-century Christian church valued human life and human equality so much that they established a community of faith where no one was discounted and no one suffered from material lack. They established a commune of equals, where value was placed not upon the accumulation of individual wealth, but upon individual sacrifices and contributions to the common good. They established a collective of compassionate contributors, and from their collective resources they distributed to everyone according to need, not greed.

Human equality. Shared resources. Public compassion. No one left behind. I am my brother's keeper. All for the common good. We are one in the spirit of Christ. The Beloved Community. The realm of God. These were the community values of the first-century Christians. These were the community values that stood as a powerful corrective to the institutionalized inequities and injustices of the Roman Empire. And these were the values that Ananias and Sapphira violated. They valued material and money over human community, and they paid a price.

PRAYER: Dear God, as we look again to the first-century mothers and fathers of our faith, help us in the twenty-first century to reclaim and renew the work and witness for human community. Amen.

THE DIVINE TIME OF "NOT YET"

Ron Buford

The God of glory appeared to our ancestor Abraham . . . and said to him, "Leave your country and your relatives and go to the land that I will show you." From Acts 7:1–16

IS GOD STILL THINKING? Does God build the plane of life as we fly it? Is creation that dynamic? Does God give us only enough of a map for the next turn? Stressful, isn't it?

Abraham left a secure life to answer God's call, traveling into the unknown, trusting only in God. Is it any wonder the scriptures call Abraham "father of the faithful"?

The magnificence of God's dreams becomes real as people with courage and faith receive and reflect them. Had Abraham required more information before leaving home, the history recalled in Acts 7 might have never happened.

Who knows what impact your words and actions today will have on the course of human history? God is still speaking, calling women, men, girls, and boys into paths God is still thinking of, still creating—based on the actions you take.

A minister tells the story of his call to ministry, saying that as a kid he was mostly bored in church. He kept coming because one older woman had a gumdrop for him each Sunday. He became a great pastor. The woman with the weekly gumdrop had a hand in shaping God's call.

PRAYER: Gracious God, help me listen for your call and respond today with openness, kindness, joy, and excellence in matters great and small. Amen.

OUR TRUE HOME

Martin B. Copenhaver

In you, O LORD, I seek refuge. Psalm 31:1a

HOME. Whether we are responding to the presence or the absence of something called home, the word itself seems to echo in the deeper recesses of our hearts. Of course, a home is so much more than a house. A house is piece of real estate. A home is a place, or a dream of a place, where you feel uniquely at home, a place in which you feel you belong. It is a place where you can seek refuge from the world and are refreshed to face the world again. Whether you live alone or with others, it is a place where you don't have to explain everything. It is a place where you can be yourself, for better or for worse, and usually it is both. And, in the home of our dreams at least, it is a place where you feel accepted, loved even. It is where, in the words of Robert Frost, "When you gotta go there, they gotta take you in."

There are not many places like that in this world, and we all need such a place. Perhaps that is why this psalm speaks of God as a home: "In you, O LORD, I seek refuge." In fact, the psalmist affirms that God is our true home. So our longing for a home in which we feel accepted, loved, and safe may be nothing less than our longing for the shelter of God, our true home.

PRAYER: O God, you have been our dwelling place in all generations, our true home. May I know in every moment that you invite me to seek refuge in you. Amen.

No More Mister Nice Guy

Lillian Daniel

Then he began to teach them that the Son of Man must undergo great suffering . . . and after three days rise again. He said all this quite openly. And Peter took him aside and began to rebuke him. But turning and looking at his disciples, he rebuked Peter and said, "Get behind me, Satan! For you are setting your mind not on divine things but on human things." From Mark 8:31–38

SOME PEOPLE PAINT A PICTURE of Jesus as the ultimate nice guy, a man who never hurts anyone's feelings and only says loving and uplifting things. It's as if they think Jesus is the world's most sensitive man. Clearly these folks have not read this scripture. Here he is in a fight with his friend Peter, and he's got the emotional gloves off. Jesus even calls him "Satan."

Peter was Jesus' real friend. You can tell that by the way they argue. It's always Peter who asks Jesus the hard questions. In this case, Peter is fed up with hearing Jesus' doom and gloom predictions. He doesn't want to hear Jesus talk about his impending death and suffering. What friend would?

But what Peter misses is the line about rising again after three days. Or perhaps he hears it but can't take it in, or simply can't believe it. So he tells Jesus to stop it. And Jesus fires back with some good old-fashioned name-calling, telling Peter to focus on God's big reality rather than his own small one.

As a human being, Jesus clearly had a temper. He told the people he loved what he thought of them, even when they were annoying him. He was no Mr. Nice Guy. He loved us too much for that.

PRAYER: Loving God, your son did not always speak gently. Sometimes he expressed anger in the cause of teaching the people he loved. Help me to understand the place of anger and honesty in my own life, and to use it carefully and caringly. Amen.

GOING AGAINST TYPE

Donna Schaper

*Moses was born, and he was beautiful before God . . . and when he was aban-doned, Pharoah's daughter adopted him and brought him up as her own son.
. . . It was this Moses whom they rejected . . . and whom God now sent as both
ruler and liberator through the angel who appeared to him in the bush.* From
Acts 7:17–40

THIS TEXT IS ABOUT HOW MOSES came to be so well versed in the Egyp-tians. It tells the beautiful story of Pharaoh's daughter picking him up out of the reeds. In other words, Moses came to be Moses by way of a miracle.

Unlike hate radio, which encourages natives to hate immigrants, Pharaoh's daughter was a version of love radio. She picked up someone not her own, of a people not her own, She behaved against type—and that, the author of Acts wants you to know, made all the difference.

It is pretty clear that God makes nations and changes worlds by using people who go against type. Henry Bester wrote an essay about living in the outermost house on Cape Cod for a full year. When asked what he learned from this time, he said that we should "Put away the vulgar fear of the night." He loved the constant shorebird migrations but even more he loved to go out at night and stare at the cosmos.

Most of us have a vulgar fear of the night. We let babies in baskets go by all the time. We are afraid of what might happen if we pick them up. We especially like to think that immigrants, those who float down our stream, are a problem when actually they are a blessing.

Our fears constitute our loss.

PRAYER: Put away the vulgar fear of the night in us and help us to save a Moses every now and then. We need him. Amen.

WHO PICKED OUT THESE CRAZY COLORS?

Lillian Daniel

Do not be wise in your own eyes; fear the LORD, and turn away from evil. It will be a healing for your flesh and a refreshment for your body. From Proverbs 3:5–12

THESE DAYS, the self-help gurus are telling you to "trust your instincts." "Go with your gut," they say. "Follow your heart." But today's somewhat cranky reading from Proverbs flies in the face of pop culture, saying, "Do not be wise in your own eyes." In other words, do not always trust yourself.

When I moved into my first parsonage, at the age of twenty-six, the church told me I could pick out any color I wanted for every room, and that volunteers would paint the house. I perused paint chips and decided that most houses were boring. Not only would I choose a different color for every room, I was going to make bold and bright choices. I couldn't wait to see the results.

Once the painting was under way, I realized I had not been wise. The little paint chips were not nearly as disco bright as the color turned out on the walls. Walking from one neon room to another was like strolling through a funhouse. I could tell the volunteer painters were skeptical, but by the time so much work had been done, all I could do was move in and live with the results of my choices, a parsonage lovingly decorated in the aesthetic of a roller rink.

PRAYER: Dear Lord, help me to know when to trust my instincts, and when to ask for help. After all, I don't know everything. Amen.

FREE

Quinn G. Caldwell

Then Jesus said to the Jews who had believed in him, "If you continue in my word, you are truly my disciples; and you will know the truth, and the truth will make you free." They answered him, "We are descendants of Abraham and have never been slaves to anyone. What do you mean by saying, 'You will be made free'?" Jesus answered them, "Very truly, I tell you, everyone who commits sin is a slave to sin." John 8:31–34

To WHAT ARE YOU ENSLAVED? What forces, institutions, people direct your energy and productivity without your consent? What are the drives, the needs, the addictions that control who you are and what you do? From what do you long to be freed?

Jesus says that the truth of God as revealed in him has the power to free us from sin. I believe that to be true, but I think Jesus was being a little too modest. I think the truth of God in Christ has the power not just to free us from sin, which is anything that separates us from God. I think it also has the power to free us from that which separates us from ourselves, and from one another, things like addiction, and overconsumption, and fear—not sins, exactly, but forces that enslave, nevertheless.

One of the ways God sets this power free in the world is the church. In the church at its imperfect best, we are reminded by good people as fragile and messed up as we are of our heritage as beloved children of the Creator of the Universe, heirs to the promises of God. We are reminded that God longs to be in control of our lives, and that we will be better—and freer—if we let it happen.

PRAYER: God, thank you for the church. Through it and in it, give me the strength to ask for the freedom I need, and the grace to accept it. Amen.

GOD IS EVERYWHERE

Christina Villa

Yet the Most High does not dwell in houses made by human hands; as the prophet says, "Heaven is my throne, and the earth is my footstool. What kind of house will you build for me, says the LORD, or what is the place of my rest? Did not my hand make all these things?" From Acts 7:1–50

I REMEMBER BEING TOLD AS A CHILD that "God is everywhere." I also remember thinking that whoever told me this just didn't know where God was and wouldn't admit it.

Today's scripture tells us that God is not located "in houses made by human hands," which could also mean God is not to be found only in the places we think God belongs.

In other words, "God is everywhere"—not just where you or I imagine God is likely to be. And anyone who says God is located "here" (in my church, my country, my way of life) but not "there" (your church, your country, your way of life) is misinformed.

Many of us speak of feeling God's presence at certain times and in certain kinds of places: church, of course, and in settings of natural beauty, or places where good deeds are being performed, but also in the midst of personal or public tragedies.

But who ever remarks on God's presence at, say, Costco, or the dentist's office, during algebra class or at a school board meeting? Spend enough time in any of these places and you may need God's presence more than you realize. This is when it pays to remember what you, too, may have been told as a child: God is everywhere, not to be reserved for grand occasions or terrible times only, not to be confined to churches or places with spectacular scenery.

PRAYER: Thank God, you're everywhere. Amen.

JANUARY 29

IN A STORM

Anthony B. Robinson

Since much time had been lost and sailing was now dangerous . . . Paul advised them, saying, "Sirs, I can see that the voyage will be made with danger and much heavy loss . . . ." From Acts 27:1–12

IN HIS BOOK, *Preaching through a Storm,* Beecher Hicks says: "You're either coming out of a storm, in a storm, or heading for a storm." Paul was heading for a storm as he traveled as a prisoner to Rome. He tried to avoid the storm by sharing his considerable experience of sailing the Mediterranean with the ship's captain. But the people in charge didn't listen to Paul. In the midst of the storm, Paul continued to offer solid counsel and was eventually heeded.

In a storm, whether literal or figurative, we can easily lose our heads and panic. Paul seemed to stay focused and centered. Perhaps this was because Paul understood himself to be making the trip in obedience to God. When we are clear about God's call to us and are obedient to that call, it's easier to stay focused and not to lose our cool in the midst of life's inevitable storms.

PRAYER: I do not pray, God, to be protected from all storms, but to protected in the storms. When the wind is high and the sea is choppy, help me to stay focused on you and your will for me. Amen.

THE ONE WHO STANDS
BY OUR SIDE

Martin B. Copenhaver

[God] . . . will give you another Advocate, to be with you forever. . . . I will not leave you orphaned. From John 14:15–21

ACCORDING TO JOHN, after Jesus concludes his public ministry, he spends a considerable amount of time with his disciples preparing them for what lies ahead. As Jesus speaks of his death and resurrection, his disciples have a multitude of questions. They sound like the questions of children just before their parents go out the door: Where are you going? Do you have to go? Can't we go with you? When will you be back? Who will stay with us while you are away? They are plaintive questions, pressing and immediate.

Jesus responds that God "will give you another Advocate, to be with you forever. . . . I will not leave you orphaned" (John 14:15, 18). He is promising them the presence of the Holy Spirit. The word translated "Advocate" (sometimes translated "Counselor" or "Comforter") means, literally, "someone who is called to one's side." The Holy Spirit is the one who stands by the disciples even after Jesus departs. And the Spirit is a constant and comforting presence for all those who follow Jesus, an advocate in times of trial, a counselor in perplexity.

The presence of the Holy Spirit, so wonderfully manifest in Jesus, continues to stand by and work through those who continue to follow him after his death and resurrection. Through the gift of the Holy Spirit we have Jesus' continued presence at our side always.

PRAYER: Wonderful Counselor, beloved Comforter, I thank you that, even as I call you to my side today, you are already there, granting me the continued presence of Jesus Christ. Amen.

JANUARY 31

PROOF

Quinn G. Caldwell

After his suffering he presented himself alive to them by many convincing proofs, appearing to them during forty days and speaking about the kingdom of God. From Acts 1:1–11

JESUS CHRIST LIVED, SUFFERED AND DIED, returned, and is right now doing stuff that matters for your life.

What would it take to believe that? Acts says Jesus presented himself "by many convincing proofs." Things, we assume, like talking with Mary Magdalene, eating with his followers, and inviting Thomas to touch the hole in his side.

But what constitutes a "convincing proof" that Christ is alive and kicking these days? What did it for you? Was it a vision? Your parents? The moment your son was born? The way you felt when they sang that one hymn on a random Sunday in 1983? Somebody you love telling you about her or his faith?

What proved it to you, not beyond a doubt—that's science, not faith—but enough for you to bend your life around it?

The Book of Acts is a story about the apostles going around presenting Jesus "by many convincing proofs" to people they thought needed reminders that God is real and hope wins. Your life, God hopes, will turn out to be about the same thing.

So, again: what first proved to you that the faith is true? And then, more importantly: how are you going to prove it to somebody else?

PRAYER: God, I am not always sure what to believe. I'm not asking for certainty here, just enough convincing to get through each day—and then for the grace to pass it on to someone else. Amen.

FEBRUARY

GET UP AND EAT

Christina Villa

[Elijah] went a day's journey into the wilderness, and came and sat down under a solitary broom tree. He asked that he might die: "It is enough; now, O LORD, take away my life, for I am no better than my ancestors." Then he lay down under the broom tree and fell asleep. Suddenly an angel touched him and said to him, "Get up and eat." He looked, and there at his head was a cake baked on hot stones, and a jar of water. He ate and drank, and lay down again. The angel of the LORD came a second time, touched him, and said, "Get up and eat, otherwise the journey will be too much for you." He got up, and ate and drank; then he went in the strength of that food forty days and forty nights to Horeb the mount of God. 1 Kings 19:4–8

HERE IS THE ANGEL OF THE LORD, like somebody's grandmother, urging Elijah to "get up and eat." It's not much—bread and water—but fortified with two such meals, plus a couple of naps, Elijah is fit for his forty-day journey.

If only we could have such faith in just the basics: three meals a day and a night's sleep. Since these are so easy to come by for most of us, maybe we take them for granted. I don't mean taking for granted our good fortune in having enough to eat. I mean maybe we're unaware of the healing power of simply eating our meals and getting our sleep.

We think that in times of disappointment or despair we require something extra to make us feel better—whether it's the large order of fries or a vacation home in Costa Rica. Yoga classes, a better therapist, free-range chicken, heirloom tomatoes.

After a death, grieving people often can't eat, so everyone brings food to the house after a funeral. At those times, the urgency of "Get up and eat" is clear. You are here in the land of the living: that's the message of all those casseroles and loaves of banana bread.

Eat and rest. Meet your basic requirements. Experiment with the sufficiency of these to make you fit for whatever journey you face this week.

And you may find yourself enjoying the French fries or the heirloom tomatoes more than ever.

PRAYER: Dear God, send us angels to remind us that if we eat, drink, and rest, we can get up and continue on our journeys, even through the wilderness. Amen.

DON'T BE AFRAID TO LOVE AGAIN

Lillian Daniel

Jesus . . . said, . . . "Very truly, I tell you, you will weep and mourn, but the world will rejoice; you will have pain, but your pain will turn into joy. When a woman is in labor, she has pain, because her hour has come. But when her child is born, she no longer remembers the anguish because of the joy of having brought a human being into the world. So you have pain now; but I will see you again, and your hearts will rejoice, and no one will take your joy from you." From John 16:16–24

I DON'T KNOW ABOUT YOU, but I remember the pain of childbirth. They say that you forget it, but I remember it. Every minute of it.

I remember that before childbirth, the women in our prenatal class mostly aspired to "natural childbirth," but not me. I was ready to take advantage of whatever science had to offer. And you know what? It still hurt. What made it possible for me to have a second child was not that I had forgotten the pain, but that joy had replaced it. It was the joy of my first child that convinced me to do it again.

Jesus spoke these words to his disciples when they were having trouble accepting that he was not going to be with them forever. He was trying to let them know that they would be broken-hearted after losing him, but that joy would return. Loss is the cost of love, but it is not too high a price to pay. Such love is priceless.

Sometimes when we lose someone, we are afraid to love anyone else again. But Jesus told the disciples that joy replaces pain, with time. People come and go, but no one can take that kind of joy from you. It is eternal.

PRAYER: Gracious and loving God, hold my pain tenderly, so that one day it can be replaced by joy. When my heart is closed, open it to love. Amen.

FEBRUARY 3

TRAVEL LIGHT

Christina Villa

Only Noah was left, and those that were with him in the ark. From Genesis 7:1–24

MANY OF US ARE PREOCCUPIED with global warming right now, but global devastation is not a new concept. It is only page 11 of my Bible when God, displeased with humanity, wipes out "everything on dry land in whose nostrils was the breath of life," and starts over with the creation, almost from scratch. God saves creation by having Noah pack up the minimum number of all living creatures and board them onto the ark.

This is as fine an example of worthwhile frugality as you're likely to find. Sons and daughters of Depression-era parents clean out their parents' houses after their deaths and dispose, in an afternoon, of a lifetime's worth of plastic sherbet tubs, defunct department store shopping bags, and TV dinner trays, all saved for decades against a flood that never came. Their houses were their arks, shortly to have a For Sale sign in the front yard.

Instead of saving, hang on to the minimum—-as God did with Noah and the ark. The two kangaroos that made it onto the ark were the two most consequential kangaroos of all time. Your life is your ark, the means of your survival. What if you could keep only consequential things in it? What would you get rid of?

PRAYER: Dear God, help me sort through everything I've gathered and send me reminders to travel light. Amen.

I'VE GOT YOUR BACK

Ron Buford

We have this hope, a sure and steadfast anchor of the soul. From Hebrews 6:13–20

AMONG CLOSE AFRICAN AMERICAN COLLEAGUES who know the risks of racism and cultural misunderstanding that can so easily and unconsciously emerge, one might say to another, "I've got your back." This is to say, I will look out for you and keep you smart, especially about ways people from the majority culture around you react to your manner, presence, and impact. It also communicates that if you need help, I will be there for you. As Americans, we are improving, but such promises are still a necessary comfort in American society where we "swim in racism." Even the best intentioned among us cannot escape it—on either side.

In this text, God, the creator, the prime mover of all that is, says, "I've got your back." This text reminds us of the assurance of God's promise to "bless us with everything God has." Wow! But wait, there's more! Jesus is described as our advocate with God. Having lived as a human, Jesus interprets our imperfect cultural context to God. When we pray and even before we pray, God takes time to know us, intimately. Should we not do the same for others? So in everything you do and say today, remember, God says: "I've got your back. Go and do likewise." Thanks be to God!

PRAYER: Gracious God, Help us to remember that we are not alone. Please help us be better at doing the things we know. For the rest, please guide, inform, and protect us so that at last we may come into your everlasting presence with joy. Amen.

FEBRUARY 5

SEARCHED, KNOWN, AND LOVED

Quinn G. Caldwell

O LORD, you have searched me and known me. You know when I sit down and when I rise up; you discern my thoughts from far away. From Psalm 139

THIS IS MY MOTHER'S FAVORITE PSALM. For her, the idea of a God this all-knowing is a source of supreme comfort. To me growing up, it was mostly just creepy. In my teenage mind, it all felt a little too much like God the Stalker, peeping at me through the windows and doing drive-bys of my house. Or maybe God as Big Brother, monitoring my library records and digging through the trash cans to see what kind of stuff I bought. I wanted my privacy—even from God.

These days, I'm less convinced that privacy is such a great virtue, at least where God's concerned. And I am very convinced that God's ways are not our ways. What's creepy and dangerous in humans or governments is actually a very good thing in a deity. I tend to think that if the people around me knew everything there is to know about me, I wouldn't be very popular. But the biblical witness is that God does know all of it—all my habits and deeds, every ugliness and act of beauty I have ever performed—and loves me anyway, completely and fiercely. These days, that feels a lot less like creepiness and a lot more like grace.

Turns out, Mom was right again.

PRAYER: Search me, O God, and know my heart; test me and know my thoughts. See if there is any wicked way in me, and lead me in the way everlasting. Amen.

IS SOMEONE TRYING TO GET BACK INTO YOUR LIFE?

Lillian Daniel

[Jacob] went on ahead of them, bowing himself to the ground seven times, until he came near his brother. But Esau ran to meet him, and embraced him, and fell on his neck and kissed him, and they wept . . . . Esau said, "I have enough, my brother; keep what you have for yourself." Jacob said, "No, please; if I find favor with you, then accept my present from my hand; for truly to see your face is like seeing the face of God—since you have received me with such favor." From Genesis 33:3–21

AS A YOUNG MAN, Jacob had stolen his brother's blessing and inheritance, and then scampered off like a chicken. But life didn't turn out to be so easy for the young con artist. He became the victim of deception himself when his father-in-law tricked him into marrying his fiancée's sister, and he had to wait years and years to marry the woman he really loved. Life matured Jacob. He grew up. He longed to reconcile with his brother, Esau.

When their tribes finally met, Jacob didn't know if Esau was bringing family members to judge him or troops to kill him. Instead his big brother greeted him with hugs and tears of joy. Sometimes the people we have hurt surprise us with their big hearts. To make himself feel better, Jacob had brought Esau all kinds of presents. Esau, a successful man, didn't need them, but in another act of generosity, accepted them anyway. Sometimes the most giving thing we can do is to accept another person's gift.

Is there someone who is trying to find a way back into your life? Is there someone offering you gifts you don't need, but gifts they need to give? Esau had every right to stay angry, but he opened up his heart instead. It felt like a miracle. That's why Jacob said, "To see your face is like seeing the face of God."

PRAYER: Open my heart to the gifts of the sorrowful, so that I can be part of your divine healing, Lord Christ. Amen.

DON'T BREAK THE BRUISED REED

Anthony B. Robinson

Here is my servant, whom I have chosen . . . . He will not break a bruised reed or quench a smoldering wick. From Matthew 12:15–21

AS HE DESCRIBES JESUS' MINISTRY OF HOPE AND HEALING, Matthew quotes from the prophet Isaiah to help us understand who Jesus is and how he goes about his business. Here he tells us that Jesus will not break a bruised reed or quench a smoldering or dimly burning wick, which is a way of saying that Jesus goes easy on and is gentle with those who have been bruised by life and those whose inner light may be flickering and threatening to go out altogether.

Maybe that's you or me? Battered by life, not burning very brightly? Maybe it's someone we will or have encountered today? We may be tempted to speak a hard word, to break off or quench a relationship altogether, to write someone off. Think twice about that. Remember Jesus, who did not break the bruised reed or quench the smoldering wick, and be as gentle and patient with someone else as he has been with you.

PRAYER: Truth is, God, we're all bruised reeds, dimly burning wicks. Thank you for being patient with me, for cutting me some slack. Help me to do that for those whom you love and for whom you hope. Amen.

A Tent, Not a House

Donna Schaper

Our ancestors had the tent of testimony in the wilderness. From Acts 7: 44–53

IF YOU'VE EVER BEEN TENTATIVE ABOUT SOMETHING, you know about tents. Tents are temporary dwellings. They are not houses. The author of Acts makes an interesting permanence out of tents when he says that our "ancestors had the tent of testimony in the wilderness." He is telling us that tents are permanent kinds of dwellings made so, even in wilderness, by the act of testimony.

I have watched so many people really want a house. My twenty-three-year-old twins, in different cities, really want an apartment, on their own, with just the right friends and just the right pictures on the wall. I, too, have house lust.

What I want more, of course, is relationship to my ancestor's testimony. I want my house to convince me that I am secure. It won't. My security lies elsewhere, in the embrace of constant permanent impermanence. In understanding the story my people tell. In understanding that Jesus secures in a way that a mortgage cannot.

PRAYER: Wake me up, O God, to the acts of genuine security and place me in the line of great storytellers who secure us by keeping us moving in and towards your love. Amen.

ONE TRICK DESERVES ANOTHER

Kenneth L. Samuel

Thus he made separate flocks for himself and did not put them with Laban's animals. Whenever the stronger females were in heat, Jacob would place the branches in the troughs in front of the animals so they would mate near the branches, but if the animals were weak, he would not place them there. So the weak animals went to Laban and the strong ones to Jacob. From Genesis 30:40–43 NIV

JACOB, OF THE FAMED "ABRAHAM, ISAAC, AND JACOB," is rightly credited for his industrious ingenuity. Serving as the hard working under-shepherd to his father-in-law, Laban, Jacob initiates a creative method of selective breeding, which brings him the ownership of the younger, stronger animals in the flock.

If Jacob's initiative had not been laced with deceit, Jacob would be worthy of our admiration. But Jacob's ingenuity falls within a long line of deception. Jacob had deceived his father, Isaac, and his brother, Esau, before being deceived himself by his father-in-law, Laban, who made him work seven years to marry Rachel, but instead gave him Leah. Jacob tricks Esau, Laban tricks Jacob, Jacob tricks Laban, and the tricks keep coming.

Think about how much effort, ingenuity, and creativity we place into the tricks, schemes, and deceptions that haunt our lives. Imagine what life would be like if we devoted as much initiative and creativity to the development of a loving human community.

PRAYER: Lord, we confess that our creative energies have served our self-aggrandizement much more than they have served the common good. Please redirect our efforts toward the aims of love and liberty for all. Amen.

When to Be Indignant

Anthony B. Robinson

People were bringing little children to him in order that he might touch them; and the disciples spoke sternly to them. But when Jesus saw this, he was indignant and said to them, "Let the children come to me; do not stop them . . . ."
From Mark 10:1–16

JESUS ISN'T ALWAYS NICE, or meek and mild. Here Jesus is indignant. "Indignation" means "anger aroused by something unjust, mean, or unworthy." I like it that Jesus got indignant, that he felt angry about things that were wrong or mean. Here Jesus was indignant with his own disciples for telling children to go away.

The psychologist Erik Erikson once cautioned, "Do not misuse one of the strongest forces in life—true indignation in the service of vital values—to justify your own small self."

Does it sometimes seem to you that today indignation is overused or used in the wrong causes? All sorts of people are ticked off and "not going to take it anymore." Someone called ours "a culture of complaint." We complain early and often. Indignation is often put in the service of our own "small self."

Jesus was indignant, not on his own behalf, but on behalf of others who couldn't stand up for themselves, for children. In expressing his indignation, Jesus bucked the conventional wisdom, surprising his disciples by telling them that children could teach them a lot. On behalf of what "vital values" ought you and I to be experiencing and expressing true indignation?

PRAYER: Dear God, help me not to misuse or overuse the strong force of indignation, but to use it sparingly and rightly in the service of truly vital values. Amen.

WILD

Quinn G. Caldwell

You, a wild olive shoot, were grafted in their place to share the rich root of the olive tree. From Romans 11:13–29

PAUL USES A FARMING METAPHOR to put you in your place.

Originally, he was writing to show how Gentiles (the wild olive shoot) had been brought into life with the Jewish God (the roots). Today, he's talking about you. In some sense, all of us are wild shoots grafted onto something older, deeper, and stronger than we are. We get our support, our sustenance, our life from that gnarled old rootstock.

We uproot it at our own peril.

Have you sometimes been a little too wild, a little too ready to uproot a little too much of our faith? Have you laughed at old hymns that gave our grandmothers strength? Have you "critiqued" and "problematized" old doctrines left and right without asking why they gave slaves and oppressed peoples daily strength? Have you officiously declared that a belief that once saved someone's life should be tossed out? Have you scoffed at ancient things that you did not understand? I have. And I have come to believe that it's a dangerous and an ungrateful thing for a new graft like me to say too lightly to too many ancient roots, "I have no need of you."

PRAYER: God, thank you for new insights, fresh ideas, and holy reformations. But thank you first for old doctrines, old creeds, old hymns, old visions, ancient hard-won truths, and the ancestors who gave them to me. Most of all, thank you for giving a wild thing like me the chance to bear fruit for such a lovely old tree. Amen.

Big Things Come in Small Packages

Lillian Daniel

[Jesus] also said, "With what can we compare the kingdom of God, or what parable will we use for it? It is like a mustard seed, which, when sown upon the ground, is the smallest of all the seeds on earth; yet when it is sown it grows up and becomes the greatest of all shrubs, and puts forth large branches, so that the birds of the air can make nests in its shade." From Mark 4:30–34

IN GRADE SCHOOL, they would always line us up in order of height. It was humiliating being the shortest one. People looked around to see where they ranked. I envied the tallest people, of course. But later, I learned that this exercise also embarrassed the tall girls, who didn't like towering over the boys and wanted to be shorter themselves.

My son, who stakes out the low end of the height graph in his medical chart, asked our pediatrician how tall he would be. Based on his chart and his parents' heights, the doctor predicted he'd reach about 5 feet 9 inches. We could see that my son was disappointed in this answer. "Sorry, kid. You chose the wrong parents," the doctor joked. I imagined that my son, like me at his age, had been dreaming of the day he would have his sudden growth spurt and shoot past them all. Just for the record, I am still waiting for my growth spurt.

So ever since childhood, I have loved the parable of the mustard seed. It is about a small thing that makes a big impact. Since it is a parable, it's not to be taken literally. Jesus doesn't mean that small things have to grow big to make a difference. You just have to live big. You have to live as though you are a part of the kingdom, the realm, of God, because you are.

PRAYER: Lord Jesus, bring me with you as you walk among the small things, noticing their greatness and claiming them for the realm of God. Amen.

Who Am I?

Anthony B. Robinson

Praise [God], sun and moon: praise [God], all you shining stars! Praise [God], all his angels; praise [God] all his host. From Psalm 148

MARTIN LUTHER DESCRIBED SIN as life curved in upon itself. The theme of today's psalm, praise, is pretty much the opposite of that. Praise is life opened out, expansive, a jubilant response to a gracious and astonishing God. What's especially wonderful about this psalm of praise is that it includes all creation in the great chorus. Perhaps this is part of the reason that many of the manger scenes we see at Christmas time aren't limited to human beings alone. They include sheep and goats, a donkey or a cow. They unfold beneath the starry sky and sheltering trees. Sometimes it can seem that all creation is somehow caught up and united in praise of God.

Such experiences tell us something about who we truly are. At one time or another, most of us wonder what life is really about and why we are here. We may think of ourselves as producers or professionals, as family members or citizens. All of these are important and have their place. But most of all we are, I think, worshipers. Whether kneeling at some manger, shouting praise unto the highest heavens, murmuring our gratitude before mystery, we are worshipers. And the reason for our praise? While we were yet sinners, Christ has come for us; while we were yet far off, Christ has come to us.

PRAYER: "Unto you is born this day in the city of David, a Savior, who is Christ the Lord." And for this we praise you this day and all our days. Amen.

DOES GOD GET MAD?

Christina Villa

For we are consumed by your anger; by your wrath we are overwhelmed. You have set our iniquities before you, our secret sins in the light of your countenance. From Psalm 90

DOES GOD GET MAD? It depends whom you ask. Some say, "No, never." For them, God is benevolent, always. When good things happen, it's thanks to God. When bad things happen, it's something else, usually unspecified . . . maybe global warming? Those of us without degrees in theology are left to wonder.

Others say God does indeed get mad and bad things happening are God's punishments. This view gets tricky whenever there's a big natural disaster: what did all those innocent children washed away by the tsunami do to make God mad? We're still wondering.

Many people firmly hold one or the other of these views of God and are deeply invested in their rightness. It's more than a matter of theology. On this question, people seem to choose the answer that's most emotionally satisfying for them. Sometimes, that's all you have to go on.

But when you want to know more about what God is like, if you're not so certain about it, it's often a good idea to read the Bible (and occasionally live your life) with your mind not made up. The Bible, like life, is a lot more revealing when you don't approach it as if it were a cable news channel—telling all its stories from one or the other point of view.

The Bible is full of people who don't know what to believe, who change their minds, and start and stop believing. When you read the Bible with your mind not made up, you find real people in there, people you can learn from. But you have to read their stories without your mind made up, or else all you'll learn is what you already believe.

PRAYER: Let me live today, or maybe just this morning, without my mind made up about every last little thing. Amen.

WEIRD ABOUT MONEY

Quinn G. Caldwell

In any and all circumstances I have learned the secret of being well-fed and of going hungry, of having plenty and of being in need. From Philippians 4:10–15

WHY ARE WE SO WEIRD ABOUT MONEY?

Why don't we talk about it more? Who decided that personal finances were supposed to be private—and just what do we gain from keeping them so? All too often in the church, the poor pretend they're not, and the rich pretend they're not, and everybody pretends that money isn't one of the great driving forces of our lives. Why?

Jesus knew that pretending money doesn't matter only leads to, at best, weird attitudes, and at worst, injustice. Other than God and God's realm, there is nothing he talked about more than money. Paul knew this, too: being rich or poor matters (ask any poor person), but neither makes one good or bad. Neither determines one's worth. Neither needs to be hidden. So what's with all the privacy?

I had a seminary professor who recommended making people publicly state their annual income before joining the church, as a way of cutting through our weirdness right up front and reminding everyone that while money matters, what's really important is the inheritance that is ours as children of God.

You, as we in the class did, are probably shaking your head and thinking, "Well, *that* would never work." And you're probably right. But what would we, what would the church, be like if it did?

PRAYER: O God, all good things come from you, and from you nothing is hidden. Give us the grace to act faithfully both in our wealth and in our lack of it. Amen.

Locked in a Room Full of Open Doors

Ron Buford

Ask, and it will be given you; search, and you will find; knock, and the door will be opened for you. For everyone who asks receives, and everyone who searches finds, and for everyone who knocks, the door will be opened. From Matthew 7:7–11

I AM TOLD THAT ALLIGATORS BRED in a fenced area for many generations won't go beyond the fenced perimeter, even after the fence is removed. It is as if they are locked in a room full of open doors.

We are not all that different, believing we can't do . . . whatever. Fill in the blank. We become certain that a mistake, influence, or limitation will determine our destiny. But it need not. God is in the business of bending time, creating new possibility from disaster, and you and I have inherited the business. Release yourself.

As a kid I heard the old ones testify, speaking metaphorically, and with excitement, "I remember the day my dungeon shook and my chains fell off. Glory!"

Are you feeling stuck or limited today? Today's text invites us to search with confidence. In God's kitchen you can always find the ingredients you need to cook up a breakthrough—if not today, perhaps tomorrow, and sometimes it takes longer. But keep looking. Finding is often connected with a determined and persistent search.

And it may not show up exactly as you imagined. You may have asked for a type of fish that would be as dangerous as a poisonous snake for you. But God has heard your prayer.

In fact, you may already have the fish God knows you need. Who has the seasoned cornmeal? Glory!

PRAYER: Gracious God, Help me never tire of looking for you, the One closer to me than I am to myself. Help me trust in and give witness to your uncontrollable, all-knowing, and perpetually transforming love. Amen.

CHEERS

Lillian Daniel

Day by day, as they spent much time together in the temple, they broke bread at home and ate their food with glad and generous hearts, praising God and having the goodwill of all the people. From Acts 2:37–47

AT ONE CONGREGATION I SERVED, potluck suppers at church did not attract many people, but when we started having them in people's homes, the attendance doubled. People loved seeing church members' living spaces, after all those years of only seeing one another at church. Was that the only reason attendance doubled? Well, in the interest of full disclosure, some people also liked meeting in homes because you could serve beer and wine. But they were drinking wine in the book of Acts, too. From the beginning, the church knew that worship is central, but it's also good to get people around the table, laughing, eating, having fun, and praising God.

To learn about the earliest Christians, who might have known Jesus and the apostles, read the book of Acts, written by the author of Luke. Like the other gospels, Luke is about Jesus. Acts is the next chapter—what happened after Jesus ascended and left regular people to build the church.

Remember: the church has not always been a building on Main Street. Acts shows the church trying to form itself, long before newsletters, building use schedules, church basement potlucks and capital campaigns. And from the beginning, the church ate together, casually. They spent time worshiping at the temple. They also gathered in people's homes, to share a good meal and a glass of wine. And that was church, too.

Cheers.

PRAYER: Help me and my church to delight in one another's presence, whether we are in the pews or around the supper table. Amen.

You're Not Alone

William C. Green

Do you not know that you are God's temple and that God's Spirit dwells in you? If anyone destroys God's temple, God will destroy that person. For God's temple is holy, and you are that temple. From 1 Corinthians 3:10–23

I WAS TAUGHT AT SUNDAY SCHOOL that it was wrong to smoke, drink, and do other bad things that violated my body because I was God's temple, and you'd better be good there—which turned out to be better advice than not. But threats of something bad happening if you do wrong things are not reliable deterrents—otherwise we couldn't so easily acquiesce to our anger and resentment, or the destruction of the environment, or the invasion of other countries.

But as those examples suggest, being "God's temple" is not just about you or me. It's about us. The Greek word here for "you" is plural. Paul is addressing the congregation in Corinth. Good faith is never singular; it's plural. It starts in relationship with others, and it grows from there—or collapses.

Weak faith often stems from weak relationships. We can feel cut off from anyone with whom we could freely share our own thoughts and be understood, or to whom we think we want to listen. This becomes a habitual predilection that undermines faith and our sense of God. And it's self-fulfilling.

In the spirit of Lent, anticipating new life in Christ, some of us may need to take a deep breath, pick up the phone or cross the room where others are gathered, and take the initiative ourselves. Sooner or later we'll connect—or reconnect. That's God's promise.

PRAYER: God, may I act more freely on my need for others and theirs for me. Together, may we grow in your Spirit. Amen.

WELCOME HOME

Martin B. Copenhaver

My refuge and my fortress; my God, in whom I trust. From Psalm 91

HOME. It is hard to think of another word with as many deep resonances. Whether we are responding to the presence or the absence of something called home, the word itself seems to echo in the deeper recesses of our hearts.

A home is so much more than a house. A home is a place, or a dream of a place, where you feel uniquely at home, which is to say a place where you feel like you belong.

Some of us have an actual place like that, a place that comforts and enfolds, a place where you can seek refuge from the world and are refreshed to face the world again. Whether you live alone or with others, it is a place where you don't have to explain everything. It is a place where you can be yourself, for better or worse, and usually it is both. And, in the home of our dreams, at least, it is a place where you feel accepted, loved even. There are not many places like that in the world, and we all need such a place.

The authors of scripture talk about God in some of the same ways, as a shelter and a comfort, as the one who accepts us just as we are, who enfolds us with care and equips us to serve. Perhaps that is why scripture speaks of God as a home. "God is my refuge and my fortress," writes the psalmist, using the words that would later inspire Luther's famous hymn, "A Mighty Fortress." Elsewhere we read, "LORD, you have been our dwelling place in all generations." Imagine: God is our home.

If the home in which you live is a sanctuary or roiled with conflict, grand or plain, a real place or merely the stuff of dreams, we all have the same gracious home in God. So welcome home.

PRAYER: O God, thank you that you have been our refuge, our dwelling place, throughout all generations and are so even now and even for me. Amen.

BODY AND SOUL

William C. Green

In the name of Jesus Christ of Nazareth . . . stand up and walk. From Acts
3:1–10

PETER ORDERS A LAME MAN to stand up and walk. The apostle carries on
Jesus' work of healing. Often in the book of Acts, Luke uses the verb "to
save" for "to heal." The spiritual and physical are two sides of the same
coin. Soul and body are one. The lame man was healed so he could be
faithful.

We can be more spiritual than God. Spirituality can be as much a
threat to the integrity of faith as materiality. Many among us can feel
judged for being insufficiently spiritual and too preoccupied with material
well-being. There are spiritual practices, and sometimes worship itself,
that, in effect, inspire detachment from material matters in the name of
faith and inner peace. But the peace and strength God gives often come
precisely amid the very things that weigh so heavily on us and make us
"lame." We can't get these things out of our minds—and God isn't asking
us to. We're simply asked to be aware of God's presence.

"The LORD is my shepherd, I shall not want" says the twenty-third
psalm. It goes on to say, even "though I walk through the valley of the
shadow of death . . . you are with me." "Walk through," the psalm says.
Walk through all that threatens or worries us. Walk through consciously,
deliberately, faithfully, no longer limping along anxiously, trying to feel
spiritual.

PRAYER: Gracious God, may each of us stand tall and walk with greater confidence
in the freedom and strength you make ours. Amen.

GOD IS STILL LISTENING,

Ron Buford

When they call to me, I will answer them; I will be with them in trouble, I will rescue them and honor them. With long life I will satisfy them, and show them my salvation. From Psalm 91:1–2, 9–16

IF YOU HAVE EVER HAD A SICK CHILD, a child afraid of "monsters," or an aged parent, spouse, or partner at risk of falling who needs help getting into and out of bed, then you know what it's like to hear the faintest beginning of a whimper or call, or the first click of a lone metal walker piercing the night's thick silence. And seemingly with one motion you throw back the covers, feet barely touching the ground . . . you fly to your loved one.

When we pray, God's heart is tuned to hear our faintest cry—even before we can say God's name . . .

The name Jesus taught us to use in the Lord's Prayer is more accurately translated, "Our Daddy." Rest assured that when we call "our daddy," before we can call, daddy is there . . . no matter who we are or where we are on life's journey . . . love is never withheld from anyone, despite the ways we kids find to withhold love from one another—no exceptions.

Imagine!

Whether you use mommy or daddy or some other word or image to harness your mind's imagery does not matter. Recall the Loving and Divine Presence you know within, the One who loves us all beyond our wildest dreams and never fails, because there is only One—too big for words or images.

Now call as if there were monsters in your room . . . again.

Remember the intensity with which you have run to save those you love. Imagine the intensity of God's love in action that makes even your best efforts seem like indifference by comparison. In God's arms, we and those we love and pray for are made whole—despite the perceived "monsters" of sickness and death, disappointment and disaster, loneliness and fear. And nothing, absolutely nothing can separate us from God's love.

PRAYER: Help, God! There's another monster under my bed. Amen.

FEBRUARY 22

YOUR ORDINATION

Quinn G. Caldwell

The angel said to those who were standing before him, "Take off his filthy clothes." . . . *So they put a clean turban on his head and clothed him with [new] apparel.* . . . *"Now listen, Joshua, high priest, you and your colleagues who sit before you!"* From Zechariah 3:1–10

ZECHARIAH HAS A VISION of a heavenly ordination, in which God makes Joshua high priest. It is short and sweet (seminarians planning their own ordinations take note: it is *not* four hours long), consisting mostly of a pronouncement of forgiveness for sins, a change of clothes, and a charge.

Perhaps Zechariah also witnessed another one of God's favorite ordinations to the priesthood: yours. Protestants proclaim the priesthood of all believers, which means that every person who loves and longs for God is, for us, a priest. Our baptisms are our ordinations.

In case you forgot the job description, here's what priests do:

They point to God in the ordinary things of the world, like water and bread and babies.

They say words of power to change the world, words like "You are beloved," "Peace be with you," and "God bless you."

They make sacrifices to please God, like sending money to Haiti instead of going to the mall, like working in the soup kitchen instead of playing Wii all day.

They show up at births and deaths, at weddings and funerals, at sickbeds and prisons, to pray and bless and make sure the people know that they are not alone.

Here's what priests do: they help the world know that God is alive, that blessings abound, that love will win. It's what you were ordained for; now go for it.

PRAYER: God, grant that I might always live up to the tasks for which you ordained me. Amen.

ANXIOUS OR ALERT?

Anthony B. Robinson

Be on guard so that your hearts are not weighed down with dissipation and drunkenness and the worries of this life, and that day does not catch you unexpectedly. . . . Be alert at all times. From Luke 21: 34–36

GOD, I AM A SINFUL MAN living in the midst of a sinful people. Way too much of the time I am, we are, filled with lizard-like anxiety, worrying about a future we can't control, frightened by rumors of the latest threat or menace the media is touting, or nurturing a slow-burning anger that we haven't received what we think is our due. And we treat our anxiety with dissipation and drunkenness. God, have mercy. Save us from fueling our anxiety, and instead . . .

PRAYER: Put me and us, Holy One, on sweet alert. Wake me, wake us, up. Wake us to the extraordinary beauty of life, to the ingenuity and goodness we encounter daily in others, to the opportunities we have to do useful work and contribute, to the mystery of your persistent grace, and to the sheer gift of being here. Make me alert like the owl, listening like the deer, and playful as a squirrel in spring. Amen.

THE TEMPTATION TO JUDGE

Lillian Daniel

Therefore you have no excuse, whoever you are, when you judge others; for in passing judgment on another you condemn yourself. From Romans 2:1–11

IN OUR FAMILY WE HAVE A RULE: Nobody can tell anybody else what they should give up for Lent.

You can imagine how we came up with such a rule. "So let's all go around the table and talk about what we're thinking about doing for Lent," quickly turned into, "I'll tell you what Dad should give up for Lent!"

Everyone's an expert about other people's spiritual welfare.

"Why give up sweets? You're already skinny."

"Cursing doesn't hurt anybody. What about global warming?"

"If you give up shopping and spending, it hurts the economy."

"You said you were giving up sweets, but I saw you eating ice cream straight out of the container after you thought we were all asleep!"

By now we are well into Lent and the things you gave up may be tempting you. Perhaps they already have. The good things you decided to do and add to your life may have proven harder to fit in than you thought.

But remember, whenever we try to get closer to God, it's only natural for the competition to show up. If Jesus had to fight off the devil's temptation in the desert, you know you'll have to as well.

Don't let other people's comments or judgments slow you down or discourage you. You know what you need to do for Lent, and God is still eager to help you do it.

PRAYER: Jesus, give me strength when the devil tempts me with ridicule and criticism. I'm trying to follow you instead. Amen.

BROKEN

William C. Green

I am God. . . . I make, who can unmake? From Isaiah 43:8–13 TM

CREATION IS SHATTERED, broken by sin and injustice, lovelessness and betrayal. But no more than oxygen can be removed from air or hydrogen from water can God be taken away from what's torn apart.

We can't easily see this. No more than parents can rest in the assurance that all will be well with their children can we bask in the belief that what is wrong, or what could go wrong, poses no threat. As Paul puts it, "not only the creation, but we ourselves, who have the first fruits of the Spirit, groan inwardly as we wait eagerly for redemption." Redemption, deliverance from the wrongs we inflict or fear, is not a simple fix. It's a process in which what is broken is brought together in ways stronger and more beautiful than before.

Lent is a time to think about all this. Too often believers jump ahead to an empty tomb and the promise of Easter. What could that really mean to Jesus, or to us, if it's a denial of the doubt and suffering that had made it so painfully unimaginable? And what can our own love and good work mean if that rests on what we alone can pull off?

This side of eternity we can't know it all. But in the spirit of Christ we can work for, and look forward to, the remaking of all now incomplete and, often enough, torn apart. Thank God.

PRAYER: Creator God, you work to remold and make us and all your creation into what you mean us to be, in the spirit of Christ. Amen.

FEBRUARY 26

LET GO OF THE DARK

Donna Schaper

The floods have lifted up, O LORD . . . the floods lift up their roaring. From Psalm 93

WHEN I TALK TO PEOPLE who are living in the dark, darkly, I often try to retrain their vision. Many people think, with the psalmist, that a flood is coming. Differing with the psalmist, they think there is no way they can get above it.

I often try to move attention to what is good. It ain't easy! Once somebody has become the prisoner of darkness instead of enjoying the night, even ice cream looks bad. It puts on weight or adds to cholesterol or shows that we are undisciplined. Some of us spiritually like the flood. We have no interest in being above it.

What would happen if we were to become re-enchanted with the world that God has made? Rather than being habitually disenchanted with it and ourselves?

Might faith not make the difference that levees cannot? Might hope not be the antidote to the complicit despair of having given up long before the rains come? Yes. But first we must let go of the dark, which we have so come to enjoy.

PRAYER: When you promise that we can rise above the floods, we hear you, O God. Give us the faith of Noah and the grace of the returning dove. Amen.

FEBRUARY 27

FAITH MADE VISIBLE

Anthony B. Robinson

And Paul, looking at him intently and seeing that he had faith to be healed, said in a loud voice, "Stand upright on your feet." And the man sprang up and began to walk. Acts 14:9–10

LOOKING AT A MAN who sat crippled by the roadside, we read that Paul saw his faith. I wonder what Paul saw? What does faith look like?

Have you "seen" faith? When someone looks at you, do they "see" faith? Does God?

I am not sure what faith looks like exactly. But I'm pretty sure it looks like trust. Trust and a willingness to take a risk. And something more, often faith has an "in-spite-of" quality to it. Trusting and getting to your feet despite being crippled; believing and going on when it's hard to do so and against the visible evidence.

Years ago, during an especially challenging time in my life, a lovely older friend gave me a three-by-five card with these words written on it: "There is, in the universe, a power forever on the side of those brave enough to trust it." I think she was telling me: despite all, keep showing up just as fully as you possibly can. And even when it's hard, even when you feel or are crippled in some way (aren't we all?), keep on trusting wildly in God. I've held those words close to my heart a long time now.

Are you living in faith, by faith these days? Can others see faith in you? Make your faith visible today. God knows, we need it. We need you.

PRAYER: God, in Jesus you have made faith visible to us and for us. Help me to make my faith visible today. Amen.

FEBRUARY 28

THE SEPARATING POWER OF POSSESSIONS

Martin B. Copenhaver

Their possessions were too great for them to dwell together. From Genesis 36:1–8

JACOB AND ESAU, THE TWIN BROTHERS whose tussles began in their mother's womb, eventually reconciled enough to be able to settle in the same neighborhood in Canaan. They prospered but eventually became the victims of their own success. The land was not able to support the herds of cattle of both brothers, so Esau had to move away. This was a matter of environmental sustainability, but also something more. As the author of Genesis put it, "Their possessions were too great for them to dwell together."

This is not an ancient problem. Today—whether it's in Canaan or New Canaan—prosperity has a way of separating us. The fastest growing segment of the housing market is exclusive gated communities, whose chief attraction is the way they separate people. If you have enough money to buy sugar in large quantities, you are less likely to have to go next door to borrow a cup from a neighbor. When you have your own car, you never meet your neighbor at the bus stop. Our prosperity can be too great for us truly to dwell with one another. There is another way of putting it: Sometimes the more wealth we have, the more impoverished our lives can become. Is there a way you can think of to keep your possessions from coming between you and your neighbor?

PRAYER: Dear God, everything I have is a gift from you. May I express my thanks by never letting my possessions create distance between me and those around me. Amen.

MARCH

GRIEF

Quinn G. Caldwell

All his sons and all his daughters sought to comfort him; but he refused to be comforted, and said, "No, I shall go down to Sheol to my son, mourning." From Genesis 37:29–36

JACOB HAS BEEN TRICKED into believing that his son Joseph is dead. His grief is huge. He cannot be comforted; he wishes he himself were dead.

Any who have lost a child will relate. They say that there is no worse pain in the world. There is something so terribly wrong, so out of order about a child dying before a parent. The pain doesn't fade with time, they say, and you never get over it. You simply hope to find a way to learn to live with it.

God also knows what it's like. "For God so loved the world that God gave God's only begotten son . . . ." God lost a child, too.

It is a strange thing, but it may be that the ones who know best the depth of God's love for us, the only ones who really know what God sacrificed in Jesus' death, are those who have lost children of their own. For they are the only ones who know the depth of the pain that God experienced in order to bring us home.

PRAYER: Great God of all mystery, before we felt the pain, you suffered it; before the burden came upon us, your strength lifted it; before sorrow darkened our hearts, you were grieved. As you walk in the valley of every shadow, be our good shepherd and sustain us while we walk with you, lest in weakness we falter.* Amen.

Book of Worship, United Church of Christ (New York: United Church of Christ Office for Church Life and Leadership, 1986), 364.

DIVINE HUNCHES

Ron Buford

And Pharaoh said to Joseph, "I have had a dream, and there is no one who can interpret it. I have heard it said of you that when you hear a dream you can interpret it." Joseph answered Pharaoh, "It is not I; God will give Pharaoh a favorable answer." From Genesis 41:14–36

THE REV. WIL GREEN, WHO WAS BOTH A PASTOR AND PSYCHOLOGIST, led a group through a series of dream workshops in which we shared our dreams. We each imagined having had the dream of one person who would share his or her dream. As we each shared the dream's meaning for us, the original dreamer took notes and identified interpretations that resonated. The group became the "Joseph" of this biblical story. The idea of the group was that God speaks though our dreams in symbols or code so that our conscious mind will not suppress them and divinely inspired messages get through.

Pay attention to those hunches; don't suppress them. Humility that hides a divine message does not glorify God, our maker. Test significant dreams, visions, or hunches with others, and then prayerfully act on them. Your dream, vision, or thought may be the difference between life and death, for you, for someone you love, for a generation, for the world. If it isn't, after discernment and prayer, know when to let go.

What is the dream or hunch God gave you? God is still sending divine hunches, many more than we acknowledge.

PRAYER: Gracious God, Help me discern and share the dreams and thoughts you give me today that have divine purpose. Amen.

GETTING ALONG

William C. Green

How very good and pleasant it is when kindred live together in unity! From Psalm 133

LIVING TOGETHER IN UNITY means different things to different people. So it was for centuries with England and France, and more recently with England and Ireland. And so today with Israel and Palestine, India and Pakistan, Syria and Lebanon, and many other places, including Iraq, where Sunnis, Shiites, and Kurds disagree on how to live together.

The psalmist was not spared the problem. His pursuit of unity was disputed by many from the north of what had been a united people. Disagreement focused on the legitimacy of priestly authority and whether Jerusalem should be the capital.

Publicly and personally, most of us would like to get along better and "live together in unity." What often trips us up is thinking this means minimizing disagreement or muffling difference. Pascal said "Unity which does not depend on plurality is tyranny." Paul's declaration of our unity in Christ hardly denies plurality. He speaks of "Jew or Greek, slave or free, male and female."

The possibility of unity grows by understanding ourselves more completely in the differences of others. None of us is defined by one characteristic or factor alone. So it was that W. E. B. Du Bois wrote: "Herein lies the tragedy of the age: not that people are poor—all know something of poverty; not that people are wicked—who is good?; not that people are ignorant—what is truth? . . . But that we know so little of each other."

PRAYER: Creator of us all, may we learn from your image in others, in the spirit of Christ. Amen.

WHAT SHOULD WE DO?

Martin B. Copenhaver

Now when they heard this, they were cut to the heart and said to Peter and to the other apostles, . . . "What should we do?" From Acts 2:22–41

MOST PREACHERS I KNOW have a collection of stories about things people have said to them while shaking hands after worship. (One of the favorites in my own collection is from early in my ministry. Someone said, "You know, Martin, every sermon is better than the next one." I thanked him. He was in his car and driving away before I realized what he had said.) Of all the things a preacher could be told, however, the words offered to Peter after his sermon on Pentecost are the most fitting response to a good sermon: "What should we do?"

A lecture can be deemed successful if it is informative or interesting. Someone giving a speech might strive to be funny or moving. A good sermon, while it may have elements of all of those things, strives for something more. It moves the listener to action. A good sermon not only prompts one to think about things differently, but also to live differently. That is why the most important response to a sermon is not what is said to the preacher at the door of the church. The most important response is what the listener does during the week.

PRAYER: God, take our words and speak through them, so that we see more clearly what needs to be done and also so that we are inspired to do it. Amen.

FAITHFUL COMMERCE

Quinn G. Caldwell

Is it not written, "My house shall be called a house of prayer for all the nations"? But you have made it a den of robbers. From Mark 11: 12–19

NEAR THE RECEPTION DESK AT MY CHURCH, we have a small display of church-related items for sale. Once I had a conversation with a visitor who was incensed that we were selling stuff in a church. He quoted the words above, which Jesus himself quoted when he turned over the tables of the money changers in the Temple.

I told him I don't think Jesus' issue was with commerce in the Temple (since Jewish law and the international nature of the Temple virtually required it). I think Jesus' issue was that that commerce was too often taking place in ways that took advantage of some and enriched others at their expense. It wasn't with buying and selling per se; it was with buying and selling in unfaithful ways—inside the Temple or out.

You will probably buy or sell some stuff today. When you do, take some time to wonder how faithful your little bit of commerce is. Who produced what you're buying or selling? Under what conditions? Were they paid enough? How good, or not, is the thing you're buying for the world? Is the person who's selling it getting paid enough? How could this transaction be more faithful to Jesus' hope for the world?

Commerce isn't good or bad. It just is. What's good or bad is what it does to the world, and its people, and to you.

PRAYER: God, as long as I live in this world, I'm going to need to do a little bit of commerce. Grant that all of it be faithful to you. Amen.

POLARITY MANAGEMENT

Anthony B. Robinson

He answered, "I was sent only to the lost sheep of the house of Israel." But she came and knelt before him, saying, "Lord, help me." He answered, "It is not fair to take the children's food and throw it to the dogs." From Matthew 15:2–26

THIS IS A TROUBLING STORY. It's difficult to imagine Jesus turning away someone in need, much less referring to her in what appears to be a derisive way. What's up with that? Jesus had, in his mind, a clear purpose and focus. His job was to renew and restore the "lost sheep of the house of Israel." That didn't mean restoring them to power and glory. It meant recalling Israel to its God-given purpose and mission as a people who had been blessed that they might be a blessing to all the peoples of the earth.

Purpose, focus, and a clear sense of calling are important. Knowing what you're about is good. We all need that. But we also need, alongside a clear sense of purpose and calling, a capacity to entertain interruptions, surprises, and the intrusions that are off our plan. So when the Canaanite women persisted, Jesus relented. "Woman, great is your faith! Let it be done for you as you wish!" Purpose/focus and surprise/interruption are not an either/or. They are a both/and. Focus or interruption is not a problem to be solved, but a polarity to be managed.

PRAYER: Grant me, God, a compelling sense of your purpose and calling for my life. Grant me as well a capacity to entertain holy interruptions that enlarge and correct my plan. You know I need both. Amen.

A MEAN-SPIRITED MEETING

Lillian Daniel

When they saw the tribune and the soldiers, they stopped beating Paul. Then the tribune came, arrested him, and ordered him to be bound with two chains; he inquired who he was and what he had done. Some in the crowd shouted one thing, some another; and . . . he could not learn the facts because of the uproar." From Acts 21:27–40

WE ONCE HELD A COMMUNITY MEETING at our church to address an issue that had made our neighbors angry with us. The lay leaders had a carefully planned introductory presentation, but they never got to give it, because when we went around the room for introductions, many attendees seized that time to tell us everything we had done wrong in the community. The introductions turned into speechifying, and, as the angry neighbors listened to each other, they got angrier at the church.

Soon there were people shouting about things that had happened long ago and had nothing to do with the matter at hand. It was one of the worst meetings I have ever been a part of and there was nothing I could do about it. Sometimes, bringing a group of furious people together is not the answer.

When the tribune arrested Paul, the city had turned into an angry mob. So the tribune put Paul in chains and asked the crowd who Paul was. They all shouted out different accusations. There was no consistent story. "He could not learn the facts because of the uproar."

There's a lesson here for us. As much as we church folk love bringing people together for meetings, there are times when it just doesn't work. You can't always get good information, or a wise outcome, from a group. Sometimes you just have to get out of there.

PRAYER: Loving God, sometimes we gather together for thanksgiving and love. Other times we get together to accuse and to hurt each other. Let your Holy Spirit guide me in either setting. Amen.

Take a Little Honey

Kenneth L. Samuel

Then their father Israel said to them, "If it must be so, then do this: take some of the choice fruits of the land in your bags, and carry them down as a present to the man—a little balm and a little honey, gum, resin, pistachio nuts, and almonds." Genesis 43:11

IN MOST INSTANCES IN LIFE, there is no easy way to do a difficult thing. Israel (Jacob) was compelled to do a very difficult thing when his sons reported that they could not purchase needed food from the Pharaoh's viceroy in Egypt without the accompaniment of their youngest brother and Israel's beloved son, Benjamin. With great reluctance and dismay, Israel allowed Benjamin to go, but he not only sent Benjamin and his other sons to Egypt with money to buy food, he also sent along with them gifts of graciousness—tokens of kindness, expressions of goodwill—to give to the mighty man in Egypt in charge of food distribution.

The sons of Israel were sent on a mission that placed their fate in jeopardy, but their father did not allow them to undertake their daunting assignment without taking with them "a little honey." A little honey—a little kindness and goodwill—can still work wonders in our lives today. It can open the door to deeper romance, respectful business negotiations, and even improved foreign relations. "A little honey" always sets the tone for better relations.

PRAYER: Dear God help us to understand that in this life good relationships require much more than money. They require that we also "take a little honey." Amen.

LITERAL

Quinn G. Caldwell

When the disciples reached the other side [of the lake], they had forgotten to bring any bread. Jesus said to them, "Watch out, and beware of the yeast of the Pharisees and Sadducees." They said to one another, "It is because we have brought no bread." And becoming aware of it, Jesus said, "You of little faith!" From Matthew 16:5–12

IN THIS STORY, we learn an important thing: overly literal people annoy Jesus.

After some rather testy remediation, the disciples learn what the reader of the story knows all along: Jesus is speaking in metaphors. He's not talking about *actual* yeast here, he's talking about false teachings that spread *like* yeast.

Jesus speaks in metaphor a lot because he knows that pulsing under and through everything we see and experience is the life and power of God. Breaking through every moment of every day, just below the surface, is the realm of God, the future shaping the here and now. Empirical observation cannot detect it. Objective testing will not uncover it. Literalism can never apprehend it. It is usually not obvious. The best we can do is to feel it, and then to talk about it in simile and metaphor.

I think that overly literal people annoy Jesus because they miss the God and the grace that are all around them. They look at bread and cup, and they see . . . bread and cup. They look at the cross, and see . . . two pieces of wood. They look at a newborn baby, and see . . . carbon. It is a dreary way to move through the world.

So, today, practice seeing in metaphors. Look deeper than the surface. Try to see the world deeply, as Jesus sees it: full of God. Today, commit to not being a literalist.

PRAYER: O God, teach me to look deep, to see your power coursing through the world. And in the looking, bring me closer to you. Amen.

GET THE DOWNLOAD

Ron Buford

Simon Peter answered, "You are the Messiah, the Son of the living God." And Jesus answered him, "Blessed are you, Simon son of Jonah! For flesh and blood has not revealed this to you, but my Father in heaven." From Matthew 16:13–20

WHEN YOUR COMPUTER BEGINS TO RUN A BIT SLOW and you get a pop-up window notifying you of an upgrade and asking if you want to download it now, do you think to yourself, "I don't have time today. I'll do it later"? You put it off . . . and off . . . and off. Eventually your application grinds to a near halt. You now have no choice but to download the upgrade.

If software engineers can design upgrades to meet ever-increasing challenges and systems to receive them, how much more likely is it that God designed us to be able to download God's upgrades so we can handle the newest challenges in the world?

In this biblical text, Peter makes the proclamation that Jesus is the Christ, the son of the Living God. Jesus responds, saying, "You got the upgrade."

Peter's upgrade resulted in an anointed proclamation that will withstand his upcoming denial, postcrucifixion depression, resurrection jitters, and a return to an old fishing career—and reemerge with power at just the right time: Pentecost.

Ultimately, Peter will be the one to publicly proclaim the mystery of Jesus as resurrected Christ. More than three thousand souls will be added to a strange new Jesus movement that will turn the world upside down and be called "the church."

PRAYER: Gracious God, I can feel my spirit grinding to a halt. I cannot handle the challenges before me today. Teach me to pray and to interpret your Word in ways that have meaning for this time, place, and situation. I need the upgrade. Amen.

THE THING THAT BIT ME

Ron Buford

As Moses lifted up the bronze snake on a pole in the desert, in the same way the Son of Man must be lifted up, so that everyone who believes in him may have eternal life. For God loved the world so much that he gave his only Son, so that everyone who believes in him may not die but have eternal life. For God did not send his own Son into the world to be its judge, but to be its savior. From John 3:14–17 GNT

FIRST-CENTURY CHRISTIANS KNEW THE STORY of Moses lifting up the "serpent in the wilderness." The Israelites were plagued by poisonous snakes after God had miraculously delivered them out of Egypt because of their endless complaints and nagging unbelief in God's power each time they faced a new challenge. The suffering close at hand always felt more real than God's sometimes distant and ineffable Presence, despite God's amazing feats of deliverance in the past.

But then, I feel that way, sometimes . . . don't you?

When the people asked God to be merciful and to forgive them, God told Moses to make a bronze serpent, put it on a pole and lift it up before the bitten. Moses did so and the people were cured.

Just so, we can derive hope and salvation—even from that which has bitten us. Though in Jesus' day this was counterintuitive, today we understand this to be the nature of antibiotics and vaccines: a bit of the venom that bit us can also save us.

Likewise, the way to true power is not by fighting back but by taking a bit of the venom and humbling ourselves even to the death of the cross.

Roman brutality would win the first round. But within three hundred years, an unarmed Jesus and twelve buddies will have toppled their great empire by . . . breaking bread from house to house; reminding one another of Jesus' mystical reappearances; reminding each other of his love and how he taught them to "be not afraid."

Jesus' followers blessed and healed those who cursed, oppressed, imprisoned, and killed them, humbling themselves as did their Jesus, reaching beyond short-term failure and disappointment; embodying the One of precious salvation, healing, and forgiveness. They overcame the deep darkness and grasped Easter hope, in a Good Friday world.

PRAYER: Gracious God, I'm bitten, but I know that venom is no match for your Divine Presence. May the sweetness of your Divine Presence oil the hinges of my heart so that the antibodies of your love, hope, and power flow freely through me . . . and out into the world. Amen.

ANNOYED BY THE RESURRECTION

Anthony B. Robinson

While Peter and John were speaking to the people, the priests, the captain of the temple, and the Sadducees came to them, much annoyed because they were teaching the people and proclaiming that in Jesus there is the resurrection of the dead. From Acts 4:1–12

ONE OF THE GREAT GIFTS of the Book of Acts is that it casts new light on old and familiar themes. Like resurrection and Easter, Acts comes to us from a very different time in the church's life, a time when the church was not part of the establishment.

For some 1,600 years now Christianity has pretty much been the established religion of western society, with churches dotting the land, crosses on their spires. In that world, Easter became a benediction on the culture-at-large, resurrection an assurance of God's blessing and comfort. Resurrection lost its power to annoy or disturb.

In the world of Acts, resurrection and the Easter message were radically different. They were a threat to the powers-that-be, reminding those powers, both political and religious, that their power was neither ultimate nor final, that a just God who had the first word would have the last word. Resurrection, as Peter and John discovered, threatened the powers of this world, unmasking their pretensions and offering the wild and wonderful hope of a new beginning by the power and mercy of God for all people.

Preaching the resurrection was a way of saying to all the god-pretenders, "Sorry, you're not in charge here, the God who raised Jesus from the dead is." Today the church is in a new time. Christianity is less the establishment, more like it was in the time of Acts. Could the resurrection again become, for us, a challenge to arrogant power and the promise of God's astonishing capacity to bring new life where it is not expected? If so, expect to annoy a few people.

PRAYER: God, I pray that I might have the courage and capacity to trust and witness to the resurrection in ways that would disturb people. Amen.

MARCH 13

WHAT'S IN A WORD?

Kenneth L. Samuel

Let no one deceive you with empty words, for because of these things the wrath of God comes on those who are disobedient. From Ephesians 5:1–6

WHOEVER SAID, "STICKS AND STONES MAY BREAK MY BONES but words will never harm me," lied. The truth is that just a few words can bring about enmity between spouses, animosity between friends, and discord in a community. And just as a few of the wrong words can wound us and cut us to our hearts, a few of the right words can heal us, lift us, and inspire us. Words like "I love you," words like "I'm sorry, please forgive me," or "You are forgiven . . . let's be friends," words like "With God, all things are possible"— these are words that save our lives.

As Christians, we are disciples of God's incarnate Word—God's Word made flesh. When we fail to make God's Word animate, active, and vibrant in the lives we live, our words become empty, hollow, and meaningless. And God, who became Word in the flesh, is never ever pleased with empty words.

PRAYER: Gracious God, please allow the words that we speak to find meaning and matter in the lives that we live. Incarnate your Word in us, so that all will know that you mean what you say. Amen.

MARCH 14

WHAT IS IT ABOUT THE TRUTH THAT SCARES US?

Donna Schaper

The coming of the lawless one is apparent in the working of Satan, who uses all power, signs, lying wonders . . . . From 2 Thessalonians 2:7–12

IN THE KING JAMES VERSION OF THE BIBLE, we are warned against "strong delusions." We are warned to love the truth. Of course, the next question is whether we can find the truth. Often I think it is suspended in air, like a dancer who really knows how to dance.

In America two different concepts of modern dance were identified by early dance pioneers Doris Humphrey and Martha Graham. Humphrey identified the theme as fall-recovery—the falling away from and the returning to equilibrium. Graham identified contraction-release as exhalation and inhalation, respectively, as the basis for all movement, and in Germany Mary Wigman used the term "die and arise." The fall, the recovery from the fall, and the suspension held at the peak of the recovery is another way that Humphrey described it.

I think truth is that moment at the peak of recovery, between fall and suspension, breathing in and breathing out—it is only there for a short minute, before it falls back into its distortions and delusions and half-truths.

How to find the truth? Learn to dance. Learn to see both sides, all sides. Learn to die and rise, to let go and hang on. Then in a few gorgeous seconds, recover. Peak. See.

PRAYER: Train our muscles, O God, to see the truth and to love it. Teach us to recover and then to move again. Amen.

MARCH 15

HE HAD A WIFE?

Martin B. Copenhaver

When Jesus entered Peter's house, he saw his mother-in-law in bed with a fever; he touched her hand, and the fever left her, and she got up and began to serve him. From Matthew 8:14–17

THIS HEALING STORY IN MATTHEW is so dramatic that we might overlook one intriguing detail. It makes reference to the Apostle Peter's mother-in-law. Wait, Peter was married? That's right. We don't know if others of Jesus' twelve apostles were married, but we know from this verse that Peter was. That means that the day he dropped his fishing nets to follow Jesus, he also left his wife and the rest of his family. Before he headed out with

Jesus, do you think he said, "Hey, I've got to go home and explain this to my family first"? And, if so, what did he say to explain why he was following this as yet little-known teacher? And what did his wife say in response? After all, not only would Peter be gone for extended periods of time, traveling with Jesus all over Galilee, but while he was away the family would not have money coming in from Peter's fishing business.

Most often, when someone takes on a challenging task or follows a call, other people are making sacrifices in order that they might do so. They are the behind-the-scenes people—family members, colleagues, or others—who keep the home fires burning, or pick up the odd chore, to make what you do possible.

Is there someone like that in your life? Can you think of a way to thank him or her for making you possible?

PRAYER: Dear God, help me to recognize those who support me in ways that I might be tempted to overlook. Amen.

MARCH 16

INSTIGATOR

Quinn G. Caldwell

God exalted him at his right hand as Leader and Savior that he might give repentance to Israel and forgiveness of sins. From Acts 5:27–32

I HAD THIS ONE TEACHER IN ELEMENTARY SCHOOL who yelled a lot. She had a whole list of words to scold us: tattletale, daydreamer, wiseacre (my personal favorite though I could never figure out what being mouthy had to do with farms). But the worst thing she could call you was "instigator." In her mind, an instigator was the one that got all the whiners, troublemakers, and bullies to ruin her life and send her to the teacher's lounge for a *lot* of furiously smoked cigarettes.

In today's story, the apostles defend themselves to the authorities while witnessing to Jesus. Peter says that God has made Jesus "Leader and Savior," but the word here translated "leader" also means—you guessed it—"instigator." This works for me partly because it's hilarious to think of Mrs. Boyle scolding Jesus in her raspy voice, but mostly because it's true. Who sent those disciples out to say things that would whip up angry mobs? Who told them God was more important than kings? Who told them to share their faith? Who made them brave?

In time, the apostles themselves became instigators. Then their followers did, then their followers did, right on down to today. And now the question is, have you done enough instigating today to make Mrs. Boyle mad at you?

If not, it's time to raise a ruckus.

PRAYER: God, grant me the grace not just to shake up the world on your behalf, but to get the people around me to do it, too. Amen.

MARCH 17

MAJORING IN MINORS AND MISSING THE MAJORS

Kenneth L. Samuel

Jesus replied, . . . "You hypocrites! Isaiah was right when he prophesied about you: 'These people honor me with their lips, but their hearts are far from me. They worship me in vain; their teachings are merely human rules.'" From Mark 7:1–23 NIV

IN RELIGIOUS CIRCLES, it is not unusual to confuse and conflate conventional traditions with eternal truth. But the danger in elevating human convention to the level of divine commandment is that the convention often obscures and diminishes the commandment. Consequently, we end up majoring in what is minor (temporal traditions), and missing what's major: eternal truth.

When Jewish religious leaders noticed that Jesus' disciples failed to wash their hands before eating, as was the tradition among the Jews, they questioned Jesus about it. Jesus' response was that they were so obsessed with religious traditions that they were missing the essential commandments of God. They were more concerned with clean hands than they were with using those hands to care for their elderly parents.

Many religious people make the same mistake today. Some of us are more concerned with school prayer in Jesus' name than we are with quality education for all in the name of equal opportunity. Some of us are more concerned with the Ten Commandments being posted on the wall of the courthouse than we are with impartial justice within the courthouse. Some of us are more concerned with condemning gay couples than we are with providing loving homes to the thousands of foster children whom gay couples could adopt, if given the opportunity.

The real consequence of majoring in conventions and missing the commandments is that while we uphold religious protocol, people suffer and even die through neglect of the essential commandments of God.

PRAYER: Sovereign God, please give us discernment, so that our traditions will not continue to obscure your truth. Amen.

SHOW SOME RESPECT

Christina Villa

Come no closer! Remove the sandals from your feet, for the place on which you are standing is holy ground. From Exodus 3:1–5

WHEN I WAS A LITTLE GIRL accompanying my mother on her errands, she would sometimes stop in at the church. Before going in, I remember her fumbling with her parcels and digging through her purse looking for a piece of Kleenex to put on her head. This was the late 1950s and we were Catholic: women wore hats or some kind of head covering in church—always. The Kleenex was obviously an emergency measure, but maybe so was stopping in at the church.

People nowadays—Catholic or not—might look back on this as another of the many impractical and pointless things from the past that we're too sensible for now, like tailfins on cars.

There are times, however, when it would be useful to be able to make some outward sign of respect for that which is greater than ourselves. That's what God is demanding of Moses: do something to acknowledge that you're on holy ground; perform this wordless gesture of humility so I know you understand your place in the big scheme of things.

Rituals of respect are helpful reminders of whom I am subordinate to —and whom I am not subordinate to. They are perspective-restorers. No matter my employer, the bank that holds my mortgage, my credit score, the people with one kind of power or another over me, I am ultimately in God's hands, just like everyone else.

PRAYER: Remind me each day of your place and mine in the big scheme of things. Amen.

ARE YOU WORTH IMITATING?

Lillian Daniel

Brothers and sisters, join in imitating me, and observe those who live according to the example you have in us. From Philippians 3:17–20

WOULD YOU BE COMFORTABLE allowing a video crew to follow you around for a month, recording your every waking moment? I know I wouldn't. But why not?

Well, I do plenty of things I do not want anyone to see. And here I am not just talking about drinking milk out of the carton, snoring in front of bad television, or wearing dirty socks because I am sick of doing laundry. I am thinking of more serious things, like speaking unkindly to the people I love, losing my temper, or being self-serving. There's a lot I wouldn't want caught on camera.

So it's hard for me to imagine how Paul could write to his fellow church members and say, "Brothers and sisters, join in imitating me." You would have to have enormous confidence in your own moral behavior to make a claim like that. Or else you'd have to have a huge ego. And my guess is that Paul had both.

But he also had a deep belief in the power of Jesus to forgive. He knew what it felt like to be cruel, to hurt others, and then to experience forgiveness. And I doubt he knew that from just one experience on the road to Damascus. Paul writes like a guy who learned it fresh every day. And still he told people to imitate him.

Perhaps they were to imitate him and his fellow Christians by being people in search of forgiveness. Not perfect, just aware and sorry.

Now, that's someone I think I could imitate after all.

PRAYER: On this day I do not pray to be perfect, but I pray to be forgiven. And remind me, Holy Spirit, that people are indeed watching what I do and say. We are all imitating somebody, and somebody may be imitating me. Help me to deserve it. Amen.

WHY ME?

William C. Green

O my LORD, please send someone else. From Exodus 4:10–13

EVERY TIME GOD ASKS MOSES TO DO SOMETHING IMPORTANT, Moses is overwhelmed by inadequacy. "Why me?" God responds in effect, "Why not you? I've promised you strength and support." But Moses found it hard to believe that what he needed to do, he would be enabled to do. That faith is hard for us, too.

As a good runner in college, I enjoyed cross-country meets—but afterwards, rarely before. Unlike those great athletes who practice imaging techniques that picture victory, I did the opposite. I began getting better when I realized that strength came when I needed it—when running the race—not while edgy and anxious beforehand.

When we are taught to pray in the prayer that Jesus taught, "Give us this day our daily bread," we are not praying for tomorrow, or next month, or next year—but for today. We're given what we need when we actually need it. This gives us hope for handling whatever the future holds, but it's hard to believe if we don't know it firsthand today.

Real or inflated, anxiety and the prospect of difficulty ahead make self-doubt inevitable. Worried, we can sell ourselves short. Let's watch out about selling God short. Strength and direction await us, however hard that can be to picture ahead of time.

PRAYER: Almighty God, who has more to give than we know how to receive, break us open to the promise of grace and guidance that always come, right on time. Amen.

SUPER APOSTLES

Anthony B. Robinson

I have been a fool! You forced me to it. Indeed you should have been the ones commending me, for I am not at all inferior to these super-apostles, even though I am a nothing. From 2 Corinthians 12:11–21

IS YOUR MINISTER A CELEBRITY? Do paparazzi dog the footsteps of your pastor, their cameras clicking and flashing? Does the face of your minister loom, god-like, on a huge video screen above your congregation's sanctuary? Is your pastor on television a couple of times a month commenting on whatever is hot and lively? Probably not. Chances are your pastor is more ordinary. He or she slogs through committee meetings with you. On Sunday mornings, your pastor doesn't do a star-turn in the pulpit but looks (and sounds) pretty human up there. Instead of being chauffeured around in a limo, your pastor is much more likely to be found driving kids to youth camp in his or her beater.

In the church at Corinth, some of the congregation preferred celebrity clergy, "super apostles" who had a lot to say about their mighty works. What they got was Paul, doggedly going about his duties, teaching, preaching, imploring, and on the side stitching tents to pay his bills. On top of that, Paul was short! God's power and beauty come to us hidden, hidden in the ordinary. In the midst of our own celebrity-crazed culture, are our eyes open to the ways God uses ordinary people to convey the extraordinary power of God?

PRAYER: Dear God, open the eyes of my heart, I pray, that I may see your extraordinary power at work in ordinary people like my pastor. Amen.

KNOW YOUR LIMITS

William C. Green

Getting into the boat again he went across to the other side. From Mark 8:1–13

SOMETIMES THE BEST WAY TO CARE for others is to walk on by.

When commissioning the disciples for his work of healing and hope, Jesus said, "If anyone will not receive you or listen to your words, shake off the dust from your feet as you leave that house or town." Jesus had done just that when he left his hometown. No one there would accept what he had to offer.

In today's passage Jesus knew it was pointless to argue with people whose minds were made up. So he just departed. It's not that he didn't love or didn't care. But he knew that whatever his miracles of love, there are times when God must do what even he could not.

And so with us. Jesus had limits. We have limits. Our trust belongs in God who can do what we cannot: reach those beyond our reach, love in ways we cannot, care for others in ways we cannot, forgive when we cannot, heal when we cannot, give hope when we cannot.

W. C. Fields said, "Try, try, try again. Then quit. No use being a damned fool about it." Yes, let's for sure "try, try, try again." But then let's watch out lest we overlook our limits. If God has no hands but our own, sometimes our hands are best folded in prayer.

PRAYER: Powerful and loving God, you far exceed my own limits in doing what needs to be done. Help me to do my part while trusting yours. Amen.

HEALING

Donna Schaper

A great number of people would also gather from the towns around Jerusalem, bringing the sick and those tormented by unclean spirits, and they were all cured. Acts 5:16

HEALING CAN HAPPEN IN THE CITY OR THE COUNTRY. Or at Sloan Kettering. Or rural spas.

Healing is less about getting the circumstances right than it is about wellness in Jesus, which is the prelude to healing. Healing can come in polluted lands or tenements, as well as by the sea. Some people have the best doctors and still aren't well.

Before the healing comes the wellness. You can be sick and still be well. You can be cured of the hold cancer has on your body by not letting it have your spirit also. Jesus' healing parables all make this clear: by faith we are made well. When the disciples carry on Jesus' pattern, people come from all around to learn the wellness of deep security, shalom, salvation. From there we commute back and forth to doctors, through trouble, and into the best environment we can find.

PRAYER: For grandmothers who don't feel well but still take care of their grandchildren, for people who battle persistent mental illness, for those who can't be bothered to bother, O God, send wellness. Cure of us our big fears, our small loves, and make us whole. Amen.

THE LONGING HEART

Martin B. Copenhaver

As a deer longs for flowing streams, so my soul longs for you, O God. From Psalm 42

I AM CONVINCED THAT WE ALL LONG for the presence of God with a deep, aching hunger, much as we hunger for food, but with this difference—we don't always know how to satisfy it. If we have a stomach hunger, we know that we need to eat some food. And, generally speaking, we have learned what constitutes nourishing food. We know, for instance, that if we are hungry it will do us no good to fill our stomachs with cotton, or even cotton candy. We know that we need food—satisfying, nourishing food—in order to live.

But if we have a soul hunger, a spiritual yearning, we are not always sure how to fill it. And people will try almost anything to fill it, to take the ache away.

Philosopher Blaise Pascal once said that each one of us is born with an empty place in our hearts that is in the shape of God. This empty space is not a square hole, or anything as simple as that, but a complex, hungering, God-shaped space where only God fits and only God can fill. We can try to fill that space with other things—human relationships, careers, or other earthly pursuits—but they will sooner or later leave us unsatisfied. After all, if that empty space implanted in our hearts is in the shape of God, then our attempts to fill it with anything else will leave empty corners that will continue to ache.

Before the fulfillment, there is the longing: "As a deer longs for flowing streams, so my soul longs for you, O God." Sometimes it is only after your hunger has been satisfied that you can see what you were hungry for all along.

PRAYER: O God, my soul longs for you, even when I don't recognize that you are the object of my longing. Amen.

PARALYZING DARKNESS

Lillian Daniel

Then the LORD *said to Moses, "Stretch out your hand towards heaven so that there may be darkness over the land of Egypt, a darkness that can be felt."* . . . *People could not see one another, and for three days they could not move from where they were; but all the Israelites had light where they lived.* From Exodus 10:21–29

ONE SYMPTOM OF DESPAIR is being unable to move. When people are profoundly low in spirit, they cannot even get out of bed, let alone get out and accomplish things. Sadness can be paralyzing, and so can grief. We have all had times when the darkness around us has made us afraid to step out. Later, we look back on such times and wonder where they came from. In hindsight, they can seem mercifully foreign. But when you are in the middle of darkness, you cannot move.

In the Exodus story, it is the Egyptians who are trapped in darkness, while the Israelites get to see the light. The Israelites were being prepared to escape from slavery. They saw light while the rest of the culture was stuck in darkness. They were heading to the promised land, while the Egyptians were unable to move. In this case, the Egyptians were the oppressors, and could not see God's light.

But sometimes we get trapped in darkness when we haven't done anything wrong. That was probably the case with some of the Egyptians. They couldn't all have been bad people, just as the Israelites could not all have been perfect. Sometimes good people get trapped in the dark, and when that happens we remember the words about Jesus from John 1: 4–5, which today will be our prayer:

PRAYER: "What has come into being in him was life, and the life was the light of all people. The light shines in the darkness, and the darkness did not overcome it." Amen.

OUT OF MY COMFORT ZONE

Anthony B. Robinson

But Ananias answered, "Lord I have heard from many about this man, how much he evil he has done . . ." From Acts 9:10–19a

ONE THING I HAVE NOTICED about how God works is that God likes to ask us to step out of our comfort zones. Darn it!

God told Ananias to step out of his comfort zone and into the presence of Paul. Paul, aka Saul, had been blinded by a revelation from God. God instructed Ananias, a follower of Jesus, to go to Paul, to lay his hands on him, and pray for him that he might regain his sight. Ananias was totally incredulous. All he knew about Saul/Paul was that he was an angry man who had hounded and jailed Christians. God had definitely called Ananias out of his comfort zone.

I have discovered a sure way to tell when God is calling me out of my comfort zone. It's that feeling in the pit of my stomach. It's the "I don't want to do this, God" feeling. I don't want to go there. I don't want to talk to that woman. I don't want to be face-to-face with that man. I don't know what I'm going to find or what's going to happen.

When I have those feelings, and fears, in the pit of my stomach, it's a pretty sure bet that God is calling me out of my comfort zone and into the life of faith.

PRAYER: God, when you call me out of my comfort zone, I seldom like it, but I do need it; thank you. When you call, help me to pay attention, and to not let my fear stop me or shut me down. Help me to trust you and go where you call me. Amen.

WHY DIDN'T JESUS TEACH ME HOW TO DO THAT?

Lillian Daniel

Peter sent them all out of the room; then he got down on his knees and prayed. Turning toward the dead woman, he said, "Tabitha, get up." She opened her eyes, and seeing Peter she sat up. From Acts 9:36–43 NIV

AS A PASTOR, when I visit the grieving and the sick, I can offer prayers and spiritual companionship, but I can't deliver a miracle. I wish I could, but thus far, the dead people I visit stay dead.

I comfort myself by thinking that Jesus could resurrect the dead, but I'm not Jesus. Yet here Peter gets to deliver the miracle. A woman presumed to be dead wakes up and lives. Why didn't Jesus teach me how to do that?

Miracle stories are tough to take in. You may find yourself going to the practical answers. Perhaps she wasn't really dead, just in a coma, and Peter got there at just the right moment. Maybe she was sleeping and Peter woke her up. Maybe, maybe, maybe . . . maybe she really did come back from the dead, not by Peter's power but by God's. But why didn't God teach us all how to resurrect each other?

Why didn't Jesus just sit still in one place his whole life and wait for all the dying people to come to him? If his main goal was eliminating all grief and suffering that would have been more efficient. But apparently that wasn't his goal.

Perhaps miracles are sprinkled lightly in the world to remind us that the real miracle is waiting for all of us after we die. If God can do a few of these here on earth, imagine what can happen on God's own turf, one day, in heaven.

PRAYER: Christ, let your healing power be known to me. Touch all who grieve with your holy hope: for a day when we will all be raised and gathered together around the heavenly banquet, where grief will be no more. Amen.

UNDERASKING

Donna Schaper

All the people saw him walking and praising God, and they recognized him as the one who used to sit and ask for alms at the Beautiful Gate of the temple; and they were filled with wonder and amazement at what had happened to him. From Acts 3:1–26

FUND-RAISERS UNDERSTAND WHAT HAPPENED. The man who used to ask for a little received a lot. Instead of a few coins, he was healed. Instead of a cup of coffee, he got the gift of motion.

Many of us underask. Fund-raisers belittle themselves and their cause when we say, "Give what you can." Once I asked a rich man for $5,000 and he responded by saying he'd like to give $50,000. Later he told me that I shouldn't be so ashamed of my organization: it needed great well-paid leaders, not anyone on the cheap. Pastors often tell their new leaders that they need to give just a "little time." Hours and days later, good leaders say they knew all along that the job was bigger than "little."

We try so hard to make realistic objectives for our days when all along we know we should be heading for large adventures, extravagant risks, and impossible dreams. The beggar in us needs to be tamed. The dreamer in us needs to be released.

PRAYER: Teach us, O God, to want more and to know we deserve it. If we can already walk, teach us to dance. Amen.

GO AHEAD!

William C. Green

By faith he left . . . unafraid of the king's anger. From Hebrews 11:23–29

THE FAITH OF MOSES was a verb, not a noun. It was less a sure belief than action. It was less a feeling than behavior. It was not an end in itself but the means by which something important happened. It's not that "by faith" Moses didn't feel afraid. But what made him afraid was not "the king's anger." It was the prospect of being thwarted by it: he knew he had to get on with what he needed to do.

So for us. Perhaps our faith is weak because we're not doing a lot with it. Perhaps we're deterred by the power of some "king's anger" in our own life in the form of what we fear: the rejection or misunderstanding of others; our own inadequacy; reprisal for what we might do wrong; being overcome by what stands in our way; punishment for sin.

We may pray for encouragement in the hope of feeling better about these matters. But chances are good we'll remain stuck until, like Moses, we accept that much we worry about cannot be resolved, at least right now, and, nonetheless, move on. By faith we can leave behind a lot that has impeded us—not forgetting the possibility of the king's anger but realizing that the greater threat is giving into it, guaranteeing a stranglehold.

PRAYER: O God, deliver us from preoccupation with resistance we face. Inspire us to live more fully in the freedom you make ours. Amen.

Build People Up, Don't Put Them Down

Lillian Daniel

Let us therefore no longer pass judgment on one another, but resolve instead never to put a stumbling block or hindrance in the way of another . . . . Each of us must please our neighbor for the good purpose of building up the neighbor.
From Romans 14:13–15:2

ARISTOTLE BELIEVED THERE WERE THREE TYPES OF FRIENDSHIP. There was the pleasure friendship, in which two people delight in one another's company, or a shared passion. A good example of this might be the golfing buddy or the friend you make in the choir. The second category was the advantage friendship, in which you are friends with someone because it may provide some benefit or profit to you. Here you might find the business friendship or the car pool connection. But the last category was the highest—the friendship of character. In this friendship, the very best in you loves the very best in your friend, and you aspire for the good in one another, even if that involves personal sacrifice. We please our character friends in order to build them up.

When Paul wrote this letter to the Roman church, he was giving them instructions on how to be a community of Christian virtue. Don't judge each other. Don't get in each other's way. Don't be consumed with your own perfection. Instead, build each other up. In your relationships, don't just look for pleasure or advantage, but be friends of character.

PRAYER: Search my heart, dear God, so that I may know if I am being a stumbling block to another person. Help me to build others up. And bring people into my life who will love the good in me and draw my virtue out, so that you can use it in the world. Amen.

Moving Mountains

Anthony B. Robinson

Have faith in God. Truly I tell you, if you say to this mountain, "Be taken up and thrown into the sea," and if you do not doubt in your heart, but believe that what you say will come to pass, it will be done for you. From Mark 11:20–25

More than a decade ago, I went off to Nicaragua on a mission trip with our youth group. As we left, a church member thrust Frederick Buechner's little book *Now and Then* into my hands. In it Buechner told this story of going to hear the Christian healer Agnes Sanford. "The most vivid image she presented was of Jesus standing in church services all over Christendom with his hands tied behind his back and unable to do any mighty works there because the ministers who led the services either didn't expect him to do them or didn't dare ask him to do them for fear that he wouldn't or couldn't and that their own faith and the faith of their congregations would be threatened as a result. I recognized immediately my kinship with those ministers."

During our trip, one of my sons became very ill, experiencing the onset of bipolar disorder there in Nicaragua. As Buechner recognized his kinship with those ministers of whom Sanford spoke, I recognized my kinship with him, seeing how timid my own faith often was. And yet in the midst of that time of danger and desperation, I came to know, as never before, God's power in Christ to heal, to uphold, and to sustain. Desperation unbound Christ's hands to hold and heal, and mountains were moved.

PRAYER: Free me, God, from my timidity, heal me of my doubt and cynicism. Help me to trust wholly in you and in your power to make all things, even me, new. Amen.

APRIL

DELIVERANCE IN DRY PLACES

Kenneth L. Samuel

He opened the rock, and water gushed out; it flowed through the desert like a river. From Psalm 105

LOCATION, LOCATION, LOCATION. It is the primary factor in determining the value of real estate, and for many, it is the primary determinant of contentment. If only we were in a better house, a better neighborhood or a better city and state. Or if only we were in a better place in regard to our career or our relationships.

So much of our lives seem to hinge on better placements. But the presence and provision of God are never subject to "better placements." In fact, God guided, nurtured, and fed Israel in the dry, desolate Sinai desert long before the Israelites even reached the desired place of the promised land. Amazing things happen in dry places: messiahs are born, hope is engendered, believers are refined, purposes are revealed, churches are renewed, rocks are opened up, and rivers flow through the desert.

PRAYER: Sovereign God, we thank you for your presence, your peace, and your provision in dry places. Thank you for allowing the rivers of your amazing grace to break through the rocks of our stubborn situation. Amen.

WHY ME?

Donna Schaper

Why are you cast down, O my soul? From Psalm 42

JIM CRAWFORD, THE RETIRED SENIOR PASTOR at Old South Church in Boston, was visiting a man in the hospital. The man was very angry that he had cancer and was not being healed of it. "Why me?" he kept saying. Crawford responded, "Why not you?" There is a turn in the process of suffering when we go from "Why me?" to "Why not me?" We tip. Elisabeth Kübler-Ross called it acceptance, at the end of all the anger and denial and bargaining. This coalescence, this shiver, is like a mountaintop experience, even though we may have it over our morning coffee.

You may also want to pray the great prayers of Psalm 42. Just say, "Deep is calling to deep, O God." Or just say, "God you are my rock." Or just say that you are panting for a stream.

Any of these sentences can tip you from the "Why me?" whining to "Why not me?" acceptance.

God rushes in to a slightly open heart, a door left ajar.

PRAYER: O God, when we suffer, we are without our diplomas, our résumés, our credit cards, our IDs. We are on our own. Teach us how to suffer as part of the human race and as your child. Amen.

VINEYARD

Quinn G. Caldwell

A man planted a vineyard, put a fence around it, dug a pit for the wine press, and built a watchtower; then he leased it to tenants and went to another country.
From Mark 12:1–12

JESUS TELLS THE AUTHORITIES A PARABLE: a man builds a vineyard, leases it out, and leaves. The tenants mismanage the vineyard pretty seriously. Jesus says that because of their mismanagement, destruction will come to them.

Very few doubt any longer that the earth's climate is changing, or that carbon put into the atmosphere by humans is the cause. There is no doubt that our mismanagement of God's vineyard is bringing destruction pretty fast. The only thing in doubt is whether the mismanagement, left unchecked, will destroy all the tenants, or only some of us. It is the most serious theological crisis of our day; if we don't get this one right, not much else will matter.

Want to learn what to do? Go to www.350.org. It's a group founded by UCC member Bill McKibben to draw attention to the climate crisis and organize us for solutions. The group gets it name because 350 parts per million is the maximum sustainable amount of carbon we can have in the atmosphere; right now, we're over 389. At 350.org, you can find out ways that you and your church can become involved.

The vineyard doesn't belong to us, it's in trouble, and it's our fault. What are you going to do about it?

PRAYER: Oh God, forgive our mismanagement and our hardheartedness. Grant that we might hear the prophets you place among us and act for the vineyard and for ourselves. Amen.

TIRED OF LEARNING THE HARD WAY

Lillian Daniel

Simpletons only learn the hard way, but the wise learn by listening. From Proverbs 21:11–16 TM

MOST OF US WOULD PREFER TO LEARN by listening, but if we're honest, most of us learn by messing up. Every deep lesson I have learned in life has come at a cost. It's only after kicking myself for my stupidity that the message registers. That really is learning the hard way.

But after I have learned the hard way, then, and only then, I will recall the wise words of people who wanted to teach me that very same lesson with some good advice. I should have listened to them. But I wasn't open to it at the time.

Maybe you have to learn the hard way, by messing up, before you can learn the wise way, by listening.

Or perhaps we are all learning both ways at the same time. When we make a mistake, we don't have to collapse and wallow in our own stupidity. We don't have to blame others. We don't have to remain simpletons. Instead we can learn by listening.

After a failure, we can listen to our own lives. We can listen for the Holy Spirit in the middle of the mess, and end up wise. Perhaps, after learning the hard way, we can listen to our own lives and learn the right way.

And that might just make us more open to listening to other people.

PRAYER: Stillspeaking God, could you adjust my lesson plan, so that I am spending more time listening and less time learning the hard way? Whom should I be listening to? Are you speaking to me through my own life? You have my attention. I'm really listening. Amen.

GLIMPSES OF THE FUTURE

Martin B. Copenhaver

I commend to you our sister Phoebe, a deacon of the church at Cenchreae, so that you may welcome her in the Lord as is fitting for the saints, and help her in whatever she may require from you. From Romans 16:1–16

SOMETIMES WE CAN GLIMPSE THE FUTURE through an individual. In some people, the future seems to arrive ahead of schedule.

In some of his letters, the Apostle Paul limited the role of women in the church. For instance, he wrote that women should be silent in church (which, you have to admit, is pretty limiting). But here, as Paul writes to the Romans, he commends a woman named Phoebe to them. She will soon be traveling to Rome, and Paul wants to make sure that she is properly received. He uses the title "deacon" (some translations render her title as "minister") in recognition of her authority. He then admonishes the members of the Roman church to do whatever she might need or ask. Whatever Paul may have thought of women's role in the church in general, in Phoebe he caught a glimpse of the future.

When my grandmother was fourteen years old, in the late 1800s, she told her Presbyterian minister that she felt called to the ministry. He informed her that she must be mistaken because God doesn't call women into the ministry. So my grandmother went in search of a denomination that would ordain her. She was ordained in 1902 in the Christian Church, a predecessor denomination of our United Church of Christ. I am proud that our United Church of Christ consistently seems to be able to catch early glimpses of the future.

PRAYER: Dear God, keep us open to the glimpses of the future, your future, that we see around us this day. Amen.

RABBLE

Quinn G. Caldwell

The rabble among them had a strong craving; and the Israelites also wept again, and said, "If only we had meat to eat!" From Numbers 11:1–9

THOSE WHO LEAD GROUPS OF PEOPLE, or who spend time in groups of people, know how just one person can have a huge impact on a gathering: Committee chairs know that a well-placed comment can change the course of a meeting for good or ill. Hosts know that a single party pooper or high-spirited guest can break or make an event. Any minister worth her salt has mastered the tricks of raising or lowering the energy in a room full of worshipers through voice and presence and, sometimes, sheer force of will.

In today's passage, the Israelites have begun their wanderings in the desert. God has provided them with manna, both delicious and nutritious. Apparently rather boring, though, at least for some. Some "rabble" begin to complain; soon everyone has joined in and the whole thing goes kaflooey. Before it's all over, God and Moses are snapping at each other, a whole new administrative system has to be set up, great piles of quails get slaughtered, and a plague sweeps through the camp. All because of those first complainers. A few bad apples . . .

What groups of people will you be a part of today? Will your presence make the party or break it, build it up or tear it down? What kind of group member will you choose to be?

PRAYER: God, guide me in every group in which I find myself today, and make me a force for the building up of your people wherever I gather with them. Amen.

THE THREAT OF CHANGE

Lillian Daniel

They seized Stephen and . . . produced false witnesses, who testified, "This fellow never stops speaking against this holy place and against the law. For we have heard him say that this Jesus of Nazareth will destroy this place and change the customs Moses handed down to us." From Acts 6:8–15 NIV

WHEN THEY REALLY WANTED TO GET PEOPLE MAD, they said that Stephen wanted to "change the customs Moses handed down to us." They knew how to get the religious crowd worked up. Stephen was in favor of change.

Stephen will end up being one of the famous martyrs of the church. He goes from here to make a long speech where he reinterprets old stories and offers a new way of thinking. He wanted them to see Jesus, but all they saw was red. They attacked this man with the face of an angel and stoned him to death.

There was an old joke around New England, where I began my ministry. How many Congregationalists does it take to change a light bulb? Three. One to change it and two to ask, "Well, what was wrong with the old one?"

We may not stone religious leaders for suggesting change any more, but we can still punish them. More than one ministry has ended over a new hymnal, a different worship style, or a new governance system. In his book *Promise and Peril,* on how congregations handle change, David Brubaker writes that congregations are most likely to go into conflict around changes in worship or governance, but a building project does not produce the same tension. Why is this?

In renovating buildings, we are dealing with changes in the concrete. But when we change our worship or our community life, it's very subjective and our emotions run high.

Still, that's no excuse for throwing stones. We're called to a higher standard.

PRAYER: When change leads to conflict in my spiritual home, let me be an instrument of your peace. Replace the human desire to win with the godly desire to understand. Amen.

THE "SWEETNESS" OF GOD

Ron Buford

How sweet are your words to my taste, sweeter than honey to my mouth. From Psalm 119:97–104

HAVE YOU EVER ENTERED A ROOM and noted the familiar sweet and pleasant smell of a perfume or cologne of a friend or lover? Sometimes you can almost taste it. Suddenly, your mind goes to happy and luscious memories. You rush to find your love.

So it can be with God.

The psalmist says this also happens by spending enough time with God — in prayer, Bible study, and contemplation. The smell, the feel, the aura, the taste of God's presence in instruction, confirmation, and unexpected calm, even in the midst of trouble, is unmistakable—even when we least expect it, and it is always right on time.

I can almost hear two of my favorite singers, Mahalia Jackson and George Beverly Shea, singing an old favorite gospel song, "I'd Rather Have Jesus."*

He's fairer than lilies in sweetest bloom
He's sweeter than honey right out of the comb
He's all that my hungering spirit needs;
I'd rather have Jesus and let Him lead
Refrain
Than to be the King of a vast domain
Or be held by sin's dread sway
Oh Lord, I'd rather have Jesus than anything
This old world can afford today.

*Words by Rhea F. Miller, 1922; tune by George Beverly Shea, 1929.

PRAYER: Gracious God, Thank you for the sweetness of your presence, lifting my head even amid difficult circumstances and changing situations. Yes! your presence is sweeter than honey! Amen!

What Tomorrow Will Bring

Anthony B. Robinson

You who say, "Today or tomorrow we will go to such and such a town and spend a year there, doing business and making money." Yet you do not even know what tomorrow will bring. What is your life? For you are a mist that appears for a little while and then vanishes. Instead, you ought to say, "If the Lord wishes, we will live and do this or that." From James 4:11–16

SOME TIME AGO, I moved to Toronto for a year to, as James puts it, "do business and make money." Not much money, as I was teaching at a seminary. I am trying to imagine how people might have heard it if every time during those months that I talked about these plans and changes, I had said, "If the Lord wills it," or "God willing," or "It's really in God's hands." I suspect I would have felt a little showy, overly pious, and maybe phony. Moreover, I imagine that a fair number of those with whom I spoke would have thought the same—that is, if they weren't wondering if I were in need of a psychiatric evaluation! We tend to think we're in charge, in control.

But however odd it may sound in the ears of a secular age, James strikes me as closer to the truth. Our illusions of control are just that: illusions. Maybe it's the people who think they are in charge of life that need the psychiatric evaluation or attitude adjustment? And life has a way of giving us those little evaluations, those attitude adjustments. Which is not to say that we shouldn't make plans or have our projects. We do and we should. And yet we don't, can't, know what tomorrow will bring. The only thing we can know for sure is that God's grace will uphold us, God's wisdom will guide us, and God's peace shall keep us. And knowing that is enough.

PRAYER: When you challenge my foolish idea that I am in charge, when you send your attitude adjustments, grant me grace to receive them graciously and learn that you are God, not I. Amen.

Forgiveness Is Bigger than We Are

Lillian Daniel

Let it be known to you therefore, my brothers, that through this man forgiveness of sins is proclaimed to you; by this Jesus everyone who believes is set free from all those sins from which you could not be freed by the law of Moses. From Acts 13:32–41

"WHY DO WE HAVE TO DO THE CONFESSION EVERY WEEK in church? It's such a downer." That's a question I hear periodically on a Sunday morning.

I'm an open-minded pastor, so I tell them we actually do not have to do it every Sunday. In fact, the first Sunday that comes up when they, and all the rest of the church members have done nothing wrong in the last week, we can skip it. But given that I am a church member who has yet to have a week, even a day, without sin, I suspect that the prayer of confession will be with us for a while.

The prayer of confession is more than admitting what we have done wrong, or what we have left undone. It is also when we receive forgiveness. Anyone who thinks this moment is a downer is not paying attention. This is the moment when, if we truly are sorry, we are granted new life in Christ. Mind you, this gift doesn't come our way because we were sorry. It is bigger than our own actions. Forgiveness in Christ comes to us as something we did not earn, but was earned for us on the cross. Laws and rules help us to live well, but divine forgiveness lets us soar into a new day, transformed.

PRAYER: Let me examine myself as you examine me, Lord Christ. Allow me to see the mistakes I have made so that I can learn from them, and to see the possibilities for my life that you have always held for me. Amen.

WATCH YOUR FEET

Martin B. Copenhaver

A man had two sons; he went to the first and said, "Son, go and work in the vineyard today." He answered, "I will not." But later he changed his mind and went. The father went to the second and said the same; and he answered, "I go, sir"; but he did not go. Which of the two did the will of his father? From Matthew 21:23–32

SAINT JEROME DESCRIBED THE PERSON OF FAITH as the one in whom the heart, the feet, and the mouth all agree. Or, to use an expression that is common in some church circles, "You can't just talk the talk, you've also got to walk the walk." We expect words and actions to be consistent.

In this parable, however, Jesus imagines two sons who are both inconsistent. One doesn't say all the right things, but does just what he is supposed to do. The other son says all the right things, but does nothing. Jesus is clear about which is preferable: he praises the one who walks the walk, even when he doesn't talk the talk.

Here Jesus is telling us something we may know already, but we still need to be reminded of on a regular basis. Words alone—even when they are all the right words—are not enough. In the end, it is actions that matter. After all, it is not a compliment to say of someone, "He is all talk and no action." But it is a high compliment, indeed, when it is said of someone, "She is a person of action and very few words."

As novelist and preacher Frederick Buechner observed, "If you want to know who you really are as distinct from who you like to think you are, keep an eye on where your feet take you."

Where are your feet taking you today?

PRAYER: Dear God, guide my feet today to where I need to be or to where I am needed. Amen.

Deep Calls to Deep

Kenneth L. Samuel

My soul is cast down within me; therefore I remember you from the land of Jordan and of Hermon, from Mount Mizar. Deep calls to deep at the thunder of your cataracts; all your waves and your billows have gone over me. From Psalm 42

FROM THE DARK DUNGEON OF A DEEP DISTRESS, the psalmist discovers something that persons who live only in the shallow plateaus of comfort and convenience may never know. The psalmist discovered that the profound depth of a person's distress causes that person to tap more deeply into the inner recesses of spirit and soul. In fact, it often takes a deep calamity to reveal to us that which is really at the core of our being.

Trouble, adversity, and trial show us who we really are by causing us to tap more deeply into the depths of energy, hope, and resilience that we never knew we had. Deep depression and deep disaster call us, beckon us and invite us to explore the depths of faith, hope, and resilience that are deeply embedded in the souls of all who cultivate faith in God. And the good news is that, like the psalmist, we can discover that our faith in God is much deeper than the disasters of our circumstance.

PRAYER: Dear God, in all our disappointments and disaster, help us to heed your call to explore more deeply the power and potential that you have placed in us. Amen.

APRIL 13

ARK

Quinn G. Caldwell

Make yourself an ark of cypress wood. From Genesis 6:5–22

NOAH'S ARK SCARES ME. It all just seems so precarious, you know? All the life on earth, every bit of viable DNA that still exists, is floating there, just one well-placed hoof-kick through a bulkhead or one escaped ember in the hay away from the end of all life forever. And only Noah and his family trying to keep it all going and alive.

Which isn't so different from the situation on this planet. Just one planet, only one, equipped by God for sustaining life as it floats a lonely path across the face of the void. Like the ark, carrying all the viable DNA in the solar system, maybe all the DNA in the whole galaxy, maybe all that there is in the entire universe. Precarious.

I believe that from time to time, God calls new Noahs to tell the rest of the family how to care for our ark, what to do to keep the life here safe and thriving. Among them: John James Audubon, John Muir, Aldo Leopold, Chico Mendes, Wendell Berry. Tomorrow is the birthday of another: Rachel Carson. I plan to celebrate it as a kind of ecological saint's day, reminding myself what she taught us and praying to live accordingly.

Why not spend today learning about these new Noahs and what God sent them to do for the ark? Why not spend today praying to see whether you might be the next one?

PRAYER: Dear God, all this life, all this life on just this one tiny planet. Show me what to do. Amen.

WHO DO YOU THINK YOU ARE, GOD?

Anthony B. Robinson

Three times in the year you shall hold a festival for me. . . . No one shall appear before me empty-handed. From Exodus 23:14–19

WHO EXACTLY DOES THIS GOD THINK HE OR SHE IS? "Three times in the year you shall hold a festival for me." Period. Just ordering, prescribing, demanding really, that three times a year we do this whether we feel like it or not, whether it's convenient or not. And, for good measure, "See that you don't come empty-handed." God in this passage sounds as sharp and direct as my grandmother, Victoria Moon Robinson. Though I was the apple of her eye, she was completely capable of setting me straight in no uncertain terms. When my words were those of a callow youth, she fixed me with the stern look of her craggy visage and said, "Mister, don't you ever think that you are any better than anyone else." Like the slap of a Zen master.

So often today, too often, we seem to construe God in ways that suggest that God's whole purpose in being is to serve us, to comfort us, to make us feel okay or peaceful or less stressed. God as a "Sleep Number Bed," adjustable to our own particular "comfort preference." God becomes another consumable, adjusted to fit our taste and needs. But what if that's not who God is at all? What if the point is not to adjust God to fit and serve us, but for us to be adjusted—transformed—to serve God? What if God is not safe but good? What if God is God?

PRAYER: Dear God, You alone are holy. You alone are worthy. You alone are God. Help me, this day, to take myself a little less seriously and take you a little more seriously. Amen.

WHICH JESUS?

Donna Schaper

Surely the Messiah does not come from Galilee, does he? From John 7:40–52

I VISITED TWO FRIENDS in their country homes last summer. During each visit, a hummingbird arrived. This summer I saw not one hummingbird at my own country place. One night I stayed on the deck for about two hours, thinking that if I sat still long enough, a hummer would come to the blooming bright red trumpet vine. None came. I made plans to sell the house. That same night I lay in the meadow and a shooting star zippered the night sky.

Finding Jesus is similar. We often look for his signs in the wrong places. We think he couldn't possibly come from Galilee, a place where we weren't looking. We figure our friends know how to find him in ways that we do not.

Jesus can be found. He is often found among the people without country homes, decks, or meadows. He is often found in an act of generosity instead of rivalry, an act of appreciation rather than envy. If you haven't checked out the night sky lately, give it a try.

PRAYER: For all the clues we miss, O God, we repent. Send us some more. We want to see Jesus. Amen.

THE MINISTRY OF RECONCILIATION

Kenneth L. Samuel

So if anyone is in Christ, there is a new creation: everything old has passed away; see, everything has become new! All this is from God, who reconciled us to himself through Christ, and has given us the ministry of reconciliation.
From 2 Corinthians 5:17–18

ACCORDING TO WHAT THE APOSTLE PAUL TELLS US in this passage of scripture, all of us who are in Christ have been changed—transformed into new creations. That's the good news! But there's also a challenge. Not only have we been changed through Christ, we are now called by Christ to be change agents in the world.

Not only have we been transformed by being brought back into right relationship with God through Christ, we are now commissioned by Christ to change the world by mediating disputes, promoting forgiveness, negotiating peace, and working to elevate the common good among all opposing persons and groups. This is what Christ has done for us, and this is what Christ calls us to do for others in this world. This is our ministry and our mandate. Let's get to it!

PRAYER: Gracious God, we pray that the change you have effected in us will be demonstrated in our commitment to change enemies into allies, factions into families, and warfare into peace, through Christ, our Eternal Reconciler. Amen.

A Respected Elder

Anthony B. Robinson

When they heard this, they were enraged and wanted to kill them. But a Pharisee in the council named Gamaliel, a teacher of the law, respected by the people, stood up and ordered the men to be put outside for a short time. From Acts 5:33–42

DO YOU HAVE WISE AND RESPECTED ELDERS IN YOUR LIFE? Who are they? What are their qualities?

Gamaliel was a respected elder in the Jewish community. When tempers flared, Gamaliel stood up and spoke. He told the people to calm down. If this new Jesus thing was not from God it would die out of its own accord. But if it were of God, they wouldn't want to find themselves opposing God. People listened to Gamaliel.

Gamaliel had three important qualities. He had perspective. He could recall examples and experiences from the past that give perspective in the present. Gamaliel also had a spirit of reverence and of humility. He wondered aloud how God was at work in what was going on and what was facing the people. God needed to be revered and respected. And finally Gamaliel had courage. He didn't sit silent. He got to his feet and spoke. Moreover, he spoke in ways that challenged the anger boiling and building around him.

Who are the wise elders in your life? In your congregation? In our nation? What makes them wise and respected? Are you listening to them? Are we?

PRAYER: Holy One, I thank you for the wise elders in my life; some whom you've called home to you (name names); some (name names) with us now. Amen.

FINDING GOD IN ALL THE WRONG PLACES

Martin B. Copenhaver

Do not follow other gods, any of the gods of the peoples who are all around you. From Deuteronomy 6:10–25

A CARTOON IN A MAGAZINE depicts a man and a woman leaving worship. The sign outside the church announces that the sermon topic for the day was the Ten Commandments. The man says, "Well, at least I haven't made any graven images lately."

The sad truth is, if the man in the cartoon is anything like us, he *has* made graven images—that is, idols, false gods.

Today, no longer are we tempted to worship gods by the name of Zeus or Aphrodite or Apollo. Now we are wooed by gods named Education or Success or Family or Money.

Paul Tillich, an influential theologian of the last century, defined God as a person's "ultimate concern." If you want to know what your ultimate concern is—or, to put it another way, if you want to know what your idols are—ask yourself these questions: Where is your ultimate loyalty? What do you consistently make time for? In what have you put your trust? Where can you be most deeply threatened?

No one ever says, "I'm going to worship an idol now." Instead, idolatry happens when we invest our fullest energy and our ultimate allegiance in those things—perhaps even good things—that are not ultimate. And if we worship idols, instead of the one true God, we will be ultimately disappointed. There is only one God worthy of our worship.

PRAYER: O God, the one true God, guide my actions and my thoughts this day so that I will not look for you in all the wrong places. Amen.

GRACE COMES FIRST

Anthony B. Robinson

Now John's disciples and the Pharisees were fasting; and the people came and said to him, "Why do John's disciples and the disciples of the Pharisees fast, but your disciples do not fast?" Jesus said to them, "The wedding guests cannot fast while the bridegroom is with them, can they?" From Mark 2:18–22

SOMETIMES WE GET THE IDEA, and give it to others, that religion is mainly about all the things you and I must do in order to draw a distant God to our side or to get on God's good side. Like the disciples in this passage from John and the Pharisees who were hard at their fasting and puzzled that Jesus' disciples weren't, we imagine that if we pray in the correct way, or fast really well, or work on behalf of all the right causes, then God will love us and take our side.

So we come up with endless programs, projects, and practices to do religion better. Church begins to seem as busy and frenetic as a major corporation. "Stop it!" says Jesus. "Stop it, right this minute! You don't need to win God to your side or complete a list of merit badges to get on God's good side. God has taken your side already." In Jesus, God has drawn near to you and will never abandon you. The bridegroom is here and the feast of life is in progress. Trust this and live! Live gratefully, joyfully, boldly, for God has taken your side in Christ and nothing in all creation shall undo that.

PRAYER: O Lord Jesus, put me in touch with the joy of your presence, mercy, and grace, and let it disturb me to life. Amen.

CHURCH FIGHTS

Quinn G. Caldwell

I urge Euodia and I urge Syntyche to be of the same mind in the Lord. Yes, and I ask you also, my loyal companion, help these women, for they have struggled beside me in the work of the gospel. From Philippians 4:1–9

THIS PASSAGE REMINDS US that church fights have been around since the beginning; they probably always will be, at least until Jesus returns to make all things new. Sometimes profound, often petty, they're usually about some hurt largely unrelated to what everybody thinks they're about. Left untended, they can escalate until they tear a church apart.

The next time a fight erupts in your church, ask yourself not how to help the "right" side win, but how this conflict might become a way to build the church up, and how you can help it to do so.

PRAYER: God, save us from avoiding every conflict and from thinking that the point of our fights is simply to win. Grant that our fights might be a way to build up your church. Amen.

THE COST OF A BAD TEMPER

Lillian Daniel

Then Moses turned and went down from the mountain, carrying the two tablets of the covenant in his hands, tablets that were written on both sides, written on the front and on the back . . . As soon as he came near the camp and saw the calf and the dancing, Moses' anger burned hot, and he threw the tablets from his hands and broke them at the foot of the mountain. He took the calf that they had made, burned it with fire, ground it to powder, scattered it on the water, and made the Israelites drink it. From Exodus 32:15–35

WHEN I WAS FIVE YEARS OLD, my mother asked me who my favorite person in the Bible was. I told her it was Moses. She asked me why, but I refused to tell her. "Was it because you remember the story of how as a baby he was put in a basket and sent down the river?" I shook my head. "Was it because he led his people out of slavery and parted the Red Sea?" No, that wasn't it.

Finally I confessed. "Moses is my favorite, because Moses got to be bad."

From a child's perspective, Moses got to do the very things I was being told not to do. He got to come down from the mountain and have a big temper tantrum. He got to throw his things and break them. And then he got to break his brother's new toy, too. Moses got to be very bad, and as a child, I was envious. As an adult, I see the story differently. I know the damage that violent adult temper tantrums can do. And Moses learned that too. Yes, the people should not have worshiped a golden calf, but Moses came to deeply regret breaking the tablets that contained God's precious Ten Commandments. Initially, Moses was right, but his violent reaction was wrong. That's the way losing your temper works. In losing your temper, you switch from the winner's side to the loser's.

PRAYER: Loving God, when I am angry but right, help me to rein in my temper, so that my righteousness will serve you, and not the devil. Amen.

CALLING ON GOD TO BE GOD

Anthony B. Robinson

But I will not go up among you. From Exodus 33:1–6

WHILE MOSES WAS UP ON MT. SINAI counseling with God, the people got a little anxious. They talked Aaron, whom Moses left in charge, into letting them make a golden calf to worship and dance around before busting out in general debauchery. In today's reading, God, having seen all this, tells Moses that he is done with this stiff-necked people. "That's it, I'm outta here," God tells Moses. "You go on, take them to the promised land, have a good time, but I'm done."

If you're the parent of a four-year-old, or a school teacher, or a pastor, or any of a number of things that have you working with people, I'll bet you may be able to relate to how God is feeling here.

But then, Moses does a most remarkable thing. In the subsequent scene in the story (33: 12–17), Moses calls God to account. Moses says to God, "Consider that this nation is your people." The unspoken here, in case you missed it, is "They aren't my people. This wasn't my idea. Remember that burning bush thing?" Moses calls upon God to be God. An incredibly courageous thing to do. Do you and I have the chutzpah, and the faith, to call on God to be God for us?

PRAYER: Sovereign God, we truly understand that there are times you wish to give up on us. Don't do it. We need you. Now more than ever. Come, be God here and now today in my life and in our church. Amen.

THE LITTLE BOOK THAT JUST WON'T BEHAVE

Martin B. Copenhaver

How beautiful you are, my love, how very beautiful! Your eyes are doves behind your veil . . . Your two breasts are like two fawns, twins of a gazelle, that feed among the lilies. From Song of Solomon 4:1–8

OKAY, IF YOU READ THE FULL PASSAGE from Song of Solomon—or, better yet, the whole book—don't be surprised if your computer screen steams up a bit. Song of Solomon is an ode to the joys of erotic love. It is so giddy with the intoxicating charms of sensual love that, like young lovers kissing in a public place, it seems not to care who else is around or what they might think of such carrying on. Song of Solomon is composed of the love songs sung by a man and a woman who can only see each other.

But see each other they do. The lovers linger over every inch of each other in voluptuous celebration, savoring all the physical characteristics of the beloved.

Those who are aware of the ways our culture can make an idol of romantic love and celebrate lust (which is romance's cruder expression) may be uncomfortable with Song of Solomon. But I am grateful that it made its way into our scripture. Were it not for this little book that just won't behave, we might conclude that we have to choose between a culture that understands only romance and a faith that leaves no room for romance. The presence of Song of Solomon in the Bible reminds us that we can have God, all the higher expressions of love, and still have our romance too.

PRAYER: Dear God, you have created us in such a way that, to be in love with someone is to find our whole being tied up with the beloved, to want to be wherever the beloved is, to want only good things for him or her. Thank you that, in such love, we can catch a glimpse of the love you have for each of us. Amen.

AWESOME

William C. Green

And everyone who sought the LORD would go out to the tent of meeting, which was outside the camp. From Exodus 33:7–11

AS A PASTOR I never liked being told by church members that they didn't need to attend church every Sunday because they could find God on the golf course, or in the state park, or quietly reading the Sunday newspaper at home. There's nothing in the Bible about golf courses, state parks, or Sunday papers. But there's much about how worship and closeness to God happen—away from daily life and in the midst of it; from a tent in the wilderness "outside the camp" to a temple in the heart of the city.

In any case, what precedes heartfelt faith is reverence and awe. We can domesticate God. Our routines can limit God to "more of the same": more of the same worship (more of the same golf!), more of what we're used to experiencing all the time, more of the same sense of ourselves and others.

G. K. Chesterton said, "The world will never starve for wonder, only for want of wonder." The real issue is not how frequently we attend church. What counts is how well we can move "outside the camp" of our own ideas and expectations and learn to love, not disregard or fear, what lies beyond our control. God's love is beyond anything we can get used to. It's awesome, making our own lives, with all their chasms and precipices, Grand Canyons of grace and beauty.

PRAYER: Almighty God, may we know your awesome love in the ways we understand ourselves and worship you. Amen.

THE KNOWN GOD

Anthony B. Robinson

For as I went through the city and looked carefully at the objects of your worship, I found among them an altar with the inscription, "To an unknown god." What therefore you worship as unknown, this I proclaim to you. From Acts 17:16–32

AS PAUL MADE HIS WAY through the sophisticated city of Athens he noticed that there were all sorts of religions, gods, and spiritualities. It was a veritable spiritual smorgasbord, perhaps much like our own time. Just for good measure one shrine there in Athens bore the words, "To an unknown god." Undaunted Paul stood up and declared boldly, "What you worship as unknown, this I proclaim to you." To be sure, there is a place for admitting that we don't comprehend God fully or completely. God remains, in some measure, unknown and beyond our capacity as human beings to fully grasp or understand. But as Christians it is important not to stop there, simply saying "who knows?" God, whom we cannot fully know, has yet revealed God's very self, God's will and God's way, in Jesus Christ. At its best the church has always had the courage, with Paul, to boldly proclaim God's revelation in Christ crucified and Christ raised. We have not been left in the dark. A light shines forth in the darkness. Remember that.

PRAYER: I thank you, Holy One, that you have not left us unto ourselves alone, but that in Jesus Christ you have searched for us and found us. Amen.

WORK THAT IS NOT IN VAIN

Kenneth L. Samuel

The Israelites had done all the work just as the LORD had commanded Moses. Moses inspected the work and saw that they had done it just as the LORD had commanded. So Moses blessed them. Exodus 39:42–43

THE "WORK ETHIC" IN AMERICA is suffering because many of us who work long, hard hours on a daily basis feel unappreciated, overwhelmed and undercompensated. So many of our busy work days end in nothing but fatigue and frustration.

When the children of Israel began the work of building a tabernacle to the glory of God in the wilderness of the Sinai desert, they knew that the work would be painstakingly meticulous and arduous. Work in a dry, desert context is always a challenge. Nonetheless, the Israelites executed their task with precision and completed their work with excellence. They were compensated not with any special bonuses or tributes, but with the blessing of God through Moses. And at the end of the day, if the aim of our work is not God's favor and sanction, are we not laboring in vain?

PRAYER: God, help us never to forget that it is you who call us to work, and it is you that we most seek to please. Beyond material compensation and social recognition, we really want to hear you say, "Well done, my good and faithful servant." Amen.

S N E A K Y   R É S U M É S

Donna Schaper

God opposes the proud but gives grace to the humble. From James 4:4–10

HAVE YOU EVER NOTICED YOURSELF sneak yourself into a conversation, sneakily? You don't really say what you are doing, you just do it. "When I was in Italy . . ." Then you go on to relate to the question of how crusty the whole wheat bread is. You are not really joining the conversation about the bread. You are doing what Carl Jung says we all, almost always, do. He says we "smuggle" our biography into everything.

We not only smuggle ourselves into the conversation; we also often are so blinded by the presuppositions of our class, race, church, parents, colleges that we don't really think. We simply react. That by itself would not be such a problem, if we would refuse to be proud about it. Nor would smuggling of our résumés into conversation be a big problem if we weren't proud about it.

Self-satisfaction is a real problem. We can learn instead to be humble about our blinders. We can also learn to talk about the bread and openly "brag" about how it is better in Italy. We can especially brag if we keep a smile on our face and a joke in our heart about how great we really aren't.

PRAYER: O God, grant us a way to see that we don't have to prove ourselves with you. Let us enjoy grace and forswear pride. Amen.

I'M NOT YOUR SISTER EDNA

Christina Villa

Now there came a famine throughout Egypt and Canaan, and great suffering, and our ancestors could find no food. From Acts 7:9–16

WHEN I WAS IN HIGH SCHOOL, I had a summer job in a convalescent home, washing, dressing, and feeding old people who talked nonstop about things that happened fifty or sixty years ago as if they were going on that very day. I just went along with them; I was seventeen and not planning on being old. Now that I am older, I have even older relatives coming out with details from our family's past that I've never heard— pieces of missing information that shed new and sometimes startling light on a family history I thought I knew. This can be entertaining, but it also reminds me that I have a history that started before I was born. The stories of how our ancestors managed to make their way through history tell us how we got here. In particular, knowing of the hardships survived by past generations of our own family makes it more difficult to take our own existence for granted, or to fritter it away.

We are each part of a long line of people—whether we know a lot or a little or nothing at all about them. Those long-forgotten realities are shaping our days and experiences while we walk around thinking we're doing that all by ourselves. Maybe those old people in the convalescent home weren't as out of it as I thought when they looked straight at me and addressed me as their sister Edna.

PRAYER: Remind me of how I am never really alone and that you know every single one of those who got me here. Amen.

LOVE AND WORRY

Lillian Daniel

As they were gathering in Galilee, Jesus said to them, "The Son of Man is going to be betrayed into human hands, and they will kill him, and on the third day he will be raised." And they were greatly distressed. From Matthew 17:22–27

LOVE AND WORRY GO HAND IN HAND. You can't love someone and not worry. Worry can turn the lights on love. Sleepless and worried in the middle of the night, you suddenly realize how much that person means to you.

"Don't worry," we say to each other, but what we may really mean is, "Stop talking. I'm tired of this." Worry is messy, and hard to listen to—especially when the person someone is worried about is you.

So isn't it good to know that the disciples worried too? They worried about Jesus' plans. They were really distressed. The miracle-working Son of God had people who worried about him.

As a child taking off for fun, I would always exit to a chorus of parental questions and instructions. "When will you be home?" "Don't forget your jacket. It's cold out." "Call as soon as you get there."

And I would roll my eyes and say, "Don't worry." I felt immortal. Their concerns seemed ridiculous.

But now, I am the one at the door, calling out last minute worries into a harsh world. "Don't worry," they tell me, but still, I do.

Worry is the cranky friend who shows up uninvited, to hold love's hand in the dark.

PRAYER: Dear God, you worry over us as a mother hen broods over her chicks. Take our worries, turn them into prayers, and let them soar to the heavens where you can hold them for us. Amen.

ON TO JERUSALEM

Anthony B. Robinson

A prophet named Agabus came down from Judea. He . . . took Paul's belt, bound his own feet and hands with it, and said, "Thus says the Holy Spirit, 'This is the way the Jews in Jerusalem will bind the man who owns this belt . . . .'" From Acts 21:21–40

PAUL WAS MAKING A KIND OF FAREWELL TOUR en route to Jerusalem. He knew, and so apparently did everyone else, that he would not be well-received in Jerusalem. To go there would be to put himself in danger. Why go?

All along the way, different warning signs flashed one after another. Here, some guy named Agabus tied himself up, hand and foot, to show Paul what lay ahead for him in Jerusalem. Despite Agabus's object lesson, Paul was determined to go.

Have you ever known someone like that? I know a young woman who was determined to go and work among the poor in the most violent city in the world, Johannesburg. I read of a man who insisted on seeking survivors in the wreckage of New York's Twin Towers, though one would collapse upon him. I know quite a number of people who keep on going places that aren't easy to go to, and are even in some ways dangerous for them. Why go? Because they have been called. Called to serve. Called to give. Called to go.

In the end, God does not care most of all about our safety or about our comfort. God cares that we live lives that matter, that we live our lives for Christ's sake. "For those who want to save their life will lose it, and those who lose their life for my sake, and the sake of the gospel, will save it." (Mark 8:35)

PRAYER: May I live this day so as to lose myself in Christ and his way, and so be truly found. Amen.

MAY

YOUR FAVORITE HYMN

Quinn G. Caldwell

Now therefore write this song, and teach it to the Israelites; put it in their mouths, in order that this song may be a witness for me. From Deuteronomy 31:14–22

WHAT'S YOUR FAVORITE HYMN? Is it one of the grand old Protestant chestnuts about God's majesty, like "A Mighty Fortress Is Our God"? A gift from the Catholic tradition about God's tender love, like "Here I Am, Lord"? One of the sweet old-time songs of personal piety, like "In the Garden"? Or something else?

Why is it your favorite? How did you learn it? Who taught it to you? What do you feel, and what do you know about God when you sing it?

My church recently had a hymn-sing Sunday. We voted for our faves ahead of time, and then we sang sixteen of the top vote-getters during that Sunday's service. I've never seen my congregation so smiley before. We grinned and grinned and just generally looked like . . . well, like we'd received some really good news.

Our hymns are some of the most powerful ways we have of teaching the truths of God, for they both tell us our faith and make us feel it as well. Try—just try—singing "Silent Night" without having any feelings while you sing. See? Impossible.

So the next time you're faced with a crisis of faith, when you're overcome by doubt or apathy, misery or unrighteous anger, fear, or even just boredom, try singing your favorite hymn. It won't solve every problem, but it'll be a start.

PRAYER: Praise God from whom all blessings flow. Praise God, all creatures here below. Praise God above, ye heavenly host. Creator, Christ, and Holy Ghost. Amen.

NO TRIFLING MATTER

Anthony B. Robinson

Take to heart all the words that I am giving. . . . This is no trifling matter for you, but rather your very life. From Deuteronomy 32:44–47

So there I was leading a wedding rehearsal on a warm and lovely August evening when I would much preferred to have been almost anywhere else. My co-officiant was an ancient African American pastor who had been wheeled into the chancel and appeared to be somewhat less than fully present. There were the beautiful young men and young women, all sexy and smart, telling jokes, high-fiving one another, and getting ready to go off to party as soon as the rehearsal ended. I played along, cracking jokes, being flip, generally encouraging them to believe that this was no big deal.

Suddenly, the old pastor, who I thought had dozed off, stirred to life in his wheelchair. In a wonderfully deep, resonant voice he growled, "This is *holy* matrimony." Those four words seemed to last about three minutes. Whether he said anymore or not, I can't recall, but spoken or unspoken the message was plain: "This has to do with God. Pay attention." I suppose the wedding party was chastened—they certainly snapped to attention. But mostly what I remember was that I was chastened, reminded that this was "No trifling matter, but rather your life." It's so easy to turn most anything into a game, to be cool, cynical, flip, and . . . dead.

PRAYER: Save me, God, from being cool and cynical and too smart by half. You have given us your truth, your way, your life that we may not lose our own. Help me heed your word and way. Amen.

WHEN NEIGHBORS ARE TOUGH TO LOVE

Lillian Daniel

"Teacher, which commandment in the law is the greatest?" [Jesus] said to him, "'You shall love the Lord your God with all your heart, and with all your soul, and with all your mind.' This is the greatest and first commandment. And a second is like it: 'You shall love your neighbor as yourself.'" From Matthew 22:34–46

I HAD A GRANDMOTHER WHO HATED HER NEIGHBORS so much that whenever she was in her yard, she would pretend to be calling out to the birds, but in a high-pitched voice she was shrieking, "Tacky, tacky neighbors." They would get mad, but she would always claim it was a legitimate yet rare bird call.

The questioner probably expected Jesus to answer with the first commandment. It was a commandment that was already well-known to the Jewish people. But Jesus didn't stop there. He added the part about loving your neighbor, and said it is "like it," in other words, just as important.

When we are worshiping, we are loving God. But it's hard to keep that going out there in the world, where people abuse us, take advantage of us or just plain annoy us.

Notice that Jesus did not say that we needed to love our friends or our family members. He deliberately chose neighbors—that group of people that we do not get to choose. You could translate that into your own life, and perhaps include as neighbors your coworkers, the other people in your classroom, or the other folks on the church committee. The point here is that we are called to love the people we get plunked down next to. And by doing that, we love God.

PRAYER: Give me the grace to love my neighbor. In loving the person who is hard to love, I'll probably encounter you, Jesus, because those are the people you stay in close touch with. Amen.

LET EVENING COME

Ron Buford

When [Saul] had come to Jerusalem, he attempted to join the disciples; and they were all afraid of him, for they did not believe that he was a disciple. From Acts 9:19–35

THE DISCIPLES WERE SKEPTICAL about Saul's conversion from persecutor to preacher and wanted to exclude him. They try to play it safe. But Barnabas advocates with the apostles on Saul's behalf to grow the circle wider. As a result, Peter ventures out to different kinds of people—even amid danger.

Sometimes it's easier to close ourselves off in fear, isn't it? Physical or emotional problems, work, finances, growing older—all challenge us. Sometimes we cut ourselves off from life trying to save it. Our world becomes smaller.

Is playing it safe worth it?

Perhaps Peter thought of Jesus' words as he left Jerusalem's inner sanctum: "Whoever would save his life, must risk losing it for my sake and the sake of the gospel." Now older and weaker, giving way to the new ways of Paul, he travels to Lydda and finds a paralyzed man, Aeneas. "Peter said to him, 'Aeneas, Jesus Christ heals you; get up and make your bed!' Immediately Aeneas got up. All the residents of Lydda and Sharon turned to the Lord."

Like Peter, like Aeneas, though life is changing, you're not through. Get up! Make your bed! Get out! Embrace life! Live in awe of the Still-speaking God who still gives life, protects, and maximizes joy into old age. And if we fall, let us fall moving forward, living in awe of God's goodness and mercy, filled with hopeful expectation, in the comfort of the Holy Spirit.

PRAYER: Gracious God, let evening come. I am not afraid. I've taken off my watch . . . for today. And when tomorrow comes, whether I see it here or over there, let's make it a blast! Amen.

Getting the Right Law Right

Donna Schaper

Mercy triumphs over judgment. From James 2:8–13

WHOM DOES GOD LOVE MORE: an industrious sinner or a lazy saint? What happens if we do the right thing for the wrong reason or the wrong thing for the right reason? In other words, how does any mortal ever know if he or she is doing the right thing, especially if we have to do the right thing for the right reasons? Thank God the writer of James helps us out. When we wonder about immigration laws, mercy is to triumph over judgment. When women broke the law to give each other contraception in the 1920s, mercy was to triumph over judgment. And what is judgment? It is getting as close to the right and legal thing as possible. When we privilege mercy, we do not disallow judgment. We just make sure mercy is an inch ahead of it in our decision-making.

Peggy Guggenheim, when asked how many husbands she had had, responded, "You mean my own or others'?" Guggenheim didn't understand James. She didn't understand the importance of keeping the commandments *and* going above and around them, from time to time. Moral decisions will never be easy. They will always be important. Real people are involved, in adultery, in immigration, in abortion, and more. Mercy is what matters.

PRAYER: O God, give us large enough hearts to privilege mercy over judgment, even when we are not sure of what is right. Amen.

SOMETHING BEAUTIFUL

William C. Green

Moses did not know that the skin of his face shone because he had been talking with God. From Exodus 34:29–35

IN THE EARLY DAYS OF C-SPAN the camera would often pan on dead space as congressional sessions or panel discussions ended. People would be seen endlessly milling about. One Sunday afternoon this happened before the performance of a community choir in Atlanta. I wondered what was about to take place as I stared at a slowly filling auditorium and an empty platform up front. Then the choir members started arriving. They obviously came from all walks of life. Some were attractive, others less so. Some looked depressed, others were upbeat and smiling. Some pushed ahead to their place on the platform, others lingered.

Then the conductor arrived and signaled for everyone to get ready for the performance. The eyes of choir members fixed on him. The music began. It was Randall Thompson's "Alleluia." The appearance and demeanor of all the choir members visibly changed. Whatever their previous states of mind it was clear that now something very special was happening. And their faces, like Moses's, literally shone. For a moment they were caught up in something that was a reminder that there is far more to life than business as usual and our own personal feelings and problems.

So with our own relationship with God. We may not often experience the equivalent of Thompson's "Alleluia." But neither is this reserved for some spiritual elite. It's there for us, too, when we take time for something beautiful.

PRAYER: Gracious God, enlarge our outlook on life with the beauty of your creation. Amen.

SAY, "THANK YOU."

Martin B. Copenhaver

O give thanks to the LORD, for he is good; for his steadfast love endures forever.
From Psalm 107

ON HALLOWEEN, when young trick-or-treaters come to our door and dip their hands into a big bowl of Butterfinger bars (because they are my favorite and I am hoping for leftovers), the adult accompanying them will almost surely remind them, "Say, 'Thank you.'" And the young voices will echo, "Thank you." It is something of a Halloween litany.

Children need to be reminded to offer thanks because no one is born grateful. Thankfulness does not come naturally to us and sometimes it does not come at all. Rather, thankfulness must be nurtured.

At almost every turn, the authors of the Psalms not only invite, but also demand that we offer our thanks to God. They understand the irony that it is by continually offering thanks that we can come to be thankful. And, obviously, children are not the only ones whose thanks need to be prompted.

So, day in and day out, in and out of season, offer thanks, perhaps at first to get the feel of it and then, only in time, because you feel it. Likewise, go to worship to offer thanks to God so that you might be nurtured in the ways of thankfulness. Sometimes words of thanks need to be on our lips before, by some slow and largely imperceptible process, they can take up residence in our hearts. As Millard Fuller once observed, "More people act themselves into a new way of thinking than think themselves into a new way of acting." And so it can be when we offer thanks.

PRAYER: Thank you, God. Thank you, thank you, thank you. Amen.

LETTING GO

Donna Schaper

Woe to you . . . for you lock people out of . . . heaven . . . and when others are going in, you stop them. From Matthew 23:13–28

THE UNIQUE IDEA IN ALL OF CHRISTIANITY is that heaven is on earth. Heaven is not above earth or over earth or opposite earth but *on* earth. Later is now. Heaven is earth. Spirit is body. There are no separations here—only those that our minds create. Many of us are still living in the idea of growth as being heavenly. The average human being needs four acres for food and bodily support. The average American uses twenty-four. Whenever we use more, we are taking food from others—particularly the unborn. Others like the idea of sustainability, but it is often the bargaining position of one who says to God, OK, I won't take any more, but could I hang on to what I have? That bargain means woe for the world's people as well. There is a third option, that of regeneration, of dying enough to live. Of letting go in order to have. Of really changing, from our metaphors on up to our behavior. Letting go of this world and its way means we open ourselves to the new. Otherwise woe is woe and it is ours.

PRAYER: Help us, O God, to see heaven on earth. Amen.

FINDING THE RIGHT WORDS

Ron Buford

If anyone says to you, "Why are you doing this?" just say this, "The Lord needs it and will send it back here immediately." From Mark 11:1–11

REV. DR. MARTIN LUTHER KING WENT to his first bus boycott rally not knowing what to say, and afraid. But God gave King the right words for the future direction of a people.

Rev. Thomas H. Dorsey, while preaching at a revival, got word that his wife had died in childbirth. Within minutes he was told that their newborn baby also died. With tears streaming, the right words came—words that have since lifted the hearts of millions "Precious Lord, take my hand. Lead me on. Let me stand. I am tired. I am weak, I am worn. Through the storms through the night. Lead me on to the light. Take my hand, Precious Lord. Lead me on." The disciples planned a processional to mock Caesar, who typically came into the city on a powerful horse, with palm branches and crowds shouting Hosanna. Just so, Jesus' disciples, with no armies or powerful horses at their command, asked some villagers to lend them a colt. That colt was a probably a precious commodity, not easily lent out, but Jesus gave them the right words.

And Jesus riding that colt became the centerpiece of celebration and political mockery, remembered for two thousand years: a celebration of God's realm of justice.

PRAYER: Gracious God, please give me the right words to say today. Keep me from saying harmful words that do not build love and trust between me and the one or ones I love. Please give me words that help many people, or maybe . . . just one. Amen.

Wanting to Believe

William C. Green

God's word . . . at work in you believers. From 1 Thessalonians 2:9–13

WE BELIEVE IN TOLERANCE AND RESPECT for views and traditions not our own. Today as in the early days of Christianity, pluralism is a reality; for us it has become a value as well. But in those early days, this reality consisted mostly of different beliefs and practices that all focused on Augustus Caesar as the supreme benefactor. Support for the church threatened Roman authority.

Paul repeatedly mentions the Holy Spirit in his letters—"God's word at work in you believers"—as a source of inspiration in the face of trouble. This power enables believers to overcome fear and find hope realistically and confidently. In our own ways today, by looking to God and no longer, as Waylon Jennings sang, "looking for love in all the wrong places, looking for love in too many faces," we become freer and more hopeful, less anxious and needy. This is what God's power makes possible—God's power, not ours, and beyond anything we believe possible.

We're far from the early Christians, but we, too, get scared and doubtful. I myself speak of divine power at work in us "not because I believe it, but because I want to believe it," as my pastor, Shawnthea Monroe, puts it. "I want to believe in God's presence, reliability, and generosity . . . I'm working on it . . . that's why we go to church. We are on our way to believing it."

PRAYER: Almighty God, may I keep on the way to believing that your power is at work in me. Amen.

ABUNDANCE OR SCARCITY?

Martin B. Copenhaver

Your wife will be like a fruitful vine within your house; your children will be like olive shoots around your table. From Psalm 128

SO MUCH OF OUR SCRIPTURE is a celebration of abundance. The first chapters of Genesis are a song of praise for God's generosity. With each act of creation, the divine refrain is, "It is good, it is good, it is very good." And it pictures the Creator saying, "Be fruitful and multiply."

Many of the Psalms, including the one for today, survey creation and catalogue this abundance in loving detail and with joyful thanksgiving.

Then, in the Gospels, Jesus multiplies loaves and fishes so that there is more than enough for everyone. At a wedding feast he turns water into wine, and more wine than could be consumed at a dozen weddings. These highly symbolic stories speak of God's abundance. There is enough, there is more than enough.

That's the biblical narrative. But the narrative by which we are tempted to live is another story entirely, a story of scarcity, where there is never enough. In fact, we are tempted to define enough as, "always something more than I have now."

In spite of all that has happened in recent months, we still live in the most prosperous country in the history of the world.

Do you live out of a sense of abundance or scarcity? That may be an economic question, but certainly it is a faith question.

PRAYER: O God, when I count your blessings, they are numberless as the sands, so I confess that I don't always get very far with my counting. So I simply thank you for sharing your abundance with me. Amen.

You Can Do It

Christina Villa

The manna ceased on the day they ate the produce of the land, and the Israelites no longer had manna; they ate the crops of the land of Canaan that year. From Joshua 5:10–12

IN THE PROMISED LAND, it turns out, there's no free lunch from heaven. God made manna rain down on the people just long enough to tide them over till they got to a place where they could do their part to provide for themselves. God gave the fertile land, and the people would now do the gathering, sowing, reaping, and all the rest to bring crops out of the ground and onto the table.

Do you remember having someone help you learn to ride a bike, holding on and running alongside until suddenly you realize they've let go and you are, incredibly, riding a bike all by yourself? The parent holds on until it's clear that the wobbly little rider has figured out the pedaling part and found his or her balance. Usually, children don't tell the parent to let go—they don't realize they can do it alone. But the parent knows, and lets go, and gives the child one of the best gifts of childhood: the exhilarating sense of pride, freedom, and accomplishment that comes with knowing you can now ride down to the corner all by yourself.

Are you waiting for manna from heaven to solve your problems? Are there challenges holding you back in life because you don't realize you can handle them? God is like the parent holding the bicycle. God has given you what you need to survive and thrive. And God knows when to let you go, even if you don't feel ready.

PRAYER: Remind me that I can ride down to the corner all by myself. Amen.

Always a Bridesmaid . . . Always

Lillian Daniel

Then the kingdom of heaven will be like this. Ten bridesmaids took their lamps and went to meet the bridegroom. Five of them were foolish, and five were wise. When the foolish took their lamps, they took no oil with them; but the wise took flasks of oil with their lamps. From Matthew 25:1–13

MOST BRIDESMAIDS WORRY A BIT about being foolish. It is easy for a grown woman to feel sheepish dressed in something she might have worn to her senior prom. But wedding attendants matter. They symbolize that this is not an event for two, but for many. The couple will need their friends and families to stand up with them through the sickness and health of the marriage, and the richer and poorer of the relationship.

In this gospel reading, half the bridesmaids think ahead about what the couple might need and bring extra fuel. This day's festivities are just the beginning. These bridesmaids are there to offer support for the long haul.

The other five bridesmaids do not bring extra oil for their lamps. They are living in the moment. (Maybe they even like their dresses. Well, I've heard it can happen.) They will be caught without enough fuel to support the couple after the big day.

In the excitement of a wedding, the thoughtful, prepared bridesmaids (and groomsmen) may be the most overlooked wedding presents. They look out ahead of the couple and provide fuel for a long, loving marriage. Couples don't do it alone. They stumble into the future, by the grace of God, getting help from a whole cast of characters, some of whom loved them enough to wear a funny-looking dress.

PRAYER: Dear God, let me never forget to pray for the people whose weddings I have attended. Open my heart to the needs of my friends whose marriages might be in need of the fuel of friendship. Let me be a blessing to someone who needs me. Amen.

BABBLE

Quinn G. Caldwell

And the LORD said, "Look, they are one people, and they have all one language; and this is only the beginning of what they will do; nothing that they propose to do will now be impossible for them. Come, let us go down, and confuse their language there, so that they will not understand one another's speech." From Genesis 11:1–9

SOMEBODY HAS PROBABLY TOLD YOU that the story of the Tower of Babel is a story about punishment. I think they are wrong.

This is how the ancients explained the diversity in the world. Reading it as a story about punishment presupposes that diversity of language or culture is a negative thing. If, on the other hand, one thinks such diversity is good, then Babel becomes the story of a gift—a fraught gift, perhaps, but a gift.

Pentecost is often paired with Babel. One traditional way of linking the two is to say that Pentecost undid Babel: at Babel, our hubris brought about the punishment of diversity, while on Pentecost, the Spirit removed the punishment and allowed us to communicate again.

I think that instead of undoing it, Pentecost completed Babel. If diversity of language and culture was the first gift, then the second was the ability to hear others' languages and understand them. At Babel, diversity; at Pentecost, the ability to harness it for the reign of God.

There are a lot of people out there who talk and think and act just like you do, but most of them don't. That diversity has never been easy to live with, but ever since Pentecost, we've known this: it's not only a gift, but the stuff that the realm of God is made of.

PRAYER: God, grant me the grace both to sing your praises and to hear others singing them in every tongue and life I encounter. Amen.

Both/And in an Either/Or World

Anthony B. Robinson

To each is given the manifestation of the Spirit for the common good. From 1 Corinthians 12:4–11

EVERY NOW AND AGAIN someone says, "If only we were like the early church, when everyone was full of faith and lived in total harmony." I suggest reading the New Testament's letters about actual early churches. Paul's to the Corinthians will do. He wrote to a quarreling, contentious congregation. Paul cautioned against spiritual arrogance, suggesting to those who thought of themselves as the enlightened that though "knowledge puffs up, love builds up."

Paul affirmed a two-sided truth: individual gifts and their expression are really important, and the life of the group, the community or congregation, is really important, too. It's not either the sacred individual or the sacred community; it's both/and. In writing, "To each is given the manifestation of the Spirit," Paul affirmed that each and every person in the congregation is given a gift of the Spirit. Amazing! No one is gift-less, unimportant, or less than. In writing, "To each is given the manifestation of the Spirit for the common good," Paul reminds us that individual gifts and their expression aren't the whole point. The point is a "common good," building up the church and its witness to God.

When our kids were teenagers we affirmed a similar two-sided truth: "You are very special, unique, and important; and you are part of a family." This Pentecost day, ponder the amazing gifts of the Spirit to each, and invite each one to use their gift to build up the church and its common life and mission. "To each is given the manifestation of the Spirit for the common good."

PRAYER: Pour out your Spirit upon us this day, O God. Remind those who think too little of themselves of the gift you have given them; remind those who think too much of themselves of the common good all gifts are meant to serve. Amen.

I'm Dying and No One Will Let Me Talk about It

Lillian Daniel

He took the twelve aside again and began to tell them what was to happen to him, saying, "See, we are going up to Jerusalem, and the Son of Man will be handed over to the chief priests and the scribes, and they will condemn him to death; then they will hand him over to the Gentiles; they will mock him, and spit upon him, and flog him, and kill him; and after three days he will rise again." From Mark 10:32–34

"I COULD BE DEAD BY NOW FOR ALL YOU KNOW!" A friend of mine called her elderly mother who answered the phone with those words. "I haven't heard from you or your brother for three days. I could be on the kitchen floor dead as a door post and you wouldn't know."

"And it's nice to talk to you too, Ma . . ."

Nobody wants to hear the people they love say things like that. It's painful.

This is the third time in the gospel of Mark that Jesus predicts his own death. The disciples must have been sick of it by now. But Jesus insists that they listen.

I heard a story about a woman who was dying, and everyone in the family refused to talk about it. Even when she raised the subject, they all shut her down, saying, "Don't talk like that!" Finally one niece sat quietly with her and let her talk. The aunt thanked her. "I know I'm dying," she said, "and no one in this family, except for you, will let me talk about it."

As a society, we're afraid to talk about death. Our culture worships youth and denies that death is on everyone's horizon.

So is there someone in your life who might actually want to talk about death? If so, instead of telling them to cheer up, you might consider that they are following Jesus, who talked about it often and honestly.

MAY 17

DON'T JUDGE

Martin B. Copenhaver

Therefore you have no excuse, whoever you are, when you judge others; for in passing judgment on another you condemn yourself. From Romans 2:1–11

THROUGHOUT SCRIPTURE GOD IS DESCRIBED as both a God of judgment and a God of love. They are both defining characteristics of God. It is important to note, however, that at every turn we are invited to reflect God's love in our relationships with one another and at no point are we asked to take on God's role as judge. In fact, we are continually warned against it. We must love, as God loves. But we must not judge. That role is for God alone. That is because we are imperfect beings. All of us may love imperfectly, but wonderful things can still be done through imperfect love.

By contrast, imperfect judgment is dangerous. It can lead to ruptured relationships, prejudice, even violence. That is why those judgments we are forced to make—such as when someone is on trial for a crime—are to be made with modesty and humility. All human judgments are provisional, waiting upon the perfect judgment that is God's alone. Human frailty does not allow for more. So love extravagantly today, in the name of the God of love. But hold back on your judgments and leave that role to God.

PRAYER: Dear God, I confess that I am tempted to judge others. I assume that I can see others clearly. When I am inclined toward judgment, give me the humility to hold back. And may I even find ways to replace my judgment with love. Amen.

MAY 18

ARE YOU SAVED?

Ron Buford

We are God's people and the sheep of God's pasture. From Psalm 100

I GREW UP BELIEVING in "salvation theology"—every sin put you in danger of hell. When asked, "Are you saved?" I always wondered.

When I joined the United Church of Christ, my sainted mother, whom we affectionately called "Queen Dorothy" behind her back, said, "You won't hear anything over there about salvation."

Years after Mom passed away, I heard Dr. David Greenhaw, president of Eden Seminary, begin a sermon, "Tonight, I am going to preach about salvation." I was shocked!

Dr. Greenhaw said the "just" live by faith in Jesus, and that is enough by itself. He called it God's safe pasture. I caught a glimpse of faith strong enough to catch us when we fall, wide enough to embrace us when we wander, loving enough to lure us back when we run from what is good.

We confess sin, not to escape hell, but naturally, whenever we think of God's unconditional love. We strive to turn from all that hurts ourselves, each other, and the world around us. God's love mystically and repeatedly transforms us.

I closed my eyes that night and whispered to Queen Dorothy, "Well, Momma, for the first time . . . I know I'm saved!"

PRAYER: Gracious God, Thank you for saving me . . . completely, and without condition. Help me believe it for myself, for all who have sinned against me in the past, and all who will sin against me this day. Amen.

MAY 19

SET FREE

William C. Green

Look, the men you put in prison are standing in the temple and teaching the people. From Acts 5:17–26

DIVINE INTERVENTION FREES THE APOSTLES FROM PRISON. Religious authorities had put them there because they wouldn't keep quiet. They kept teaching in the spirit of Jesus—and the people were often persuaded by what they taught.

We see here the two essential components of divine assistance: freedom and commandment. The apostles are let out of jail for a reason. They are to carry on God's work. Faith is private. But ultimately it involves others and is meant to be shared. After all, that's how we learned it—from parents, friends, colleagues, or church. We didn't just dream up faith on our own any more than did the apostles. And we, too, are called to pass it on.

It's easy to get so used to feeling locked up by oppressive circumstances that we can't believe the cell door has been opened. It's our responsibility to get going and walk the talk of faith. This, then, becomes a lesson for others, too.

How am I, how are you, exercising this freedom and responsibility? How am I stuck when the only hindrance to moving on is me and my own self-imprisoning habits of doubt? What justice and dignity do I withhold from others by thinking I can't do enough, or give enough, to make a difference? What are we teaching others by our own example? What do our lives say about God?

PRAYER: Help us face these questions, God, knowing you will deliver us from what holds us back if we'll take the first step. Amen.

WHAT DO YOU WANT?

Martin B. Copenhaver

They called the blind man, saying to him, "Take heart, get up, he is calling you." So throwing off his cloak, he sprang up and came to Jesus. Then Jesus said to him, "What do you want me to do for you?" From Mark 10:46–52

A BLIND BEGGAR NAMED BARTIMAEUS calls out to Jesus as he passes by. The people in the crowd tell Bartimaeus to be quiet, but Jesus asks to see him. Bartimaeus springs to his feet and is directed to Jesus. There he stands before Jesus, obviously blind and just as obviously eager for what will come next. Jesus says, "What do you want me to do for you?"

It is a simple question, but a remarkable one under the circumstances. Most healers would assume that what Bartimaeus would want is a restoration of his sight. And, in fact, that is what Bartimaeus asks for. But Jesus does not presume that this would be his most urgent desire. He waits for Bartimaeus to tell him so.

Folks with disabilities often express frustration that others seem to define them by their disabilities. And when people are in need, we often presume to know what is good for them, what they most want, or should want. Jesus' question makes it clear that he does not view Bartimaeus as a beggar defined by his blindness. Instead, Jesus engages him as a human being—that is, as a person with hidden needs, hopes, and desires that no one can presume to know without being told.

And so Jesus asks each of us: "What do you want me to do for you?" When Jesus is the one asking, it is not a hypothetical question or a casual one. It is worthy of our deepest reflection and most considered response.

PRAYER: Jesus, thank you for inviting me to bring my deepest needs, hopes, and desires to you. Amen.

IN THE UPS AND DOWNS, GOD LEVELS THINGS OUT

Lillian Daniel

A voice cries out: "In the wilderness prepare the way of the Lord, make straight in the desert a highway for our God. Every valley shall be lifted up, and every mountain and hill be made low; the uneven ground shall become level, and the rough places a plain." Isaiah 40:3–4

PEOPLE WHO ARE FACING A SERIOUS ILLNESS tell me they have a new respect for how changeable life is. Suddenly, they realize how precious the ordinary moments are. One man once told me what many others have said in different words: "I used to complain about being bored. But I could use a little boring right now."

These words from Isaiah seem to predict the divine future God wants for us. God does not want us laboring up steep mountains one minute and down in a ditch the next minute. God wants to level things out.

But life on earth doesn't work that way. Life delivers wild fluctuations in the stock market, our love lives, our health, and even our sanity. The ground we travel is uneven and rough.

It is God's grace, working through the passage of time, that evens out the terrain. We look back in hindsight and don't just see a lot of ups and downs. As we learn from our mistakes and our heartbreaks, some of those past mountains get laid low.

It's good preparation for the real moment of understanding, when we meet Jesus in the afterlife and finally understand that all this was just the prelude. Until then, let's hold on to the image of God watching us in our ups and downs, and using grace and mercy to turn the rough places into a fertile plain.

PRAYER: When my heart is a desert, make straight a highway through me, and remind me that one day every mountain I am climbing will be made low and every valley will be lifted up. Eventually. Amen.

MAY 22

CHURCH AS FAMILY

Anthony B. Robinson

Jesus replied, "Who is my mother, and who are my brothers?" and pointing to his disciples, he said, "Here are my mother and my brothers! For whoever does the will of my Father in heaven is my brother and sister and mother." From Matthew 12:46–50

IN MY WORK WITH CONGREGATIONS I often hear people speak of their church as a "family." "We're like a family." They may even say, "This church is my family." It's the kind of thing that sounds great, but lately I've begun to wonder if it really is.

Too often church-as-family congregations seem pretty inwardly focused and difficult to break into. Somehow, the large transformative purposes of the church, like hearing and doing the will of God, seem to have been eclipsed by ensuring the comfort and satisfaction of the congregation's members. Moreover, keeping folks happy seems to have replaced the higher calling of transforming both individuals and society to be more Christ-like.

Our purpose as the church isn't the comfort and satisfaction of members or being a happy family. It is hearing and doing God's will, and in doing so becoming a whole new kind of family, one that is salt to the earth and light to the world.

PRAYER: For your disturbing word, Lord Jesus, we are grateful. May it disturb us to life. Amen.

MAY 23

BELIEF AND FAITH ARE DIFFERENT

Martin B. Copenhaver

The LORD is my strength and my shield; in [the LORD] my heart trusts. From Psalm 28

PEOPLE SOMETIMES USE THE WORDS "belief" and "faith" as if they are synonyms. They do have much in common, but they are different, as well.

Imagine that you are at a circus. A skilled high-wire artist has accomplished many marvelous feats that inspire awe in the audience. Then the ringmaster addresses the crowd: "Ladies and gentlemen, if you believe that this daring man can ride safely over the high wire on his bicycle while carrying someone on his shoulders, please raise your hand." Seeing an almost unanimous vote of confidence, the ringmaster then says, "Very well, then, now who would like to be the first to volunteer to sit on his shoulders?"

The difference between belief and faith is the difference between raising your hand and getting on the high-wire artist's shoulders. Faith is not passive or merely intellectual. To believe in God all you need say is, "True," but to have faith in God you must go on to say, "Yes."

Belief, in itself, is not enough. We may believe that God "has the whole world in his hands," but faith is the act of trust by which we put ourselves into God's hands. The real synonym for faith is "trust." You can sit back and believe, but faith requires that you get out of your seat. Faith is the active expression of trust.

PRAYER: O God, whatever I might believe or not believe about you, help me to entrust myself to your care, at every turn and in every hour this day. Amen.

MAY 24

NOT JUST THE STUFF OF HORROR MOVIES

Lillian Daniel

Then another angel, a third, followed them, crying with a loud voice, "Those who worship the beast and its image, and receive a mark on their foreheads or on their hands, they will also drink the wine of God's wrath . . . . There is no rest day or night for those who worship the beast and its image and for anyone who receives the mark of its name." . . . And I heard a voice from heaven saying, "Write this: Blessed are the dead who from now on die in the Lord." "Yes," says the Spirit, "they will rest from their labors, for their deeds follow them." From Revelation 14:6–13

TODAY'S READING HAS SPAWNED too many horror movies. It is an apocalyptic vision of the end times, or the second coming of Christ. It is also a theological interpretation of the political situation produced by the early church on the island of Patmos in the first century. Revelation is where we meet the beast, or the Antichrist, whose followers have a mark of some kind. In Revelation 13:8, the mark is revealed to be the number 666, which some scholars believe was code for a political figure, perhaps the Emperor Nero, whom the early Christians may have believed was the Antichrist. In 2005, scholars at Oxford University, newly able to read an ancient fragment, suggested that the number was actually 616. Would that make the Antichrist one of Nero's subordinates? And will that little baby who appeared in the horror classic *The Omen* have to get a tattoo removal?

As odd as all this may sound, perhaps we should stop and consider how hard the lives of these early Christians were. Granted, they engaged the world with a certain supernatural suspicion, but they also risked their lives to follow Jesus. That's something people are still doing around the world. So as long as we have the freedom to go to church where we please, we ought to say a prayer for those who do not.

PRAYER: Gracious God, allow me to take a fresh look at this mysterious book of the Bible. Allow Revelation to open my imagination, not to horror, but to a heavenly future, where justice, kindness, and mercy reign supreme. Amen.

MAY 25

Torn Heavens

Anthony B. Robinson

O that you would tear open the heavens and come down. From Isaiah 64:1–9

O THAT YOU WOULD DISTURB our committee meetings, break in upon our congregational gatherings, and take hold of our conference and synod meetings; O that you would trouble our placid worship, intrude upon our tidy rituals, intervene in our sacraments; O that you would surge into our bland Scripture reading, strike dumb our wordy prayers, and lay your hands upon our feckless preachers; O that you would tear open the heavens and come down. It is you we need, O God, you alone.

PRAYER: We praise and thank you, Holy One, that in Jesus you have torn the heavens in two and come down. Grant us eyes to see, ears to hear, your fresh advent. Amen.

MAY 26

HOPE OF THE RIGHTEOUS

Ron Buford

They do not know the thoughts of the LORD; they do not understand God's plan. From Micah 4:6–13

I WAS TAUGHT THAT RIGHTEOUSNESS is simply having a "right" perspective and acceptance about one's relationship with God and one's fellow creatures and creation, and about one's powers and limitations. Such perspective does not come from ordinary human knowledge alone but through attentiveness to life's "holy moments" amid the mundane and the frightening. Such attentiveness reveals things we do not know, precisely when we need to know them. Such light and revelation, coupled with human knowledge, is the Stillspeaking God continuing creation.

We may not always know God's "thoughts" or understand God's "plan." At times, we ask God, "What's going on? Why?"

But as we remember past victories, some a long time coming, they become midwives birthing increased faith from the womb of our being. Pilots learn to trust instruments that guide them through clouds when flying. Just so, we remember to trust God's presence, persevering through challenging times. Despite travail, we deliver. Despite turbulence, we arrive.

The hope of the righteous is that no matter how things look right now, God's realm will certainly come, for us, our children, and the world. Somehow our work, our presence in creation, our lives by the grace of Almighty God will have been for a blessing. We may not live to see it, but it will be so in the midst of our weakness, unbelief, and imperfection. God is faithful, holding us, never letting us go because we belong to God. Believe it!

PRAYER: Gracious God, Thank you for the confidence we have in your presence and that we belong, body and soul, in life and in death, to you. Amen.

MAY 27

SOBER UP

Lillian Daniel

Be on guard so that your hearts are not weighed down with dissipation and drunkenness and the worries of this life, and that day does not catch you unexpectedly, like a trap. From Luke 21:34–35

AT MY FATHER'S FUNERAL, the minister opened up the service for anyone who wanted to come up and speak. She did this because so many of the people in attendance were members of Alcoholics Anonymous, and she wanted to offer them the chance to share in the way they did at meetings. I believe her pastoral sense told her that this would be a tough time for everyone, but in particular for the crowd who must decide day by day to stay sober.

I attended some open AA meetings with my dad, and I heard some wild stories, some of them sad, others darkly funny. The stories were not meant to glamorize drunkenness; they were meant to help the alcoholic stay sober for one more day. They helped us all to pay attention to the gift of the present.

In the Advent readings, Jesus tells us in many different ways to be present. He tells us to stay alert, to wake up and, here, to sober up. I don't think Jesus was making a statement about alcohol but about life. After all, Jesus drank wine himself. But he could see when drinking got out of control, and he cared enough about it to say something. I have no doubt that Jesus is as present around the tables of AA meetings as he is at the communion feast.

Why do people get dissipated and drunk? We turn to that kind of behavior when we are at the end of our rope. We mistakenly think that it will ease our worries, but that kind of behavior can bring worries of its own.

PRAYER: God grant me the serenity to accept the things I cannot change; courage to change the things I can; and wisdom to know the difference (Reinhold Niebuhr). Amen.

MAY 28

REAL PROPHECY

Donna Schaper

I do not know how to speak . . . for I am only a boy. From Jeremiah 1:4–10

WHAT IS A REAL PROPHET OR REAL PROPHECY? What if we are all puerile when it comes to prophecy? The spirit is so willing and the résumé is so weak.

A real prophet understands how distant the efforts are from their realization. Sending and returning hundreds of e-mails a day must have some resemblance to a prophetic hoarseness of old. Results, we don't have.

Prophecy is often real by its very detachment from outcomes and deliverables. We reach toward heaven on earth when we prophesy. We don't touch heaven so much as reach toward it.

We are in a real bind. In response to grace, we can only foresee heaven on earth, for all, especially the poor. We can't drag heaven down to earth. If anything, we are the exhale of God's inhale: we breathe God's will and Jesus' promise. God makes the justice. We are God's rhythmic promise. Simultaneously, we cannot rest. We must send better e-mails, make more engaging phone calls, write better newsletters, preach better sermons, and run better meetings. All can be done prophetically. These things are up to us. Heaven on earth is up to God.

PRAYER: Grant us the grace to be real, if boyish, prophets, O God, and tend to our frustration. Let it not disable us. Amen.

MAY 29

"CAN YOU HEAR ME NOW?"

Kenneth L. Samuel

God, who at sundry times and in divers manners spake in time past unto the fathers by the prophets, hath in these last days spoken unto us by his Son, whom he hath appointed heir of all things, by whom also he made the worlds. From Hebrews 1:1–4 KJV

HOW MANY TIMES have we abandoned all efforts to communicate with persons who were nonresponsive? After a few unanswered messages or e-mails we've had it! After all, who would even want to communicate with someone who obviously doesn't want to talk and couldn't care less about building any kind of mutual relationship? What kind of person would keep reaching out and trying to establish dialogue with people who are obviously not interested?

That kind of person would be God. Our whole history is a chronicle of God's patient and persistent attempts to open up a divine-human dialogue with those of us who isolate and insulate ourselves by talking only among ourselves. The advent of every prophet was an invitation for us to dialogue with God; the rejection of every prophet was a refusal of that invitation. And just when we thought God might have abandoned the effort, God, instead, turned up the volume, wrapped the message up in human flesh, and spoke to us in the living language of sacrificial love personified in Jesus. Can we hear God now?

PRAYER: God, after all of our dismissals and rejections of your call, thank you for never giving up on us. You have spoken clearly to us through your Son and we hear you now. Amen.

MAY 30

LEARNING FROM CRITICISM

Lillian Daniel

And when Jeremiah had finished speaking all that the LORD *had commanded him to speak to all the people, then the priests and the prophets and all the people laid hold of him, saying, "You shall die!" . . . Then Jeremiah spoke to all the officials and all the people, saying, ". . . As for me, here I am in your hands. Do with me as seems good and right to you. Only know for certain that if you put me to death, you will be bringing innocent blood upon yourselves and upon this city and its inhabitants, for in truth the* LORD *sent me to you to speak all these words in your ears." From Jeremiah 26:1–9, 12–15*

NOBODY WANTS TO BE THE BEARER OF BAD NEWS. Have you ever heard the expression, "Don't kill the messenger?" It became an expression for a reason. People hate to be told off.

Here Jeremiah criticized the people and they turned on him, violently. With courage, he admitted that his life was in their hands. He called them to conscience, and his life was spared when some of the elders spoke up and told the community that Jeremiah was worth listening to.

Who is the hero of this story? Jeremiah, certainly, but I also nominate the elders, who were willing to hear criticism and own up to it. If it's hard to be the bearer of bad news, it is even harder to receive it.

Here's a real test of spiritual maturity. How capable are you of learning from criticism? God uses critics to set us straight. When we can't hear God, God has to engage a third party: a prophet, family member, trusted friend or colleague to sit us down and tell us off.

We've all experienced unfair criticism. So our first response is to ask ourselves if this is justified. But if there's even a small part of us that thinks it could be, we need to stop, listen, and pray. The best way to learn from criticism is to pray over it, and that takes time.

So the next time you want to shoot the messenger, remember the elders who held back the crowd, protected their critic and called the community to conscience.

PRAYER: Bless me with an open heart, to learn from the words of others, even when it is painful. Make me an elder who can grow and change. Amen.

TAKE TWO

Anthony B. Robinson

Then Jesus laid his hands on his eyes again; and he looked intently and his sight was restored, and he saw everything clearly. From Mark 8:22–30

IT TOOK TWO TOUCHES for Jesus to cure the blindness of the man at Bethsaida. One application of spit and hands didn't do it. A second shot was required. What's up with that?

This little story is the front bookend for a section on what it means to follow Jesus. The back bookend is another story of blindness healed (Mark 10:46–52). What it meant to follow Jesus is something the disciples didn't quite get the first time around. Initially they thought that following Jesus would mean the wide road to glory and positions of power and prestige in his new administration. Time and a cross would give them deeper insight and a different vision: following Jesus isn't just about getting what I want or fulfilling my ambitions, it is about becoming what God wants.

We sometimes think that Christian faith or being part of the church is mainly about enriching my life and meeting my needs. We may even complain that church "isn't doing anything for me." When we think it's all about us, we need a second touch, too. We need things cleared up so that we learn to ask a better question: Today, how am I to follow Jesus, to serve God, and to be an instrument of God's purposes and grace?

PRAYER: Gracious God, may I so lose myself today that I may be truly found; found anew in your life, in your service, in your love. Amen.

JUNE

BAPTISM

Donna Schaper

They brought him up to Jerusalem to present him to the Lord. From Luke 2:22–40

MY LITTLE BROTHER'S LINEN AND FRILLED BAPTISMAL ROBE hung in the coat closet at my house for decades. He is now past fifty. One day he called and wanted it. I said, your children are grown, so are mine. Why?

Because, said he, I want it near me. Why? I said again.

I want to remember that I was presented to God and that God took me in. But why now? Because, he said, life has become very hard for me. My first wife and my first child are angry with me again. My second wife just hit my only son. My third wife is tired of hearing me talk about my first and second wives.

Aha. Life becomes too much for many of us, many times. At Christmas, we realize that we not only have to rely on a child for salvation (!) but also have to rely on our own childhood. It is never too late to have a happy childhood, I have quipped often.

It is also never too late to remember our baptism—*Baptismatus Sum*—as a touchstone of all of God's promises. We too have been presented to God. And God accepted the present of us.

PRAYER: When life becomes too much for us, O God, let us remember whose we are. Amen.

THE PLANET IN PRAISE

Kenneth L. Samuel

Praise the LORD *from the earth, you great sea creatures and all ocean depths, lightning and hail, snow and clouds, stormy winds that do his bidding, you mountains and all hills, fruit trees and all cedars, wild animals and all cattle, small creatures and flying birds, kings of the earth and all nations, you princes and all rulers on earth, young men and maidens, old men and children.* From Psalm 148 NIV

MAKE NO MISTAKE ABOUT IT, the entire earth is a declaration of God's awesome power to create and sustain life with wondrous beauty and fathomless splendor. Every leaf on a tree, every crystal in a snowflake, every feather of a bird, every pebble on a mountain, every leg on an ant and every whisper of the wind is a testament to the great care and "attention to detail" of the Creator.

According to the psalmist, humanity is not distinct from, but very much a part of the earth's natural symmetry. When we violate the planet through global warming, toxic contaminants, and environmental neglect, we interrupt the planet's praise to God. And in so doing, we pollute our own praise to God as well.

PRAYER: Gracious God, let our praise to you be reflected in our care for the planet, and let our love for you resound throughout this wondrous world. Amen.

THE POOR ARE NOT LUCKY

Lillian Daniel

Listen carefully to what I am saying—and be wary of the shrewd advice that tells you how to get ahead in the world on your own. Giving, not getting, is the way. Generosity begets generosity. Stinginess impoverishes, Jesus said. From Mark 4:24–26 TM

A WELL-DRESSED WOMAN AT A RELIGION CONFERENCE told me that she had learned that it was harder for rich people to experience God's love than the poor. "The poor," she explained, "have so little that they have to rely on God's love so much more. They just seem so much happier." This was presumably why she delighted in mission work overseas, where the poor were "just so grateful."

She was inspired by the people she served, saying, "They offer me so much more than I offer them." Well, at least that last part I could imagine to be true, but not for the reasons she imagined.

She continued to explain that the people who have less, have less to worry about, and that was why they were closer to God. "In some ways, I truly envy them," she said. "It is just easier for them to experience God's grace." For that reason, she believed that it was more worthwhile for her to offer her presence than her money.

I have heard rich people say that the poor are lucky before. But I have yet to hear a poor person say it.

Yes, Jesus does say that we get closer to God by giving away what we have. But the poor do not get closer to God by having less. Most people in the world are not poor by choice. They are poor because other people have more than their fair share. Whole nations steeped in poverty are not an accident of fate. Whole nations who enjoy most of the world's wealth are not God's will.

"Generosity begets generosity," Jesus says. Generosity ought to inspire others to be generous. Mission trips are miraculous faith-filled pilgrimages when they alert us to the injustice in the world and inspire us to be generous and to change things. Mission trips are self-serving vacations when we come back thinking that the poor we met overseas are the lucky ones.

We can admire the poor people we meet, and we can respect them, but to call them lucky is ridiculous. When generosity begets stupidity it wasn't really generosity to begin with. But when generosity begets more generosity, it is the real thing.

PRAYER: Dear God, give bread to those who are hungry and a hunger and thirst for justice to those who have plenty. Amen.

JUNE 4

THE TWENTY-THIRD PSALM

Donna Schaper

The LORD is my shepherd, I shall not want. He makes me lie down in green pastures; he leads me beside still waters; he restores my soul. He leads me in right paths for his name's sake. Even though I walk through the darkest valley, I fear no evil; for you are with me; your rod and your staff—they comfort me. You prepare a table before me in the presence of my enemies; you anoint my head with oil; my cup overflows. Surely goodness and mercy shall follow me all the days of my life, and I shall dwell in the house of the LORD my whole life long. Psalm 23

MORE PEOPLE KNOW THIS ONE BY HEART than any other—and well they should. Watching people mumble it at funerals is one of life's great joys. Maybe you or your children haven't memorized it yet. You'll want to.

Maybe I can tweet it to you. "Intention to leave wanting behind: I shall not want. God, guide, green pastures, still waters, souls restored, right paths, then the trouble, the turn. Enemies arrive. Dark valleys abound.

Evil. There in the trouble, we will not fear. Not back to the peace but forward to the peace. Then the Eucharist, the table set up in the wilderness. Then the overflowing cup after the trouble, after the fearlessness. Then dwelling in the house of God forever. Peace then, peace now, joined by peace in the future, right in the middle of the trouble." Pretty nice. And I have some characters left.

PRAYER: Teach or twitter us, O God, to mumble your words and memorize your peace and always to know that we have some characters, some spaciousness left. Lead us in the paths beyond cramped, into righteousness. Amen.

LOOKING AND SEEING

Anthony B. Robinson

The Israelites groaned under their slavery, and cried out. Out of the slavery their cry for help rose up to God. God heard their groaning, and God remembered [God's] covenant with Abraham, Isaac, and Jacob. God looked upon the Israelites, and God took notice. From Exodus 2:23–25

IS THERE A DIFFERENCE between looking and seeing? Or between seeing and really seeing?

Here, as the Exodus story begins, we read that God "looked," or "took notice." The Hebrew word is *ra'ah*. It does not refer to a mere glance. It means to begin to move toward another with kindness or sympathy. God really saw the suffering slaves in Egypt. He moved toward them.

In a novel I was reading recently a woman who had been a waitress for fifty years, which is an awful long time to be on your feet like that, was asked about her memories of a particular customer, a naval officer. She says,

"He actually saw me, if I can put it like that." The implication was that few of her customers, few of the other high-ranking officers where she worked, did actually see her. She was not seen by the others as a person.

There's seeing and there's really seeing. There's eye contact and there is moving toward another with kindness or sympathy.

Often privilege and power, rank or status, as well as plain old self-centeredness, keep people from really seeing or really hearing another person

How remarkable, then, that our God and God's power is not like that at all. Our God sees, really sees, the suffering and the lowly. Our God's power is not manifest as distance or not getting involved or sending orders. Our God enters in, moves toward us, in kindness and sympathy. God doesn't just look, God sees.

PRAYER: God, forgive me for the many times when I only look but do not see. Grant me grace today to really see and to move toward another person in kindness. Amen.

JUNE 6

FOR THE THIRSTY

Christina Villa

For I will pour water on the thirsty land, and streams on the dry ground. From Isaiah 44:1–5

AFTER GYM CLASS when I was in elementary school, we would all line up at the drinking fountain, sweaty and dying of thirst, and wait our turn for a drink of water. I remember that my fifth-grade teacher would stand next to the fountain and turn the handle briefly for each kid, so we only got as much water as she decided we needed. We all left the water fountain still thirsty. When you're really thirsty, you can't think about anything else. Thirsts of the spirit are in a class apart from ordinary passing hunger. People get parched, like the ground in a drought. Nothing will grow in them. Loneliness and every kind of grief are droughts for the spirit. People can become parched for love, for company or a kind word, even a smile.

In the Bible, blessings are poured like water onto people because the spirit's need to be blessed is as urgent as the body's need for water. "For I will pour water on the thirsty land," says God. Try being more like God (and less like my fifth-grade teacher). Just assume that everyone you encounter is thirsty, somehow or other. Pour water on the dry ground to revive and bless someone's spirit today.

PRAYER: God, let me pass along your blessing freely like water. Amen.

JUNE 7

MULTITASKING LEADS TO MINILIVING

Lillian Daniel

If you pay attention to these laws and are careful to follow them, then the LORD your God will keep [God's] covenant of love with you. Deuteronomy 7:12

REMEMBER THE DAYS, decades ago, when multitasking was hailed as the greatest invention time management had ever seen? Well, decades later, most of us know that it really doesn't work

We still do it, check our e-mails while we're on the phone, balance laptops on our laps when we watch television, sometimes two channels at once. But we've learned the hard way that it's not all it's cracked up to be.

Maybe in haste you sent the wrong e-mail to the wrong person, because you were moving too fast. More seriously, people have crashed cars and trains because they've been distracted by multitasking. But now comes the scientific backup for what we are beginning to suspect is true.

Executive coach Vickie Austin devoted a newsletter to the folly of multitasking. She cited an article from *NeuroImage,* a science journal, which determined that managing two mental tasks at the same time significantly reduces the brainpower available to concentrate on either task, ultimately damaging the quality of the final product. Scientists reporting in the *Journal of Experimental Psychology* found it takes our brains four times longer to recognize and process when we switch between tasks. So if we just showed more patience and stuck with one thing at a time, we might actually be more efficient.

There's a story from London's East End where they have new lampposts designed to protect those who are not paying attention from banging into the posts. This trial program began after a survey revealed that one in ten people were harmed by focusing on their cell phones instead of where they were walking. So they've padded the lampposts. Padded the lampposts? There has to be a better way.

PRAYER: Gracious and attentive God, if I can't pay attention to the people in my life and the tasks at hand, how can I pay attention to you and your teachings? Help me focus on the small things, so that I can focus on the big ones. Amen.

WHY HERE, WHY NOW, WHY YOU, WHY ME?

Donna Schaper

You yourselves know that it is unlawful for a Jew to associate with or to visit a Gentile; but God has shown me that I should not call anyone profane or unclean. So when I was sent for, I came without objection. Now may I ask why you sent for me? From Acts 10:23b–33

PETER ASKS CORNELIUS A PRETTY TOUGH QUESTION. What is a nice Jewish boy doing in a place like this?

God has told us that we are not to call anything or anyone profane or unclean. When we find ourselves on something that feels like another planet, with seeming zombies or aliens, we can follow these guidelines in the great soap opera of life.

We can slow down and really notice what we think we have already seen. We can ask the questions of what and why and avoid the tyranny of the technical, the hegemony of the how. Often we don't know how to do something until we really know what it is and why we are doing it.

Maybe we are here to separate the chaff from the wheat. Maybe we are here to learn the desirability of certain difficulties. Maybe we are here to forget about whom we can blame and learn whom we can trust. Maybe we are here to build hate-free zones. Maybe we are here for the soap and the opera.

PRAYER: Send us on a sacred search for the profane and the unclean parts of life. Make sure we know our part in the great soap opera. Amen.

MAD AS HELL

Christina Villa

Though I walk in the midst of trouble, you preserve me against the wrath of my enemies. From Psalm 138

CATCHING UP WITH AN OLD FRIEND from childhood, she told me the tale of her divorce. It was a sad story, but she brightened up when she came to the part about how she put a long and deep scratch with her car keys on her ex-husband's car on her way out of divorce court. She clearly loved telling this part of the story, dwelling on the details with glee. When did this happen? Twenty-three years ago.

All those years, and her recollection of that act of revenge was still fresh in her mind, cheering her up, distracting her from her troubles, and entertaining her friends.

It seems that in the minds of many divorced people, their ex-spouses function as the enemy, if not the devil.

The advice on this is that dwelling on past injuries inflicted by enemies—people we hate—gives them the power to run our lives. Let it go, we're told. Easier said than done, since seething anger can, in fact, cheer us up, distract us from our troubles, and energize us. But when it does, we're being our own personal demagogues, perpetually and repetitively riling ourselves up against some person in our lives—or, politically, against some group of people in the world. We are our own demagogues, and those ex-husbands or ex-wives—or whoever we're mad at—are merely our scapegoats.

PRAYER: Dear God, preserve me against my own righteous wrath when it feels too good. Amen.

WELL, SHUT MY MOUTH

Lillian Daniel

As in all the churches of the saints, women should be silent in the churches. For they are not permitted to speak, but should be subordinate, as the law also says. If there is anything they desire to know, let them ask their husbands at home. For it is shameful for a woman to speak in church. From 1 Corinthians 14:26–40

I WAS TEMPTED TO SKIP this particular reading, or to follow it with nothing but a blank screen, the visual version of a woman being silent in church.

But instead, I'd like to have my say. "Sit down and shut up" is not the final word of the God.

I once led a Bible study for some well-educated clergy on a reading from Paul. A woman minister interrupted me right off the bat, saying, "Sorry, but I just have to say, I have a real problem with Paul." And I responded, "Well, the feeling's mutual."

But despite her "problem" with Paul, I continued. Paul's letters, while not perfect, are still wonderful and rich. I have no trouble believing that someone can be right on many spiritual things and still get stuck in the cultural norms of his day.

I approach texts like this with a spirit of humility. What statements of mine will people read one day and ask, "What was she thinking?" I know I carry the prejudices of my world around with me, just like Paul. And like him, I may be blind to many of them during my own lifetime.

For that reason, I am grateful to all the people who were told, "Sit down and shut up," and didn't. Because of them, we read Paul differently today. He's fallible, as we all are, and the church is richer for it.

PRAYER: Still Speaking God, have I shut down someone else's speech? Still Speaking God, have I allowed myself to get shut down? Have I been sad and silent when I should have been loud and proud? Have I been proud and loud when I should have listened in humility? Amen.

SURRENDER

Anthony B. Robinson

Master, we have worked all night long but have caught nothing. Yet if you say so, I will let down the nets. Luke 5:5

As LIFE GOES ON, some words seem to change their meanings, or acquire more or different meanings than they once had. For me, it's been like that with the word "surrender."

"Surrender" was always something to not do. "Stay in the game, don't give up, never surrender." Like that. There's certainly a place for that. A place for persistence. A time for tenacity. I sometimes observe that ministers who are working on change in the life of a church and encounter resistance give up too soon. You have to be persistent.

But "surrender" has acquired another meaning that is not negative, but positive. Like Peter in the scripture story of fishing but catching nothing, I had been working very hard for what seemed a long time and didn't have a blessed thing (that I could see) to show for it. I was frustrated, angry, and depressed. Very slowly, I realized there was another meaning to surrender and that I needed not to give up on the work, but to trust God more, to surrender it to God, and to let God be God for me. Instead of insisting on the outcomes I had in mind or the schedule I kept in my head, surrender to God, as ridiculous as it sounded, was the only sane path. A friend likes to say, "When you're at the end of your rope, there's a reason you're there; let go." That doesn't mean giving up. It means remembering who's on first, and that it's not you (or me).

PRAYER: Sovereign God, grant me this day the courage to fight the right battles and not give up, and the grace to surrender to you. Amen.

LOOKING INTO THE FACE OF GOD

Kenneth L. Samuel

As for me, I shall behold thy face in righteousness; when I awake I shall be satisfied, beholding your likeness. Psalm 17:15

IT IS THE LIFELONG DREAM and solemn hope of many to behold the face of God in all of its glory, majesty, and power. We dream about it, meditate upon it, and celebrate it in joyful anticipation of its expected manifestation.

What we don't look for with quite as much enthusiasm is the face of God that is revealed in our everyday acts of righteousness, compassion, and love to one another. Often, the supernal hope that compels us to anticipate the glorious revelation of God's face "in the by and by" allows us to miss countless opportunities "in the here and now" to reveal the face of God by how we choose to relate to people in our world who were created in God's image.

The psalmist looked for the likeness of God in human acts of righteousness; and the psalmist found that, in itself, to be quite satisfying.

PRAYER: God, never let us forget that we disclose your glorious face in our daily interactions with others. May our actions and attitudes reveal the true likeness of you. Amen.

Thank-you Notes

Martin B. Copenhaver

How can we thank God enough for you in return for all the joy that we feel before our God because of you? From 1 Thessalonians 3:6–10

No one is born thankful. Gratitude is something that is learned, and perhaps the best way to learn gratitude is by repeatedly expressing it. It is by offering thanks that we can come to something like thankfulness. When our children were young we would often prompt them to express gratitude ("Say 'thank you' to the nice gentleman."), not merely to teach them manners, but also so that they might learn gratitude. After all, thankfulness takes practice.

As adults we can easily fall out of the practice of gratitude. So I was intrigued by a book by John Kralik, *365 Thank Yous: The Year a Simple Act of Daily Gratitude Changed My Life.* During a dark time in his life, Kralik resolved to write a handwritten thank-you note each day. When he had written to all of his family members, friends, and coworkers, he expanded the list. Once he wrote a brief thank-you note to the barista at his local Starbucks. That one almost wasn't read because the young man behind the counter assumed it was a letter of complaint. After all, who would write a thank-you note to someone for making you a cup of coffee each morning?

Over time Kralik found that this practice was changing his life. He started viewing aspects of his life differently, not as occasions for despair or complaints, but as a source of gratitude.

So, thanks to Kralik, I am resolving to practice gratitude by writing more thank-you notes.

PRAYER: O God, the source of every good and perfect gift, thank you, thank you, thank you. Amen.

EVEN STONES DON'T LAST

Donna Schaper

As he came out of the temple, one of his disciples said to him, "Look, Teacher, what large stones and what large buildings!" Then Jesus asked him, "Do you see these great buildings? Not one stone will be left here upon another; all will be thrown down." From Mark 13:1–31

THERE IS NOTHING LIKE A CRUMBLE to get our spiritual attention. Western civilization, our Sunday school building, Americans speaking English only—all these have the crumbling sound of the old temple. The sound is frightening, even if the future is not.

We build walls to keep people out of the country—and some pass a communion wafer to loved ones through the holes in the walls. In the history of the American west, there was a big fight between those who wanted to fence and control the land and those who wanted free and common grazing land for their herds. Some want open space, others want to close it, worship it once and for all, and get a temple that lasts. Many historians say that the emergence of cheap barbed wire mattered mightily to this debate.

What if we found a good way to construct temples that didn't last? Would that help us be less afraid of the sound of the crumbling? What if walls were built of disposable material and self-destructed, like the Berlin Wall, after ten years of people needing their so-called security? What if the world roamed free and safe, grazing with gratitude?

Imagine what Jesus was saying as good news: the old is crumbling. It is on its way out. Even stones don't last, not to mention barbs on wire.

PRAYER: Spirit of the Living God, you who love the temple and even know that good fences make good neighbors, but love humanity in its rubble and its bubble more, draw near. Help us to know when to hold 'em and when to fold 'em. Amen.

DEMENTOR JESUS

Quinn G. Caldwell

Your face, LORD, do I seek. Do not hide your face from me. From Psalm 27:7–14

THE MOST BEAUTIFUL PART OF THE CHURCH I grew up in was the great Christ Window over the rear balcony. Kindly face, outstretched arms, glowing, flowing robes: to me, this window had it, and said it, all.

There was only one problem with the Christ Window: nighttime. Each evening, as the light began to fade, so would Jesus' face. Of course all stained-glass windows fade as the light behind them does, but I'm telling you that that face disappeared a good half hour before the rest of him did, leaving behind a black hole surrounded by glowing white robes: Dementor Jesus. It was terrifying.

As I got older, I stopped being creeped out by that window, and actually came to appreciate the transformation, for it's a pretty good symbol of how I understand him—or don't. Some days, the light streams through and I can see, clear as day, who he is: Glowing Jesus, Open Arms Jesus, Forgiving Jesus, Come-unto-Me-My-Yoke-Is-Easy Jesus. Other times, it's like the sun has gone down early. His face disappears. I lose track of who he is. What kind of savior says things like, "I have come not to bring peace but a sword"? What kind of friend is forever calling me "Ye of little faith" and "viper"? What kind of God promises to come back soon and then stays away for a couple of thousand years—and has he stayed away, or am I just missing something?

PRAYER: Lord Jesus, don't hide your face from me. Reveal yourself, and give me the grace to reveal you to the world. Amen.

GREAT QUESTIONS

Ron Buford

Give to the emperor the things that are the emperor's, and to God the things that are God's. And they were utterly amazed at him. From Mark 12:13–17

SOMETIMES WE THINK the Bible is mainly a book of answers. And sometimes we think that Jesus, or other leaders, are people who have the answers for us. But at least sometimes good leaders are effective because they ask good questions. And in some ways the Bible is really a book of great questions.

In this passage from Mark a couple of different religious factions try to trap Jesus with a trick question. "As Jews, should we pay taxes to the Roman Emperor or not?" Whichever way he answered, Jesus would displease someone. But he didn't give an answer so much as a question. He said to those who demanded an answer, "Give to the emperor the things that are the emperor's, and to God the things that are God's." The implicit question Jesus asked them was, "What things belong to the Emperor, and what things belong to God?" That's an important question. What do I owe my country and what do I owe God?

The Bible is full of other, equally important, questions. "Who is my neighbor?" "What is truth?" "Why are you here?" "Who do you say that I am?" "Am I my brother's keeper?" Perhaps you are struggling with some big questions now in your life. That's not a bad place to be. Jesus is someone who asks us worthy questions and walks with us as we seek to answer them in our lives.

PRAYER: God, I thank you for a faith that is as complex as life itself. I thank you that Jesus is someone who faced and asked important questions. Amen.

Here Comes the Judge

Kenneth L. Samuel

Behold my servant, whom I uphold; mine elect, in whom my soul delighteth; I have put my spirit upon him: he shall bring forth judgment to the Gentiles. He shall not cry, nor cause his voice to be heard in the street. A bruised reed shall he not break, and the smoking flax shall he not quench: he shall bring forth judgment unto truth. Isaiah 42:1–3 KJV

I REMEMBER THE FIRST TIME I was summoned to appear in traffic court for a speeding ticket and some unpaid parking violations. I could have just mailed in the fines, but I'd failed to do so in a timely way. I had never been to court, and being in my early twenties I wasn't quite sure what to expect. All the horror stories I'd heard raced through my mind as I sat in the crowded courtroom waiting for the appearance of the judge.

Upon the judge's entry, I breathed a deep sigh of relief. The judge was a member of the church I attended while I was a seminarian at the Emory School of Theology. He was a kindly gentleman, always greeting me with a smile, a firm handshake, and words of encouragement. Surely he, who knew me so well, would grant leniency, or perhaps dismiss my violations altogether.

But as he looked down at me from his high and lifted-up position, I heard him say: "Kenneth Samuel, you are guilty as charged. You will pay the maximum fines with interest, because I know that you know better. You've got to be an example for other young people." That was it. Such a nice man, but such a stern judgment. Still, I could not deny the truth of his words or his judgment. After his ruling I was determined to never have to appear in traffic court for neglected violations again.

In the Christian faith, the judge described in Isaiah can be seen as a prototype of Jesus Christ. This judge is first and foremost a servant with a special endowment of discernment. This judge is not boisterous or self-promoting in the streets. This judge possesses a gentleness that will not allow him to even crush a broken reed. Yet the judgments he renders are righteous, true, and abiding.

This judge knows us very well. In fact, he loves us dearly. But he has a tendency to chastise those whom he loves, and to hold those of us who know him to even higher standards. His judgments are much more than our punishment. His judgments are really our salvation.

PRAYER: Jesus, you are our friend and our judge. Help us to find blessing and correction by relating to you fully as both. Amen.

COMMANDING LOVE

William C. Green

I give you a new commandment, that you love one another. Just as I have loved you, you also should love one another. From John 13:1–17, 31b–35

JESUS DOES NOT COMMAND FEELINGS. He commands duty, first to God, then to others.

It's often hard to love what needs doing, like pay attention to those we disagree with, or forgive someone as we have so often been forgiven, or love "enemies" in our own midst or beyond, as Jesus admonished.

But the commandment to love is not a commandment to condone or agree; it's a duty to respect. I can't find help and hope apart from respecting a world bigger than my own feelings. The church is meant to be a model and an entry into that larger world, one made up of people we have to be with, not people we choose to be with. Jesus commands us to pass on the love and respect we have already received. Without this, any personal difference or grievance is magnified and distorted, and we're lost in ourselves with no way out.

This scripture passage makes us remember the first communion, the Last Supper. Here was love beyond personal feeling, not thrown by the betrayal of a close follower and impending death. This is God's love for us. Not even the disciples understood it. But they were changed by it, and given the duty to pass it on. They did so, however imperfectly. And so can we.

PRAYER: Gracious God, may I not make a god of my own feelings, and pass on the deeper love you make mine. Amen.

JUNE 19

LESS BOASTING

Donna Schaper

Your boasting is not a good thing. Do you not know that a little yeast leavens the whole batch of dough? From 1 Corinthians 5:1–6

LESS IS USUALLY MORE. Subtraction is a good spiritual strategy. A little often means a lot. And yet, many of us spend a lot of time on our résumés or on social networking. We present or we represent. We may be warned against boasting but that doesn't mean we don't boast! Carl Jung says we sneak our biography into just about everything we say.

Many of us want to be recognized more even than we want to be known. We want to be seen for who we are. We want people to know what we've come through. This hunger for recognition is Human Being 101. If you don't believe me, feel the warmth you know after a good conversation with a friend.

Paul is advocating recognition and being known. He wants the good bread to rise. Perhaps less boasting and more yeasting would achieve the results of recognition we so very much want. And deserve.

PRAYER: O God, understand how much we want to be seen and known. And then lead us to a good batch of dough and let us sprinkle our yeast upon it. Amen.

LOOK WHO'S WATCHING

Martin B. Copenhaver

Put these things into practice, devote yourselves to them, so that all may see your progress. Pay close attention to yourself and your teaching; continue in these things, for in doing this you will save both yourself and your hearers.
From 1 Timothy 4:6–16

I WAS ONCE ASKED to recruit some folks to stand outside the entrance of our local supermarket on a December Saturday to solicit contributions for the Salvation Army. All the volunteers were asked to do is stand beside a red bucket and ring a bell. I thought I should take a turn myself. It was fascinating to see how people responded.

I noticed that there were two groups that responded in extraordinary numbers: First, there were the members of my church. I like to think that they would have responded that way no matter who was ringing the bell, but all I can say for sure is that every church member who passed me put a contribution in the bucket.

The others who responded in extraordinary ways were adults with children at their side. And the reason seems clear enough: they knew that there were very important eyes on them—the eyes of their children. Knowing that they were being observed by their children helped them draw on the better angels of their nature. They became more generous than they would have been otherwise.

That experience also was an important reminder to me, and to parents and grandparents and to all who have some special tie to a child: there is nothing we can give our children—no toy, no trip, no tuition—that is more important than the gift of our generosity to others. It is the one thing that will not and cannot be taken away from them.

PRAYER: God, help me to seize an opportunity to be more generous today, as if young eyes were trained on me because . . . well, they are. Amen.

NOT JUST MY PEOPLE

Donna Schaper

On the second day, as they were drinking wine, the king again said to Esther, 'What is your petition, Queen Esther? It shall be granted you. And what is your request? From Esther 7:1–4

I WONDER IF QUEEN ESTHER used the king's power well in asking for security for herself and her people.

Every time I go through an airport checkpoint, I become naughty. It seems we will do anything a person in a uniform tells us to do. "Take off your sweater." "Take off your belt." I fantasize that one day I will make a parody of obedience and just take everything off and walk through the gates of electronic insecurity, unadorned. Obedience to security is making me insecure, in the same way that ads warning me about diabetes or heart disease flood me with worry that I might be sick.

My people are not just my people, in the same way that Esther's people weren't just her people. There may be no genuine difference between self and other, host and guest, Jew and Greek. Or so I have come to think in my imagined nakedness and real fear.

I want to learn to want something worthy—and it is not just being safe.

PRAYER: O God, when we overdo our personal security, undo us and redo us, into people who want salvation and shalom and not just security. Amen.

BREAKDOWN OR BREAKTHROUGH?

Anthony B. Robinson

Now as he was going along and approaching Damascus, suddenly a light from heaven flashed around him. He fell to the ground and heard a voice saying, "Saul, Saul, why do you persecute me?" Acts 9:3–4

SOMETIMES BREAKDOWNS BECOME BREAKTHROUGHS. There's a breakdown. All heaven breaks loose. Life falls apart. We end up on our knees wondering what hit us. We cry out. We can't see clearly, if at all. It's not fun. It can be terrifying.

But at least sometimes what feels like a breakdown can become a breakthrough. What sounded like death knocking turns out to have been a wake-up call. What looked like the end proves to be a new beginning, one we would never have planned or devised for ourselves.

So Saul had a breakdown on the road to Damascus. Lights flashed around him. Voices called to him (though others heard nothing). He lost his sight. He sank to his knees.

But it wasn't the end. It was a beginning; so much so that his old name no longer seemed to fit him. Saul became Paul.

When things break down in our lives, with the end of a job, the crash and burn of an identity, a knock-down-drag-out at the congregational meeting, or a family blow-up, God can take these things and do a new thing. The breakdowns can, and sometimes do, become breakthroughs.

PRAYER: Oh God, when things fall apart in us and around us, help us to know that you are still God, that you are still at work, and that by your grace and in your time, we will know new and deeper life. Amen.

A Prayer from the Pit

Kenneth L. Samuel

In [God's] great power God becomes like clothing to me [and] binds me like the neck of my garment. [God] throws me into the mud, and I am reduced to dust and ashes. From Job 30:18–19 NIV

THE ONLY THING WORSE than the deep dark agony of desperation and suffering is silence. Out of the abysmal cauldron of his condition, Job speaks, but not just in rants to those around him who would listen. Job speaks in faith to God, for there is no other way to speak to God. Prayers from the pit of painful predicaments are nevertheless acknowledgements of God's presence.

And even though Job expresses great disappointment that God had not alleviated his distress, he nevertheless acknowledges God's power—for the God who has the power to throw us into the mud and reduce us to dust and ashes is the same God who has the power to lift us out of the mud and give us new life. Any prayer out of any condition that acknowledges the presence and the power of God has potential to unleash new possibilities for life. Ask Job. He would tell you that the God of his deepest dejection is also the God of his greatest deliverance.

PRAYER: Sovereign God, even in the midst of our deepest distresses, we are grateful that you hear us. Help us to never forget that your presence has the power to make our lives new. Amen.

SING ANYWAY!

William C. Green

They sing a new song . . . they will reign on earth. From Revelation 5:1–10

WE'RE MEANT TO ENJOY OUR LIVES because that's what God wants. "To make injustice the only measure of our attention is to praise the Devil," writes the poet, Jack Gilbert. "We must have the stubbornness to accept our gladness in the ruthless furnace of the world. There will be music despite everything."

That's the note that resounds amid the commotion in the last book of the Bible. Oppressive rulers are overthrown; evil itself is destroyed. The book concludes as it says the world will—with Amens . . . and song.

This has guided and sustained many who knew a lot about "the ruthless furnace of the world"—the slaves under Pharaoh; all those enslaved thereafter and right now, including women and children who are still chattel; those with barely a chance to work who see that financial well-being is a right for the wealthy but a privilege not all deserve; those who find it's okay to be gay as long as they don't try to get married.

We're all caught up in this when we're not doing what God wants and enjoying our lives. What is the evil that has a grip on me? What oppression do I suffer, sometimes at my own hands? How much of this do I inflict on others without knowing it? Is injustice the only measure of my attention, especially as I experience it? Or can I, too, sing despite everything? God wrote the song.

PRAYER: God, teach me to sing all over again, no matter what I face. Amen.

WHAT WOULD JESUS DO?

Christina Villa

And he was transfigured before them, and his clothes became dazzling white, such as no one on earth could bleach them. From Mark 9:1–13

A SMALL REPRODUCTION OF RAPHAEL'S PAINTING of the Transfiguration hung in my grandmother's house when I was a child. Apart from family photos and a picture of Pope Pius (not a family member), there weren't many pictures in that house, so as a child I used to like to look at this one. It featured Jesus in a white robe floating amid illuminated clouds in the top half of the picture. In the bottom half, there was a knot of distressed-looking people, all pointing in different directions, some of them kneeling or lying on the ground. It looked like the immediate aftermath of a hit-and-run accident. Perhaps Jesus was floating down to take care of this mess, I thought. On the other hand, he might be floating up to get away from it.

What would Jesus do? Surely both options were open to him. As it turns out, Jesus does come down from on high and instantly heals a stricken boy on the ground, to everyone's relief. One problem with asking ourselves "What would Jesus do?" is that quite often what Jesus did was perform a miracle. I'm not up to that, myself. But more often than I choose to recognize, there probably is something helpful I can do, even though it's usually something I'd really prefer not to, something inconvenient or unappetizing or dull, something I won't even get any credit for. Or I can float somewhere above the mess on the ground and let somebody else deal with it, which Jesus did not do.

PRAYER: Dear God, don't let it take a miracle for me to notice when you want me to go out of my way and pay attention to something I'd rather let slide. Amen.

FIRST THINGS FIRST

Anthony B. Robinson

And do not keep striving for what you are to eat and what you are to drink, and do not keep worrying . . . Instead, strive for [God's realm], and these things will be given to you as well. Luke 12:29, 31

I WAS SPEAKING AT A CONFERENCE where teams from a bunch of congregations had gathered. After a while, someone said, "Listen, the question for us is survival. Will our church survive? We don't have many members. No young people. Our pews are emptying out and so is our bank account. We need you to tell us what to do to survive."

I had to respect the pain and the earnestness. I knew the feeling was real, and the anxiety genuine. I said, "I understand, I do. And yet, 'How can we survive?' is the wrong question. And I suspect that worrying it to death isn't helping you."

"Well, what should we do?" said that worried, good man.

"I'd suggest that you ask God to show you God's purpose, God's calling and mission for your church. What is God calling you to do? Call on God to show you that and give you what you need to be about it, and leave the other things to sort them selves out. I suspect it was something like that Jesus had in mind when he said, 'Seek first God's realm and these things will be given to you as well.'"

There are so many congregations today worrying and wondering if they will survive. Trust me—better, trust Jesus. It's the wrong question. The right one is "What's God's purpose/mission for our church today?" Discover that and go after it with holy love and wild abandon. Nothing else matters.

PRAYER: God, give us the courage to seek your will and way for us. Let your purpose and call so take hold of us that we lose ourselves for your sake, and thus are truly found. Amen.

TELL NO ONE

Martin B. Copenhaver

They brought to [Jesus] a deaf man who had an impediment in his speech; and they begged him to lay his hand on him. He took him aside in private, away from the crowd, and put his fingers into his ears. . . . And immediately his ears were opened, his tongue was released, and he spoke plainly. Then Jesus ordered them to tell no one. From Mark 7:31–37

WHY DID JESUS, after performing this marvelous miracle of healing, order the witnesses not to tell anyone about it? Most of us, if we do something praiseworthy, are happy to let the world know, or, even better, to have others spread the word. And if we say, "Don't tell anyone about this," usually it is in a circumstance when we have done something embarrassing or shameful.

Throughout Mark's Gospel, when Jesus performs a miracle, he gives similar instructions. Why does he want to keep these miracles secret? Why not shout out the good news? Well, for one thing, Jesus probably did not want the people to be distracted by the spectacular. The word miracle literally means "a sign that points to God." But if people began to focus too much on the miracles Jesus performed, it might distract them from his message.

There may be another reason in this instance. Perhaps Jesus wanted to make sure that the healed man got to tell his own story. Formerly he could not speak in a way others could understand. Now he gets to tell the news of what has happened to him. It is his story to tell and now he can use his own tongue to tell it. And then he can use that same tongue to praise God that his own life has become a miracle, a sign that points to God.

In what way is your life a miracle?

PRAYER: Dear God, give me a tongue that can tell of your mercies toward me and that can offer you praise. Amen.

I'll Take the Short Version

Lillian Daniel

One of the scribes . . . asked him, "Which commandment is the first of all?" Jesus answered, "The first is, 'Hear, O Israel: the Lord our God, the Lord is one; you shall love the Lord your God with all your heart, and with all your soul, and with all your mind, and with all your strength.' The second is this, 'You shall love your neighbor as yourself.'" From Mark 12:28–34

SOMETIMES, WHEN I ASK SOMEONE A QUESTION, they will respond with a sigh. "Well, do you want the short version or the long version?" I know that pastors are supposed to be good listeners, and that the long version will have the most depth, but to be honest, sometimes I just want the short version.

It may be that time is short. Perhaps I'm just not in the mood for a long story. Or perhaps I have an urgent need for some small piece of information. But let's be honest. There are some times when you just don't want the long version—for example, when awaiting the answer to this question: Where is the bathroom?

Well, periodically people would try to pin Jesus down and get him to give a simple answer to a complicated question. And usually Jesus refused. They wanted the short version and he responded with an even longer story, or, to make matters really confusing, with a parable. They were looking for deliverables. He was trying to make them think for themselves.

But today's scripture is a rare instance in which Jesus agrees to give the short version. He tells us what it all boils down to. Still, when asked to tell them one commandment, he ends up giving them two. And we're left to consider how to balance loving both God and our neighbor, since Jesus isn't willing to separate them.

So even the short version makes us think for ourselves.

PRAYER: Almighty and complex God, we cannot begin to understand you in your mystery. Thank you for sending your son Jesus to earth, to break it down for us, in words that we can ponder all our lives. Amen.

BACK TO OUR MAKER

Kenneth L. Samuel

Know ye that the Lord . . . is God: it is God that hath made us, and not we our-selves; we are God's people, and the sheep of God's pasture. From Psalm 100 KJV

WHEN I AM PARTICULARLY FRUSTRATED with the complications and vexing annoyances of life, I am encouraged to remember that my life is not a product of my own manufacturing or maneuvering. The bottom line is that I am not a self-made individual. The origin and the essence of my life are in the hand and in the will of my Creator. While I try desperately to take my life where I want it to go, it strengthens me to know that God is my source and my supply.

We would do well to remember what some of us teach our children: "God made me, and God doesn't make junk!" In fact, according to the book of Genesis, all that God makes is good and very good. Isn't it refreshing to know that at the basis of everything we do in life there is the good work and the good will of our good God? And is it not up to us to make sure that our daily actions reflect the goodness of our maker?

And even if life for us today is not as good as we believe our Maker intended, is it not good to know that our Maker is also our Redeemer? Isn't it good to know that nothing that we or anyone has done or will ever do can erase the basic goodness of our lives? No matter how troubled, torn, or tormented we may be, our lives have basic enduring, eternal value and goodness. There is nothing wrong with us today that cannot be redeemed, rescued, and renewed by our Creator!

There is such a thing as a manufacturer's warranty. If something is broken, and not performing as designed, don't try to fix it all by yourself. Take it back to the one who made it.

PRAYER: "Come ye disconsolate; where 'ere ye languish. Come to the mercy seat, fervently kneel. Here bring your wounded heart; Here tell your anguish. Earth has no sorrow that heaven cannot heal."* Amen.

*Thomas Moore, "Come Ye Disconsolate," in *Sacred Songs*, 1816, changes by Thomas Hastings, in *Spiritual Songs for Social Worship*, 1831.

YOUR HEART WILL FOLLOW

Martin B. Copenhaver

Where your treasure is, there your heart will be also. From Matthew 6:19–21

JESUS' STATEMENT, "WHERE YOUR TREASURE IS, there your heart will be also," may sound familiar, but if we don't read it with care we might reverse the statement through a kind of scriptural dyslexia. We might read it to say, "Where your heart is, there will your treasure be also." That would make sense to us because much of the time our dollars follow our heart's lead. We give to what matters to us. But that isn't what Jesus said.

That's the appeal you hear over and over again from, say, National Public Radio or your alma mater: If you care about this institution, you will write a check. In other words, "Where your heart is, there will your treasure be also." But Jesus didn't say that.

Jesus is speaking of a different dynamic: Give and spend where you want your heart to be, and then let your heart catch up. Don't just give to those things you care about. Give to the things you want to care about. Ask yourself, "If I were the sort of person I long to be, then what would I do? How would I spend my money?" Then do what you would do if you were that sort of person. Put your treasure where you want your heart to be. And if you do, says Jesus, your heart will go there. If you want to care more about the kind of car you drive, buy an expensive one. If you want to care more about property values, remodel your house. But if you want to grow in your faith, bring an offering to God. Wherever your treasure is, your heart is sure to follow.

PRAYER: O God, fashion my spending and my giving in ways that refashion my heart. Amen.

JULY

"Put Me in, Coach!"

Lillian Daniel

Then I heard the voice of the LORD saying, "Whom shall I send? And who will go for us?" And I said, "Here am I. Send me!" From Isaiah 6:1–8

IF YOU WATCH LITTLE KIDS PLAYING BASKETBALL, you see a lot of different attitudes from the kids on the bench. Some of them look relieved to be there, glad for a bit of rest. Others seem anxious, wondering when they might get put in and if they are ready. And then there are the enthusiasts, the ones who seem unable to sit still on the bench, ready to spring to their toes, eagerly making eye contact until they just can't stand it, and finally they blurt out, "Put me in, Coach!" They are dying to get in the game.

Isaiah didn't want to get in the game at first, but when he finally got to the point when he was ready, he didn't say something passive to God, like "Ok, I'll go." He said something much stronger: "Send me." Saying, "Ok, I'll go," is reactive. Saying "Send me," is active. It's like saying, "Put me in, Coach!"

A lot of people will feel called to something but the most they can muster is an "Ok, I'll go, God." Then they sit back passively and wait for the pieces to fall into place, and when they don't, they say, "Oh well."

But to really follow your calling, you need energy and action. Once you say, "Here I am. Send me," you're on the record. You can't look back and say you didn't know what you were doing. You are like the kid on the bench who says, "Put me in, Coach." You may miss a few baskets, but at least you've got your heart in the game.

PRAYER: God, give me an active and passionate approach to whatever you want me do in life. Here I am. Send me. Amen.

A New Thing

Quinn G. Caldwell

Now those who were scattered because of the persecution that took place over Stephen traveled as far as Phoenicia, Cyprus, and Antioch, and they spoke the word to no one except Jews. But among them were some men . . . who . . . spoke to the Greeks also, proclaiming the Lord Jesus. From Acts 11:19–26

THE APOSTLE STEPHEN HAD BEEN PREACHING in Jerusalem. As good Christian preaching sometimes will, his sermon angered his audience. They stoned him, and that understandably scared many of the other apostles out of town.

Not being timid people, they kept on preaching. And since they were Jews talking about the impact of the Jewish Jesus on the Jewish faith, they naturally talked about their faith only with other Jews. This was a sensible course of action—in theory. Problem was, it actually didn't work very well.

But then some of them started doing a new thing nobody had really thought of before: talking to the Greeks, the non-Jews. The story says that it worked so well that apostles came running from all over the Mediterranean to check it out.

There was nothing wrong with the apostles' first instinct; it just happened not to work very well, and a new thing was called for. Is there a place among the apostles you know, in your church, where a new thing is called for? Is there a way of doing things that made sense at the time, but just isn't working so well, but that you keep on doing anyway? And if so, what are you going to do about it?

PRAYER: God, give me the courage and vision to do a new thing for your sake when the old things stop working. Amen.

DRAWN OUT TO DRAW OTHERS

Kenneth L. Samuel

When the child grew up, she brought him to Pharoah's daughter and she took him as her son. She named him Moses [meaning "to draw out"], "because," she said, "I drew him out of the water." From Exodus 1:22–2:10

IS THERE ANY CONNECTION between the debacles from which God saves us, and the duties to which God calls us? So often, the deliverance from tragedy and trouble in our lives ends only with relief; but that sense of relief is not always translated into a sense of responsibility.

The infant Moses had been drawn from the Nile River, out of the claws of male genocide mandated by the Pharaoh of Egypt. Moses could easily have grown up to simply revel in his good fortune and bask in the wonder of his amazing rescue. However, at some point in his development, Moses came to understand that "to whom much is given, much is required." He was able to connect his personal deliverance from disaster with a sacred duty to serve others.

Moses, the one "drawn out" of danger, became the one to draw the nation of Israel out of Egyptian bondage. And Israel, the nation drawn out of bondage, has certainly drawn the world to a more vivid revelation of God's unfailing love.

PRAYER: God, we do thank you for rescuing us from many dangers, toils, and snares. Now let the relief of our rescue be translated into a responsibility to love, lift, and liberate the oppressed. Amen.

IS NOTHING SACRED?

Christina Villa

Don't be flip with the sacred. Matthew 7:6a TM

ONE SUNDAY AT A CHURCH I was visiting in New England, the time had come in the worship service for "Joys and Concerns." People stood up one by one to request prayers for successful outcomes to minor surgeries and a few actually serious life situations.

Then one lady stood up and said, "When will the shutters be put back up?" The exterior of the church had just been painted, and the shutters hadn't been put back up yet. "I have no idea!" replied the minister brightly before moving on to the next concern like a politician taking a reporter's question.

When will the shutters be put back up? She could grill the pastor about her petty concerns pretty much any hour of any other day of the week. But she chose now, the supposedly sacred hour.

Whatever happened to the sacred? People seem suspicious of it. It's not accessible, or transparent. It thinks it's better than, well, everything: it's elitist. It asks us to treat it with humility and reverence, and some of us have too much self-esteem for that. It expects us to put all else aside and prepare our hearts to encounter it. And sometimes I just don't feel like it. I have too many concerns.

A friend of mine used to dread taking his mother to church because she always complained about the Mexicans filling up the pews where once it was all Italians, like her. Finally one Sunday, he couldn't take it anymore and said to her, "For Christ's sake, Ma, this is a church! It's not the Sons of Italy!"

One of the purposes of the sacred, I think, is to relieve us—if only for an hour—of our petty concerns and prejudices, our obsessions with trivia and things we're going to forget about soon anyway. I'm pretty sure those shutters went back up eventually, and I know my friend's mother now sits happily in church with Mexicans, as if it didn't even matter.

PRAYER: The shutters, the disappearing Italians, the fact that I think the pastor should start dyeing her hair again—take my mind off all of it, please! Remind me where I am, and what this hour is for. Amen.

THIS DAY

Martin B. Copenhaver

This is the day that the LORD has made; let us rejoice and be glad in it. From Psalm 118

I AM A VERY FUTURE-ORIENTED PERSON. I have a calendar that contains pages for the present year but also two years ahead. I can tell you now what I am going to preach about in Lent. I have a special drawer where I keep tickets to plays or games or trips I look forward to. When that drawer is empty, I get almost panicked.

None of that is bad, I suppose, but being such a future-oriented person sometimes prevents me from appreciating the only day I can live in, and that is today.

Those of us who are farsighted—both literally and figuratively—can see things at a distance but have a hard time seeing what is under our noses.

That is why, when I read this from Psalm 118, I tend to emphasize the very first word: "*This* is the day that the Lord has made . . ."

That single word "this" is often the reminder I need. This is the day that God has made and given to me, to all of us, as a gift. This is the day that will have the power to bless, if I let it. This is the day I can make a difference in the world, even if only one small corner of it, if I choose to. This is the day to enjoy, if I will allow myself to.

Not tomorrow. Or next year. This day.

PRAYER: God, thank you for the gift of this day. Open my heart to receive its blessings and to find in this day ample reason to rejoice. Amen.

JULY 6

GOODBYE

Quinn G. Caldwell

"And now I commend you to God . . ." When he had finished speaking, he knelt down with them all and prayed. There was much weeping among them all; they embraced Paul and kissed him, grieving especially because of what he had said, that they would not see him again. Then they brought him to the ship. From Acts 20:17–38

NOBODY LIKES GOODBYES, and we go to many lengths to soften or avoid them. A colleague leaves or a friend moves, and we say it's not goodbye because we promise to have lunch, or to write, or to communicate through Facebook. Sometimes we avoid the moment altogether: even though I barely knew her, I once hid in the bathroom for half an hour at a co-worker's goodbye party to avoid the moment when she actually left.

When Paul says goodbye to the Ephesians, he gets it right. He remembers what they did together, he tells them what they mean to him, he commends them to God. The word "goodbye" is a contraction of "God be with ye." Saying it is a reminder that even when we're apart, God is with us both. It's an act of faith that, if God is with you and with me, then somehow we're still together and that, in the end, we'll join each other at a reunion in God's heart. It's a promise that even when I can't be with you, God will be, and that that will be sufficient.

Sometime soon you'll have to say goodbye to somebody. It's worth doing well, for it's all about faith.

PRAYER: Oh God, all these partings are hard. When I have to say goodbye, help me to cling fast to the faith that you are with us always, and that all of us will one day be reunited again in you. Amen.

WINTER SHALL PASS

Anthony B. Robinson

For now the winter is past, the rain is over and gone. The flowers appear on the earth; the time of singing has come . . . . Song of Songs 2:11–12a

WINTER IS A SEASON but also a metaphor for a season of the spirit. Wintry times come to all. We lose someone we love and who loves us, and everything goes grey and bleak. Or we lose our way, our path in the world, and feel like a child lost in a dark wood, frightened and alone.

Winters of the heart can come even in July. The loss of a job takes away not only income and security, but role and relationships. A depression or a manic episode disorients us or someone we love. Or a time of crisis engulfs and threatens our family, our church, or our community.

When we are in the midst of such a winter of the heart, it seems it will never end. It feels as if there will never be any new day, never again a time when life will be joy-filled and glad. That's not true. Both scripture and experience testify, this winter too shall pass. A time of singing shall come.

As a theological concept, "grace" has other and deeper dimensions, but it means at least this: winters of the heart do pass, a new spring of the spirit will, by God's mercy, come. Where snow now lies heavy, flowers shall bloom. Where branches appear dead, there will again be abundant fruit.

Even though we have, as we ought, done things to prepare this new season, planting seeds and the like; still it is grace. It is gift, strange and wondrous. We rejoice and utter, "Thank you."

Trust this; winter shall pass, the time of singing shall come.

PRAYER: "When our hearts are wintry, grieving, or in pain, Christ's warm touch can call us back to life again, fields of our hearts that dead and bare have been: Love is come again like wheat that rises green."* Amen.

*John Crum, "Now the Green Blade Rises," *The New Century Hymnal*, 238.

JULY 8

ATHEISTS

Quinn G. Caldwell

When Gentiles, who do not possess the law, do instinctively what the law requires, these, though not having the law, are a law to themselves. They show what the law requires is written on their hearts. From Romans 2:12–16

I LIKE ATHEISTS. They tend to have considered the issues. They tend to have asked themselves the holy questions about the origins of the universe, about happiness, about what constitutes the good life, about good and evil, injustice and mercy, about how to live.

Of course they and I disagree on at least one fundamental point. Of course many are grumpy, judgmental, and dogmatic (certain public intellectuals come to mind). Of course many have chosen atheism out of laziness. Then again, those things are true of many Christians, as well.

By and large, my experience has been that the average atheist has arrived at her position through careful thinking at some cost to herself, and lives a life marked by kindness and generosity. Which is saying something in a world where many people's vision of the good life is spending half their time watching TV and the other half shopping—precisely so they don't have to think about big questions or make sacrifices.

Paul wanted to convince his coreligionists that God is at work everywhere, even in those with religious convictions different from Paul's. So it is, I believe, with atheists—though most would not thank me for saying so.

If what Paul says is true, then God is shown forth more fully in the life of a careful-thinking, good-living atheist than a lukewarm Christian-by-default. If what Paul says is true, God might even prefer the latter to the former.

PRAYER: God, thank you for working through all kinds of strange people—even me. Amen.

JULY 9

SALTY LANGUAGE

Martin B. Copenhaver

Let your speech always be gracious, seasoned with salt. From Colossians 4:2–18

WORDS MATTER. Words can either inspire or discourage, heal or hurt, offer a blessing or a curse. As someone once told me, "Whoever said, 'Sticks and stones can break my bones, but words can never hurt me,' must have lived among deaf mutes." As it says in Proverbs, "Rash words are like sword thrusts, but the tongue of the wise brings healing" (12:18).

So the Apostle Paul counsels us to mind our tongues, to act as if words matter: "Let your speech always be gracious, seasoned with salt." He is not advocating "salty language" in the way we use the term. In the Bible salt means many things. It preserves food, keeping it pure. Salt also is treasured as a source of healing. So Paul wants us to tend to our words as if they have that kind of power.

When I served First Congregational Church (UCC) in Burlington, Vermont, one of my colleagues was Thelma Norton, a great saint of the church. In her role as Parish Visitor she had intimate access to the lives of hundreds of people and yet I never heard her speak ill of a single person. When, in the course of conversation, she came even close to speaking a harsh or judgmental word, she would stop herself and say, "Well, I'll just say, 'Amen' to that," and then move on. Her speech was always gracious in a way that inspires me still. Her language was salted in the way Paul had in mind. She was the kind of "salt of the earth" whom Jesus praised.

PRAYER: Dear God, help me to tend to my words as if they matter. Because they do. Amen.

JULY 10

BLAMED, SHAMED, AND FRAMED

Lillian Daniel

Jesus said... "I do not judge anyone who hears my words and does not keep them, for I came not to judge the world, but to save the world." From John 12:44–50

MY GRANDMOTHER HAD A BADLY BEHAVED DOG named Amos, who was known to knock over her neighbor's trash cans in the middle of the night, leaving them to clean up a mess of tin cans and old food. She denied it was her dog, but there were witnesses. The neighbors were relieved when Amos finally passed away. There would be peace in the valley.

But just two days after Amos's death, the neighbors awoke to find trash and garbage everywhere. And then about a week later, the same thing again.

Clearly, this was not Amos. The community, in their smug superiority, had been so quick to judge the eccentric woman with the odd habits, and in turn her eccentric dog.

In those weeks after Amos' death, when they cleaned up their garbage, they began to wander over to her driveway one neighbor at a time, and speak a few awkward words of apology. "We were just certain it was Amos," they said. "I mean, we saw him out there once or twice."

Years later, someone in our family actually spied the creature that was knocking over trashcans. It was a Pall Mall-smoking, lace bathrobe–wearing grandmother, sneaking out every few months at three o'clock in the morning to knock over her neighbor's trashcans and avenge the memory of Amos, years after his death.

For she would not be judged. Even though she was wrong. She would make them wrong, too. But of course, none of that made it right.

And it didn't work for her in the end either. I mean, who wants to be out at three a.m. knocking over garbage? There have to be better things to do with our time.

PRAYER: Lord Christ, I pray that you will help me to love my neighbors, and even their garbage-eating dogs, for you came not to judge the world but to save it. When we get into the cycle of blame and shame, save us from one another. Amen.

ANIMALS, HUMAN AND OTHERWISE

Quinn G. Caldwell

Then God said to Noah and to his sons with him, "As for me, I am establishing my covenant with you and your descendants after you, and with every living creature that is with you, the birds, the domestic animals, and every animal of the earth with you, as many as came out of the ark." From Genesis 9:8–17

DID YOU CATCH THAT? In today's story, which comes near the end of the whole ark episode, God makes a covenant not just with Noah and his descendants, but with every living animal, everywhere.

How does one make a covenant with an animal? A covenant is a contract, pure and simple, an agreement between two parties that spells out how they will behave with one another. "If you give me X, I will give you Y." "If I do this, you will do that."

So what is the birds' quid to God's quo? What is it that God needs, or even wants, enough to make a contract with zebras? What could dinosaurs or dolphins possibly do that's enough to pay for God's offer of a future?

It turns out that what your cat can offer God for her salvation is just what you can offer: exactly nothing. It turns out that covenants with God aren't quite the same as covenants with everyone else. It turns out that with God, it's not so much a quid pro quo as a quid pro nil. The promise, the salvation, the future on offer to every living thing is free, and there's nothing you or your cat can do to earn it, or to lose it.

So why don't you go find an animal you know, and celebrate?

PRAYER (best said while holding or snuggling your favorite animal): God, I thank you that in you, through you, and with you, the world, the animals, and I have a future. Amen.

A Gift with No Strings Attached

Ron Buford

For by grace you have been saved through faith, and this is not your own doing; it is the gift of God. From Ephesians 2:1–10

SOMEONE ACCUSED ME OF PREACHING "CHEAP GRACE." He suggested that I somehow made God's grace seem so accessible, so without requirement, that I cheapened God's grace.

I thought for a moment and said, "Thank you. God's grace is so cheap, it's free!"

Many well-meaning religious teachers taught us that there are requirements for God to love us. But Jesus says this is a lie.

It is a lie that fits our human desire to earn and accomplish, for order and control. And while these traits can be good for successful living and moral discipline, they are not requirements to receive God's grace. Jesus called people who teach such things about God, "thieves and robbers."

Receive God's really good news. Hear and accept God's gracious invitation, "Just love me." God says. "Love me with all your heart, all your soul, and all your mind. See how that feels and then share the love that wells up within you with everyone until they feel it too—no exceptions. Hanging out with me changes everything!"

When I have trouble loving anyone or am looking for excuses to make it right for me to judge others, this only lasts as long as I am not mindful of God's inexhaustible love for me. The two states of mind cannot coexist in me. How about you?

PRAYER: Gracious God, help me stop trying to save myself. I repeatedly fall in and out of trying. Thank you for loving me no matter what. Help me grow in mindfulness of your presence, your love, your grace. May the overflow of your presence, love, and grace in me touch others, even those closest to me. Amen.

PADDY WAGON BLESSING

Lillian Daniel

Do not repay evil for evil or abuse for abuse; but, on the contrary, repay with a blessing. From 1 Peter 3:8–18a

THIS IS REALLY HARD TO DO. Who wants to repay abuse with a blessing?

When someone hurts us, we want to hurt that person back. We may not admit that, to them or to ourselves, but underneath we want them to know what it feels like to be hurt. We may not actually plot to hurt them, but let's be honest; we usually do not plot to fill their lives with blessings.

Yet some of the most important social justice movements have done exactly that. People practicing civil disobedience during the civil rights movement knew that they had to break the cycle of violence. They had to deliver a blessing, which was peaceful resistance, not more cruelty.

One time when I was arrested for civil disobedience, I had sat alone for a long time in a paddy wagon that smelled of urine. I had been with a group of clergy who were supporting striking workers. As the police arrested us, we sang "Amazing Grace." But stuck alone in that stinky paddy wagon wasn't feeling like grace to me.

The police officer finally spoke to me. "You know, when you guys were singing in there, it was real pretty. I liked it."

"Thanks," I said, suddenly aware that I was not alone.

His voice was kind. "I know it smells awful, but are you ok in there?" he asked.

And from there, we moved into some real conversation; two people separated by steel bars, trying to exchange blessings in a broken world.

PRAYER: Christ, take my hurt and my resentment and transform it, so that I can repay it as a blessing. Amen.

WHAT IS SIN?

Donna Schaper

For there is no distinction, since all have sinned and fall short of the glory of God. From Romans 3:21–31

WHAT IS SIN? It is to fall short of the glory of God. It is to miss the mark of our ideal humanity. It is to be distant from God. Jesus, as the ideal human, might be defined as one who never doubted the full presence of his Father. What made him so special was how close he stayed to the one he called "Abba."

Often we mistake sin for its disguises in right and wrong behavior. Smoking, drinking, and eating too much come to mind. Abuse of our body becomes more important to us than abuse of our souls. Glory, as well as health, is our destination as a human. When we miss the mark of our best humanity, we sin. Smoking, drinking, and temple disregard are surely sins, but they are the outer sign of inner conditions. Glorious souls rarely abuse the temple in which they are housed.

We are in good company! Apparently all of us are in this boat together, this place of minimal glory and maximal distance from our mark as God's creatures. What might be different? We might learn to live in the deep water instead of the shallow. We might try to get closer to God by the practice of prayer or by raising our hands in worship to touch the Spirit of the room. We might work less on the outside and more on the inside. We might become inner actives.

PRAYER: O God, you who are the source of any glory we might ever have, draw near. Help us know what it is you meant us to be. Amen.

FORSAKEN WITH JESUS

Martin B. Copenhaver

My God, my God, why have you forsaken me? From Psalm 22

"MY GOD, MY GOD, WHY HAVE YOU FORSAKEN ME?" These first words from Psalm 22 are most familiar because they are words that Jesus subsequently uttered on the cross. It can be difficult to find these plaintive words on the lips of Jesus. But Jesus came to live among us, not as God in a human costume that could be shed whenever things get hard and rough. Rather, in Jesus, God came as human to the bone, which means human enough to experience bone-deep despair and even the perceived absence of God. If Jesus never experienced these emotions, that would mean that he never experienced the kind of life we live, which is filled with such things.

The Apostle's Creed contains this affirmation: "Jesus Christ was crucified, dead and buried. He descended to hell." The last part of that statement always used to trouble me, until one day someone told me that, for her, it was the most treasured part of the creed. When I asked why, she answered: "Because hell is where I spend much of my life." Hell—a sense of being forsaken, a place of despair. We have been there. And Jesus has been there. He has been with us. And, having been there, Jesus transforms it by his presence. And he still has the power to transform the experience of any and all who have been in the darkest regions. So this word of despair ends up being good news, indeed.

PRAYER: Oh precious Lord Jesus, accompany me into the darkest valleys of my life, that I might know that I do not journey there alone. Amen.

THE GIFT OR THE GIVER?

Anthony B. Robinson

Take your son, your only son, Isaac, whom you love, and go to the land of Moriah, and offer him there as a burnt offering . . . . From Genesis 22:1–9

WHETHER IT'S "THE TESTING OF ABRAHAM" or "the sacrifice of Isaac," this story is not an easy read. Even after all the centuries, it trembles with power and leaves us trembling.

Is it a perverse story of a hopelessly primitive God? Some say so. Or is it a powerful text trembling with deep truth? The latter, I'd say. And what is that abiding message and eternal truth? It's a question: "Where does your trust lie—in the gift or the Giver?"

Isaac was a wonderful gift. A boy whose very name meant "laughter," and more, the long-awaited first child for a people whom God had said would be as numerous as the sand on the seashore. But now God asked Abraham, "Where does your trust lie, in the gift or the Giver?"

We, too, are tested. A commitment to Christ and his way can mean giving up a great job or putting our reputation at risk. Or, say, your beloved church building burns or is sold. What then? Where does your trust ultimately lie, in the gift (job, reputation, or building) or in the Giver (God)? When we trust in the Giver, we stand on a very firm foundation.

PRAYER: When the testing comes, help me, God, to put all my trust in you. Amen.

FEELING SMALL

Martin B. Copenhaver

The heavens are telling the glory of God. From Psalm 19

A FRIEND ONCE TEASED that my idea of a picnic is to go to a French restaurant and open the windows. And it is true that, for the most part, I am a lover of the great indoors. That is where I most often encounter God, in human community, through art and books, and one book in particular. So when I hear, "The heavens are telling the glory of God," I do not immediately picture a star-bejeweled night. Rather, I hear Haydn's wonderful musical setting of that psalm.

But there are times when I have been overcome with awe in God's creation. For instance, when I stand at the lapping fringe of the ocean, gazing at the seemingly limitless horizon, it serves as a living reminder to me of the greatness and power of God.

I gather that when Theodore Roosevelt was president, he used to entertain naturalist William Beebe at his home at Sagamore Hill. After the evening's conversation the two would go out on the lawn and gaze up at the sky. Then one or the other would ritually recite, "That is the Spiral Galaxy of Andromeda. It is as large as our Milky Way. It has a hundred million suns, each larger than our own." After an interval, Roosevelt would grin at Beebe and say, "Now I think we're small enough. Let's go to bed."

Every once in a while it is good to be reminded of just how small we are. But there is a second reminder that is just as important: God loves small things, perhaps most of all.

PRAYER: God, today I thank you for the way your creation bears witness to your greatness, and yet you care for each of your creatures, including me. Amen.

POLITICAL CHRISTIANS

Quinn G. Caldwell

Then the LORD said to [Moses], . . . "I have surely seen the mistreatment of my people who are in Egypt and have heard their groaning, and I have come down to rescue them. Come now, I will send you to Egypt." From Acts 7:30–40

I BELIEVE THAT THE AMERICAN PRINCIPLE of the separation of church and state is designed to protect religion from the state, not the state from religion. You might argue this particular point, as many do. What's harder to argue is this: that the entire story of the people of God from the Exodus on, from the prophets to Paul to Jesus Christ himself, derives from this: a story in which God sent the prophet Moses to Pharaoh, a head of state, to advocate on behalf of the poor and oppressed. God told Moses to get political.

In the days before his inauguration, then President-elect Obama reminded us that voting should be the beginning, not the end, of Americans' political involvement. He told us to organize, to write letters, to advocate for what we believe needs to happen. He reminded us that politicians' hands are tied without the will of the people behind them.

So I say, let's give him what he asked for, and let's do it as Christians. Ask yourself: how does God want me to be political? What does God want to happen in the nation or the world?

The poor and oppressed are still here, the realm of God is not, and God needs you to get political.

PRAYER: God, until only you rule everywhere, show me what I can do to make the realm I live in more like yours. Amen.

DON'T BE A JERK

Ron Buford

God is God not of the dead, but of the living. From Mark 12:18–37

THEOLOGIAN MARCUS BORG SAYS IT IS CORRECT to replace the word "commandment" in verse 28 with the word "relationship."

So our first or greatest relationship is to love God with all our heart, soul, mind, and strength. The second great relationship is to love our neighbors as ourselves. There is no relationship in life, law, or eternity greater than these.

Borg goes on to say, "You can keep the commandments and still be a jerk. But you cannot be in relationship with the living God without be continually transformed." Jewish scholars interpret God, the great "I am," to mean, "I will be what the future demands."

Our God is not a God of outmoded rules and laws, keeping people separated. People do that. By contrast, the rule of God's living love is to always take another look and see your relationships with others and with God as primary. You will find God, Jesus says, where the love of God bends toward making each person's life as wonderful as God wants it to be.

PRAYER: Gracious God, we are grateful that you are a God of innovation in all things, shaping human and divine relationships in view of your ever-unfolding and always embracing present. May we remember that and grow into it—even when we do not fully understand it. Amen.

FOOLISH WORDS

Lillian Daniel

For God's foolishness is wiser than human wisdom, and God's weakness is stronger than human strength. From 1 Corinthians 1:18–25

WHEN I WAS A TEENAGER, I was not allowed to swear. So when I was really mad, I had to choose alternate words that had equal power to insult and infuriate. The word I chose was "fool."

"You're a fool," I would say, with my lip curled and my eyes rolled.

And my mother would hit the roof every time. "You can't say that to me," she would say.

"Why not? It's just another word in the English language." My nasty tone made the word "fool" sting a lot more than a swear word. The word "fool" has many layers of hurt to it. It implies stupidity, hopelessness, and mocking disdain.

So that is why Paul was so brilliant to turn the word on its head. He said that what we think of as foolishness might be Godliness. The person we call a fool may be the wise one. And Christ works through the ones the world calls foolish.

I was so sure, at the time, that my teenage disdain was wisdom. But now that my mother lives with God in the seat of wisdom, I wish I could take every sneering, disdainful expression back. I was the fool, not her.

Now as a parent I understand the message of the cross a little better. We bear a lot of pain in the name of love. When people tell us we are foolish, we keep on loving them. As Christians, we do that for one another, in order to remember that God is doing it for us.

PRAYER: Guard our harsh tongues and critical thoughts, so that we do not dismiss as foolish the ones you have chosen to show your love. Amen.

FAITH AND FEAR

William C. Green

Do not be afraid, for I am your God; I will strengthen you, I will help you.
From Isaiah 41:8–10

WE'RE TOLD NOT TO BE AFRAID precisely because, in spite of faith, so often we are afraid. However spiritually minded we are, it's hard to worry— without getting upset! And worry we do, about money, health, family, the future, including all that's so blatantly wrong in the world.

It would be nice if faith resolved hard feeling like doubt and anger— and fear. It would be nice if God meant not having to get upset. Or so it's easy to suppose.

But where would that leave us in relation to anyone else? And what of God? We wouldn't need God, we'd be God—and we certainly wouldn't need one another's support and understanding. And what of ourselves? Is all hard feeling simply weakness, or can't it, too, make possible strength and wisdom we would otherwise lack?

Faith draws us together in a world at once beautiful and flawed. What Jesus and the disciples were not spared, we're not spared. Their own togetherness and closeness to God while challenged by all that was profoundly upsetting was also made necessary, and possible, by it.

And so with us. "For I am your God" means something greater is at work than what truly is disturbing. And we are told not to be afraid, not because we will be spared hard feeling, but because amid it all we will find the strength and help we need.

PRAYER: Almighty God, we praise you for the power you make ours, whatever we feel or face. Amen.

GOD'S DWELLING PLACE

Donna Schaper

For a day in your courts is better than a thousand elsewhere. I would rather be a doorkeeper in the house of my God than live in the tents of wickedness. From Psalm 84

LIVING IN THE COURTS OF THE HOLY is a great understanding of an ordinary day. We go in, we go out. Doors mark our time. We are not stuck anywhere. We are people on the move, from one holiness and one strength to another. We go from strength to strength.

Unfortunately we are habituated to living courtless lives. We find ourselves spending time in the tents of wickedness, whether we want to or not. We imagine that our 401K's ups and downs define our security. They do not. We imagine that having health insurance is the key to having health. It is not. We imagine that very little can be done to stop crime or properly reform criminals. Indeed, when we stand at the gate of the holy, we are filled with ideas for forgiveness, reparation, renewal of those, including us, who have "gone wrong." There is nothing permanent about the tents of wickedness for us or for criminals. What is permanent is the court of the holy. We can spend every day there.

When we imagine our lives as doorkeepers to the courts of the holy, we let go of what we think is the norm on behalf of a new normal. We live a different way, as people who "wake up and smell the possibility," in the great words of Alice Walker.

PRAYER: Spirit of the Living God, tell us what it is that keeps us from being good doorkeepers. Give us detail. And then send us to the gates and there let us move in and out of holiness with joy and gratitude. Amen.

CONSIDER BREAKING A RULE

Christina Villa

He heard a voice saying, "Get up, Peter; kill and eat." But Peter said, "By no means, Lord; for I have never eaten anything that is profane or unclean." The voice said to him again, a second time, "What God has made clean, you must not call profane." This happened three times . . . . While Peter was still thinking about the vision, the Spirit said to him, "Now get up, go down, and go with them without hesitation, for I have sent them." From Acts 10:9–23a

PETER IS HUNGRY. He has a vision and hears God tell him what to do: "Get up, Peter; kill and eat." Wait a minute, Peter says, I'm not going to just kill any old thing and eat it! That's against the rules, and apparently even having God tell him it's OK—not once, not twice, but three times—isn't enough for Peter. He's still "greatly puzzled" by what he's heard. What could it mean? What should he do about it? He's still thinking about it later, when the Spirit, sounding exasperated, has a job for him to do, but has to prod him into action: "Now get up, go down, and go with them without hesitation, for I have sent them."

Sometimes we get so used to following rules that our obedience to them gets in the way of our obedience to God. Sometimes we follow rules in order to avoid challenge or risk. In the process of staying safe, and perhaps congratulating ourselves for being good rule-followers, we never do anything that might be considered divinely inspired—or even very important to us. In this scripture, Peter actually refuses to do what God tells him to do—he tells God, "By no means, Lord"—because he's let the rule become his god. But God is changing the rules here, as if to illustrate the old saying that rules are made to be broken.

What "rules" are you busy following while the Spirit is repeatedly trying to make you "get up" and do something else, something you were meant to do, something God has in mind for you?

PRAYER: Thank you for never giving up on trying to get my attention. Amen.

UNSTOPPABLE

Ron Buford

That day a severe persecution began against the church in Jerusalem, and all except the apostles were scattered throughout the countryside of Judea and Samaria. . . . Now those who were scattered went from place to place, proclaiming the word. From Acts 8:1b–8

UNSTOPPABLE IN THE FACE OF HORRIFIC PERSECUTION, early Christians continued proclaiming the Jesus story. Persecution seemed to stimulate Christianity's spread, farther and faster, to Judea and Samaria.

Jesus promised! "You shall receive power after the Holy Spirit is come upon you and you shall be my witnesses." No, it did not free them from suffering, imprisonment, and death . . . but from the prisons of powerlessness and fear. Their unstoppable acts became an unrelenting witness to a skeptical world.

Saul's seemingly unstoppable energy for persecuting Christians eventually collides with the energy and light of the Jesus of the persecuted. He later writes to Timothy, "God has not given us a spirit of fear, but of power, love, and of a sound mind."

Are you afraid today? Fear has no power over us as it does not come from external circumstance, but from our internal disconnect from the God of all power. May the Holy Spirit rest and abide within you today, granting you unexplainable, unstoppable power.

God did it for me and will do the same for you.

PRAYER: Gracious God, help me believe, release, grasp, and conduct your possibility power . . . not only for myself, my love, my family, but as one of many witnesses to your power at work in the world. Thank you. Amen!

GET READY TO CELEBRATE

Martin B. Copenhaver

Keep awake—for you do not know when the master of the house will come.
From Mark 13:32–37

IN THIS PASSAGE Jesus says that we are to live as if he will return any time. He says that we are to act as if we are servants who do not know the exact moment when the master will come home. So we are to keep alert and be ready, treating each moment as if he is about to walk through the door.

When I was a teenager and my parents left me on my own while they took a trip out of town, sometimes they would be coy about the time of their return. They wanted to keep me wondering when they would be back so that I wouldn't get into mischief while they were away. Is that something like what Jesus is saying here?

Well, perhaps, in part. Jesus does expect us to live in an upright manner. But, in the end, preparing for his return also means being ready to celebrate. When our children were young, we always kept party hats and noisemakers in our dining room because we never knew when the events of the day would be cause for celebration. Birthdays one can prepare for, but other kinds of celebrations require a more constant preparedness. And when Jesus shows up in big and small ways in our lives, it is cause for great celebration. Will you remember where you have put your party hat and noisemaker? Will you be prepared to whoop it up?

PRAYER: Jesus, help me to prepare for your appearance in our world and in my life with a heart that is tuned for joy. Amen.

NOTHING GOOD WITHHELD

Kenneth L. Samuel

For the LORD *God is a sun and shield; the* LORD *will give grace and glory: no good thing will [God] withhold from them that walk uprightly.* From Psalm 84 KJV

I HAD JUST PURCHASED a brand new Dell Computer from the Best Buy store. I was frustrated because I couldn't get the thing to work right. I had wireless Internet from Verizon and I had a brand new computer, but I still couldn't access cyberspace or check my e-mails. In an agitated flurry, I put the computer back in the box and took it back to the store. Surely some device or some cable had been omitted from my computer package.

The "Geek Squad" tested it and politely informed me that all I needed was in the package, but that with the new configurations of a new computer I needed new procedures to access the Internet. The store had not withheld anything I needed; I just needed to learn how to use it.

When I think of the goodness that seems to be lacking in my life, I am often tempted to believe that for some reason God is holding back and holding out on me. But in light of my computer experience, the problem may not be God's lack of provision, but my failure to fully access all that God has provided. For me, this is the promise of Psalm 84:11—God is not a withholder of anything that is good. And this is the blessed assurance of goodness in my life—the goodness that has been revealed, and the goodness that is yet to be accessed.

PRAYER: God, give me the faith to trust in your goodness that I cannot see, and to depend on your provisions that I have not yet realized. Amen.

GOD SHOWS NO PARTIALITY

Martin B. Copenhaver

Then Peter began to speak to them: "I truly understand that God shows no partiality, but in every nation anyone who fears him and does what is right is acceptable to him." From Acts 10:34–43

IN JESUS' DAY there was great enmity between Jews and Gentiles. So perhaps it is not surprising that, in the earliest days of the church, there were many who thought that the good news of Jesus was for Jews alone. Peter was particularly fervent in his belief that in order to be a follower of Jesus one had to conform to Jewish practices. But then Peter was touched by the faith of a Gentile named Cornelius and he received a vision in a dream that showed him otherwise. Peter said, to everyone's astonishment (and perhaps his own), "I truly understand that God shows no partiality."

Given what Peter had previously believed, it would have been remarkable if he had said, "I truly understand that God does not want us to hate one another." It would have been startling if he had said, "I truly understand that God wants us accept one another." It would have been revolutionary if he had said, "I truly understand that God wants us to be in relationship with one another." But Peter says more than any of those things, and more than all of that combined. Peter says, in essence, "No one is in and no one is out. We are the same in God's sight."

That story is such a pivotal one, not merely because it traces an important moment in the history of the church, but also because it reminds us that that history continues. God is still extending a wider welcome than we would be inclined to give.

PRAYER: God, we affirm that you are still speaking. May we still listen. Amen.

A LOVING CHALLENGE

Anthony B. Robinson

He came to Jesus by night and said, "Rabbi, we know you are a teacher who has come from God. For no one could perform the miraculous signs you are doing if God were not with him." In reply Jesus declared, "I tell you the truth, no one can see the kingdom of God unless he is born again." From John 3:1–13 NIV

WELCOME TO THE WEIRD WORLD of the Fourth Gospel, where conversations can give you the feeling of ships passing in the night. A religious leader, Nicodemus, dropped by for an after-hours conversation with Jesus. Two experts talking shop. "How do you do it, Jesus?" Perhaps Nicodemus hoped to learn Jesus' secret and get some of that power himself?

Nicodemus did learn Jesus' secret, and he was never the same again. "I tell you the truth, no one can see the kingdom of God unless he is born again." Nicodemus was stunned and confused. He had wanted a little knowledge, maybe some advice—not a whole new life. Jesus said, "You must start all over again." Jesus dared to challenge Nicodemus.

The thing about the challenges that come from Jesus is that they are rooted and wrapped in love. He challenges us because he loves us. Sometimes our love of others is empty of challenge or the invitation to grow. And often our challenges are short on love. "Those whom we would change," said Martin Luther King Jr., "we must first love."

PRAYER: God, thank you for loving me enough to challenge me. Grant that I may offer the gift of a loving challenge to someone else today. Amen.

On the Way to the Springs and Palm Trees

Ron Buford

He cried out to the LORD; and the LORD showed him a piece of wood; he threw it into the water, and the water became sweet. From Exodus 15:22–27

THE TRIP WAS GOING BADLY as he led the children of Israel out of Egypt. In his moment of desperation, Moses did the three things we should all do. First: call on God—in good times and bad. Second: Be open to God's answer when we sense an answer—even when it seems . . . well, strange. And, finally, we should act on what God reveals through the sacred texts, prayer, and impressions or hunches we get on our daily prayerful walk with God.

It's not always easy. Would you have thrown that piece of wood in the water? I doubt that I would have. I might have been more afraid that I'd look desperate or foolish.

How does one know the will of God? Sometimes you don't know. Sometimes you have to take the risk, the leap of faith. And after taking the risk, you will know because the bitter undrinkable water in your life will become sweet or healthy. If it doesn't work, don't be too proud to change course. But notice how Moses' temporary solution eventually leads the people to an abundance of water.

So it is in life. In conflict, add a little sweetness. In time, it will lead you and those in conflict to a greater abundance of peace.

PRAYER: Gracious God, help me bring calm and peace to a troubled situation in my life, my family, my community today. Help me take the risks needed to make peace. Bless the effort and help it lead to an abundance of peace. Amen.

NAKED DREAMS

Lillian Daniel

And before [God] no creature is hidden, but all are naked and laid bare to the eyes of the one to whom we must render an account. From Hebrews 4:1–13

I KNOW I AM NOT THE ONLY ONE to have had this dream, but I may be the only one to admit to it in a widely read devotional. You know the dream. You are trying to get to an important event, only to realize you are missing some key items of clothing. Like pants. And even more essential items. Sometimes all of them.

In the dream, I look around, wondering if people in the crowd have noticed that I have taken the television show "What Not to Wear" way too literally. And oddly enough, the people have not noticed, at least not yet. The nightmare commences with me trying to get from point A to point B without anyone noticing I have no clothes on.

Did I mention that in these dreams, I am often en route to a professional gathering? For me that would be church. But I have also had the dream about elementary school, violin recitals, and even one where I'm competing in the Olympics.

So this passage about God seeing us naked makes many of us a little uneasy. It's like a bad dream we want to wake up from.

But here our anxiety is misplaced. God isn't checking out our tan lines. God means to express that we are totally known, for better and for worse, even in ways that we would not want the world to know us. And even in that state, we are loved. We will be examined of course, but we will also be loved.

PRAYER: If anyone should see my soul naked, I would choose you, God, because you have seen it all. And still, you sent me Jesus. Amen.

HONEST TO GOD

William C. Green

Let us therefore approach the throne of grace with boldness, so that we may receive mercy and find grace to help in time of need. From Hebrews 4:14–5:4

DURING THE TIME that I served a congregation with many farmers in it, there were seasons of drought. City boy that I was, and not comfortable with the idea that God can make it rain, I got around the drought by thanking God for our many blessings. Besides, the days when it didn't rain were beautiful.

Jesus said, "Ask, and you will receive. Knock, and the door will be opened." He did not say, "Be realistic, and you might get what you're requesting," or "Tap on the door, and someone might answer."

Jesus was bold, and urges us to be bold, because God is bold. What counted for Jesus is what counts for us: not prayer, but God, who works through our prayers. Maybe that means rain amid a drought. Who are we to doubt what God can do? If it doesn't mean rain it means something just as life-giving—power greater than our own that can see us through the worst circumstances. But if we don't ask for it, how can we really receive it?

One preacher put it well when he said, "Some of our prayers need to be cut short at both ends and set on fire in the middle." Honesty is the match.

PRAYER: God, make us bold. And keep us honest. May we ask for what we really want, not just for what we think might be possible. Amen.

AUGUST

MANY MEANINGS

Anthony B. Robinson

Now there were some Greeks among those who went up to worship at the Feast. They came to Philip . . . with a request, "Sir," they said, "we would like to see Jesus." From John 12:20–33 NIV

AT JESUS' BIRTH Gentiles, magi, came seeking him. Now, as a kind of bookend, Greeks—Gentiles—came once more just before Jesus' death, also seeking him. "Sir, we would like to see Jesus." What powerful words!

Their words have more than one meaning. On a literal level, they request an audience, an appointment, a little time with Jesus. On another level, "We would like to see Jesus," is to say we want to become disciples of Jesus. We want to see and follow him. And at an even deeper level, they are saying we want to have a spiritual blindness healed and truly to see.

Perhaps not in so grand a way as this, but many of our words and conversations too have layers and levels of meaning. There's a literal level. But often there's more, much more. Do you listen for "the song beneath the words" in the words or requests of others? Do you listen to the longing that our own words, as well as the words of others to us, both hide and reveal? Have you experienced being heard, deeply and truly, by another human being? It's an incredible experience. When it happens, it feels holy. We feel that we have been in God's presence, that in some way we have seen and been seen by Jesus himself.

PRAYER: Okay, Lord Jesus, two ears, one mouth. Now I get it, listen twice as much as you speak. Help me hear, really hear, someone today. Amen.

AUGUST 2

SPIRITUAL SPONTANEITY

Lillian Daniel

As they were going along the road, they came to some water; and the eunuch said, "Look, here is water! What is to prevent me from being baptized?" He commanded the chariot to stop, and both of them, Philip and the eunuch, went down into the water, and Philip baptized him. From Acts 8:26–40

TODAY, IF SOMEONE WANTS to get a baby baptized, they first call our church and check some dates against the church calendar. Then they may call around to family, godparents, and friends to see who might be available for the brunch. Perhaps next they see if the baby fits into the prepurchased little baptismal outfit, and if he or she suddenly looks like a ten-pound sausage in a five-pound bag, they might choose that earlier date. But it all takes a lot of planning.

Unlike the early church leader, Phillip, I have never been stopped by a eunuch and talked into performing a baptism on the side of the road. But I think it might be good for me.

Churches are complex institutions. They have rules and procedures and calendars, and we don't need to apologize for that. That's how we weave together the fabric of community, and make possible our communal worship of God.

But we must never let the rules and regulations become the object of our worship. If the winds of the Holy Spirit can't blow through them, the fabric is knit too tight.

Healthy churches have room for the question: "What is to prevent me?" And their leaders are careful not to answer that question too quickly with a list of things like the bylaws, our tradition, or the schedule.

If we can hold our tongues when the newcomer asks "What is to prevent me?" we might find ourselves realizing that indeed the Holy Spirit is trying to blow through us with a little spiritual spontaneity. And we might say, "Well, why not?"

PRAYER: God, what is to prevent me? What is to prevent me from doing the thing I have not yet imagined? Well, why not? Amen.

Can I Get a Witness?

Kenneth L. Samuel

I will say to the north, "Give them up," and to the south, "Do not withhold; bring my sons from far away and my daughters from the end of the earth— everyone who is called by my name, whom I created for my glory, whom I formed and made." Bring forth the people who are blind, yet have eyes, who are deaf, yet have ears! Let all the nations gather together, and let the peoples assemble. Who among them declared this, and foretold to us the former things? Let them bring their witnesses to justify them, and let them hear and say, "It is true." Isaiah 43:6–9

SECOND-HAND EXPERIENCE AND INFORMATION have only so much credibility. There is nothing as compelling and convincing as a firsthand testimony. Everyone strains to hear the eye-witness account. In the cosmic courtroom of human judgment, God's defense does not rest on hearsay. From every sphere of the globe there are witnesses, ready and willing to stake their lives on the testimony of their own personal experiences with the God of Israel. No need for endless debate or prolonged deliberation. Those who do not know God can listen and learn of God's trustworthiness from those who've been baptized by the fiery trials of life, and yet continue to live by faith.

The mothers and fathers of the African American church put it this way: "You can't make me doubt him, 'cause I know too much about him!" This is the kind of witness that will move personal skepticism and shake the rafters of institutional indifference. This is the kind of witness that will inspire hope among the disconsolate and command the attention of the world.

PRAYER: Sovereign God, I thank you for all that you have allowed me to experience in your Spirit firsthand. Now make me a witness to the power of my own testimony. Amen.

GOD DOES NOT LIKE WHINERS

Martin B. Copenhaver

Why have you brought us up out of Egypt, to bring us to this wretched place?
From Numbers 20:1–13

ONE OF THE MESSAGES FROM THIS PASSAGE from the Book of Numbers is easily summarized: God does not like whiners. God had just led the people of Israel out of slavery in Egypt when they started whining about where they ended up, in a land where there was little vegetation and no visible source of water. In response, God told Moses to strike a rock and water poured out of it, but God was not too happy about it and said, in essence, "This group of whiners is never going to make it to the promised land."

God doesn't always expect us to be cheery. In fact, it is evident from scripture that God welcomes lament and even complaint as legitimate responses to the hardships of life. The difference is that whiners always find a way to whine, regardless of circumstances.

They tell a story in Vermont about a farmer who always moaned about his crop yields. Every harvest seemed to fall short. Then, one year, after a spectacular bumper crop, a fellow farmer said, "Well, even you will have to admit that this was a good year." To which the whining farmer replied, "Yes, but terribly hard on the soil."

Whiners always find reason to whine. And those whose lives are marked by gratitude always find reason to give thanks. It is clear which kind of person God expects us to be.

PRAYER: God, please hear my complaints when life is difficult, but, dear God, please don't let me become a whiner. Instead, trace my heart with gratitude. Amen.

THE BLOOD OF THE LAMB

Christina Villa

They have washed their robes and made them white in the blood of the Lamb.
From Revelation 7:13–17

HOW DO YOU WASH SOMETHING IN BLOOD and have it come out white? Well, you can if it's symbolic. It's not real blood. Or a real lamb. Or even a real robe. And it's not literally "white" either. The blood, the lamb, the robe, and the color white symbolize other things. Once we're taught what those other things are, we can think about them. We can think about the ideas of suffering, sacrifice, innocence, and redemption.

We are not fundamentalists; we don't take the Bible literally. This leaves us, sometimes, not quite knowing what to do with robes washed in the blood of the lamb. We usually rush straight to the meaning of the symbols, so we can think, discuss, conclude, and move on. Next idea, please! Ideas are great because, unlike real things, they go away if you stop thinking about them.

There is so much real blood of so many real innocents flowing in the world. Literally flowing in the gutter, soaking into the ground, and collecting on the floor in emergency rooms. Surely the blood of the Lamb is a real thing.

At the beginning of the Iraq war, a widely printed photo showed an American soldier with a stricken look on his face carrying the dead body of a very small child, her head hanging back at an unnatural angle. Such a picture always has the last word, I think, on the subject of bloodshed. People often say they don't need the graphic detail to understand such things. Maybe not. But why should we be spared them? Who are we to avoid dipping our robes in the blood of the Lamb?

PRAYER: Keep me from turning away, from turning real things into ideas, from thinking the world into harmlessness. Amen.

Should I Stay or Should I Go?

Anthony B. Robinson

Stay here in the city until you have been clothed with power from on high.
From Luke 24:44–53

THE GOSPELS OF MATTHEW AND LUKE CONCLUDE in quite different ways. In Matthew the disciples are told, "Go and make disciples." "Go." In Luke, they are told to "stay," sit tight, wait in Jerusalem, stay put until you are clothed with power from on high. I don't imagine that the band the Clash had the New Testament in mind when they sang, "Should I Stay or Should I Go?" but they could have.

Generally, I am more of a Matthew type than a Luke type. I prefer to go, to get on with it, to move, to do, and to act. But there is a time for waiting. Waiting until the time is right. Waiting until some gift of power and grace, not our own, comes upon us to make it possible for us to do what cannot be done in our own strength alone.

"Stay" said Luke, wait. But it's not just waiting. It's waiting for the Spirit, for a power not our own to come upon us, to clothe us. There are things that need doing in this world that are beyond our ability to accomplish solely by our own effort. God's word, God's incursion, God's Spirit are required. "Stay in the city until you have been clothed with power from on high."

PRAYER: Veni Sancte Spiritus: Come, Holy Spirit, come. Teach me to wait and to pray. To wait for you, to call upon you, to be clothed by your power from on high. Amen.

MOSES AT A DEAD RUN

Quinn G. Caldwell

Then Moses went up from the plains of Moab to Mount Nebo, to the top of Pisgah, which is opposite Jericho, and the LORD showed him the whole land . . . Then Moses, the servant of the LORD, died . . . . From Deuteronomy 34:1–7

AN OLD STORY IMAGINES what happened after Moses died. Abraham, Isaac, and Jacob are sitting in the afterlife, when they look up and see Moses in the distance. He's headed their way at a dead run, his long white beard flowing behind him, his robes hiked up, and his skinny old-man legs flashing. He skids to a stop in front of them, and as soon as he catches his breath, he blurts out, "I have seen it! I have seen the promised land! The oath that the Holy One swore to you? He has fulfilled it!" Their faces light up and they begin to praise God.

It's such a great image: Moses like a little kid running up to his parents, bursting with news, and the Patriarchs, having lived, and labored, and waited long for God's promise, hearing that it has finally been fulfilled.

Here's an even better story: Moses has taken his place next to Abraham, Isaac, and Jacob. They look up, and there, sprinting toward them in the distance, bursting with news about God's faithful action on earth is . . . you. And you run up to them, and you catch your breath, and you open your mouth, and say . . .

Well, I'll let you decide what you'll say.

PRAYER: Faithful God, help me to keep my eyes open for the fulfillment of the promises you made to the ancestors. Let me never miss a single one of your blessings, and give me the grace to never stop telling people about them. Amen.

Every Time I Remember You

Ron Buford

I thank my God every time I remember you. From Philippians 1:3–11

WHEN THOSE CLOSE TO US DIE, simple things remind us of them—a smell, a song, a flower, the gathering of family and friends. And we remember . . .

Sometimes their memory breaks in on us like an intruder, without ample time for us to prepare and brace ourselves. And so, we cry. We miss them. At other times we laugh. Either way, it is a good thing to not hold back. Experience your range of emotions but do not stop there. Give God thanks for your having had them in your life. Acknowledge their presence as a gift from God; this will always put your heart in the right place.

Sometimes, we are like children who want more ice cream. "We did not have them long enough," we say. And that is always true of those we love most dearly—especially those who had, from our perspectives, untimely deaths. Let us instead give thanks that we had them, remembering, we have them still. They were never our possessions. They were companions God placed into our life's journey . . . for a while. Best of all, they surround us now, so many as to be like the stars of the Milky Way, a cloud, all witnesses to love, to faithfulness, to the hope and mystery that we shall see them . . . again.

PRAYER: Gracious God, Sometimes I miss someone so much I cannot seem to bear it. Still, I thank you for placing such a great person in my life. I remember her perfume, his crazy laugh, the way he looked at me that let me know I was loved, for the great things she accomplished, for the things we saw together. Thank you for these special lives and times, and for ways they helped shape me to be the person I am today. Give them blessed rest and peace and confidence in knowing they left us well and continuing on with life until we meet them again. Amen.

ONLY WONDER

Anthony B. Robinson

Listen, listen to the thunder of [God's] voice, the rumbling that comes from [God's] mouth. Under the whole heaven [God] lets it loose, and [God's] lightning to the corners of the earth. From Job 37:1–13

EVERY YEAR, IT SEEMED, sometime during the week of Summer Family Camp, there was a thunderstorm. Before the storm, it was strangely still. Still and heavy, as if some invisible weight pressed down on us. In the late afternoon the wind would start, gusting up out of the south. Whitecaps soon spiked the lake's placid waters. The sky darkened into swirling shades of gray, black, and blue. Suddenly, a crack of thunder, then another, and then a rolling rumble. Lightening ignited in the heavens.

And we, happy campers, did nothing. Nothing but watch, watch and wonder. Mostly silent we beheld the spectacle of a summer storm from the deck of the lodge or a cabin porch. What was so powerful about this annual array of thunder and lightning? Why did it so often feel as if it were a kind of worship service? The desert father, Gregory of Nyssa, wrote, "Concepts create idols; only wonder comprehends anything." Wordless in wonder, we heard. "Hear this, O Job; stop and consider the wondrous works of God." The storm stilled us and stopped us. The storm said, "Be still and know that I am God." Only wonder comprehends anything.

PRAYER: Holy One, I thank you for summer storms and every gift or sign that reminds me that there is a God and it's not me. Amen.

ALIENS

Quinn G. Caldwell

When Pharaoh calls you, and says, "What is your occupation?" you shall say, "Your servants have been keepers of livestock from our youth even until now, both we and our ancestors"—in order that you may settle in the land of Goshen, because all shepherds are abhorrent to the Egyptians. From Genesis 46:28–47:6

JACOB AND HIS SONS AND THEIR FAMILIES immigrate to Egypt because conditions in their home country have become untenable. Son Joseph, who has gotten there ahead of them, advises them to take up shepherding, honest work that needs to be done, but which the Egyptians don't want to do.

What was true then is true now: those who move to another country in search of a better life, unless they are highly skilled or educated, will likely end up doing the jobs that the natives avoid.

Who mows your lawn?

Who cleans your mother's nursing home?

Who does your manicure?

Who picked the oranges for the juice on your breakfast table?

Have you taken time to meet them, or are they wallpaper to your life? What do you know about their wages? Their health-care coverage? How sure are you that what you buy, or eat, or wear isn't breaking their bodies or minds on its way to you?

These questions of justice are worth thinking about because if the story that we tell is true, then the aliens in our midst aren't cheap labor; they're God's chosen people. For our own good as well as theirs, it's worth treating them well.

I mean, look what happened to Pharaoh in the end.

PRAYER: God, you were once an alien residing in this land, and we did not treat you well. Give us the grace to learn from our mistakes, and to treat the aliens in our midst as we would treat our own family. Amen.

WANTS AND NEEDS

Kenneth L. Samuel

The LORD is my shepherd, I shall not want. He makes me lie down in green pastures; he leads me beside still waters; he restores my soul. He leads me in right paths for his name's sake. Even though I walk through the darkest valley, I will fear no evil; for you are with me; your rod and your staff—they comfort me. You prepare a table before me in the presence of my enemies; you anoint my head with oil; my cup overflows. Surely goodness and mercy shall follow me all the days of my life, and I shall dwell in the house of the LORD my whole life long. Psalm 23

I DON'T KNOW ABOUT YOU, but I've been wrestling with Psalm 23 for a long time. As a boy, I used to read the first line of this psalm as one complete thought, with no comma or semi-colon. Then my mother kindly instructed me that it would make no sense to worship God if I didn't want God. After I separated the two thoughts of the first line, I then had to wrestle with the reconciliation of those two thoughts. I eventually came up with this: "Because the Lord is my shepherd, I shall not be in want."

This resolution seemed pretty clever to me, and certainly in keeping with church orthodoxy. The only problem I had then was that as much as I affirmed God as my shepherd, I nonetheless could not deny the fact that I still had some rather serious wants. So, was I to understand the first line of Psalm 23 as a declaration of hope, or eschatological expectancy? I couldn't determine if Psalm 23 was a distant hope or a present-day assurance.

It could be a bit of both, but I have elected to pull it more into my present context. In light of all my present wants, what does it mean to say, "'The Lord is my shepherd"? The answer for me has been in linking the two thoughts of the first line more consistently. Instead of jumping so abruptly from the shepherd to my wants, I've learned to linger and live in the simply profound declaration: "The Lord is my shepherd." With my focus on the shepherd's care, the shepherd's guidance, and the shepherd's sacrifice for me, I have come to understand that because the Lord is my shepherd, I have everything I need. Now those are two thoughts that I can reconcile and relate to my present-day situations, my wants, still notwithstanding.

PRAYER: Caring, shepherding God, we do thank you for being our good shepherd. And we do thank you for being all that we need right now and forever more. Amen.

You Have What It Takes!

William C. Green

Whatever you ask in prayer, believe that you have received it, and it will be yours. From Mark 11:20–25

JESUS DID NOT SAY believe that you will receive what you pray for. He said, "believe that you have received it."

So often we pray for what we already have. Time and again the psalmist says "God is my strength," not "God, grant me strength." The same with all kinds of help and healing, forgiveness and guidance, an ability to keep the faith and to pray. "God is my rock and redeemer." Not please, God, give me something I need and don't have.

So why pray? Because our petitions rightly understood are not requests but praise. The dreariest from the Psalms, full of neediness and despair, almost always move seamlessly into declarations of what God has done and makes possible.

We are created in the likeness of God's goodness and strength—"little less than God."

True, we fall away from this and abuse our God-given endowments. But we are not stripped of them. And prayer recalls us to who we are in the first place. It's an awakening, or reawakening, to what's still ours.

Often enough I've felt like some bottomless pit that no amount of encouragement or reassurance could fill. At those times I'd always pray for strength I lacked. I've now taken to praying another way. "God, make me aware of the strength you've given me." That's proven a good way to respect God, and others. When I quit looking elsewhere for what I already have, I find it!

PRAYER: O God, I praise you for the strength and hope you give us. Amen.

AUGUST 13

SHEEPISH

Lillian Daniel

I am the good shepherd. The good shepherd lays down his life for the sheep.
From John 10:11–18

IF GOD IS THE SHEPHERD, then who are we? I have some bad news. We are the sheep.

If I were to pick an animal to be, my mind would go to some of the more exciting animals, like an eagle or a lion. I'd like to be something that can fly or at least pounce.

Next, I might consider the animals I already know and love, like cats and dogs, who seem to have pretty good lives. At least they do in my house. Judging by who gets the best seat on the sofa, they are clearly in charge.

But a sheep? Who wants to be a sheep?

I don't really know any sheep, of course. I have only seen them from a great distance, as I zoom by in a car. They always seem to be milling around with their noses in the grass, doing nothing at all exciting.

But perhaps that's what we look like from the perspective of heaven. At our worst, we just mill around the earth, with our noses pointed down, unaware of what's going on around us. At our best, we have a shepherd, who nudges us, makes sure we are fed, and takes us to higher and better ground.

I may not want to be a sheep, but I am grateful that the Lord Jesus is my good shepherd.

PRAYER: The Lord is my shepherd, I shall not want. Amen.

AUGUST 14

ADDRESS: 5715 BROKEN SPIRIT

Anthony B. Robinson

For thus says the high and lofty one who inhabits eternity . . . I dwell in the high and holy place, and also with those who are contrite and humble in spirit.
Isaiah 57:15

WHERE DOES GOD DWELL? Where is God to be found? If you're looking for God, where should you look? Isaiah, the prophet, gives a two-part answer. One part is no big surprise. God dwells in "The high and holy place." That's sort of God's expected address, "High and Holy." But God has another primary dwelling, a second address, and one that comes as a surprise. God dwells "With those who are contrite and humble in spirit." God makes his home at 5715 Broken Spirit Drive.

We might imagine, and there seem to be plenty of people who will tell you that it is the case, that God resides with those who are full up, on top, and standing out—those who have arrived. God is with the winners. God is with those who are doing good and doing well, who know what the right side is and that they are on it. But sometimes people who dwell at that place are so full of themselves that there's just no room for God.

God finds room with people who aren't full, but who are empty. God finds a dwelling place with those who aren't totally satisfied with themselves, but who experience some godly sorrow, some wish that they had done better and some knowledge that they haven't. God dwells with those who know their need of God. When that's where we live, when our address is "Broken Spirit" or "Contrite Heart," God can and will find a dwelling place with us.

PRAYER: "The sacrifice acceptable to God is a broken spirit; a broken and contrite heart, O God, you will not despise" (from Psalm 51:17). Amen.

AUGUST 15

RISKY

Quinn G. Caldwell

What is your petition, Queen Esther? It shall be granted you. And what is your request? From Esther 7:1–10

ESTHER IS A JEWISH WOMAN living in the Persian Empire. Through beauty, intelligence, and luck, she becomes queen. Then, not knowing his wife is Jewish, the king declares that all Jews in the empire be put to death. Esther is in a tight spot: she can keep her heritage secret (and thereby betray her faith), or she can out herself as a Jew and try to stop the murder (and thereby risk death). She chooses the latter, saves the people, defeats her enemies, and becomes a hero.

As with Esther and her faith, it can sometimes be difficult to out our-selves as Christians to friends, coworkers, even to family. Will people think we are superstitious? Backward? Stupid? Will they make assumptions about our political leanings? Will they still like us? It's not death we risk, to be sure, but the risks are—or at least feel—real nonetheless.

But perhaps the question is less about the risks we take in telling of our faith in God, and more about how the telling might help those around us. Who knows who among your friends might be saved from aimlessness, from despair, from loneliness by hearing what you believe? Esther used her position as queen to say something good about her faith; perhaps you can use yours as friend, coworker, or family member to do the same.

PRAYER: God, help me to remember with Esther that, though the risks of talking about you can be real, the joys you grant will always be greater still. Amen.

AUGUST 16

THE DRY BONES OF DEPRESSION

Lillian Daniel

The hand of the LORD came upon me . . . and set me down in the middle of a valley; it was full of bones . . . and they were very dry. He said to me, "Mortal, can these bones live?" I answered, "O LORD God, you know." From Ezekiel 37:1–14

A WOMAN SITS AT HER KITCHEN TABLE after the children have left for school. She was barely able to muster a goodbye smile, and now that there is no one else to perform for, she gives into the absolute loss of energy that sweeps her every morning. There are dishes to do and errands to run, but it will be an accomplishment if she spends the school day awake and does not give in to the overwhelming temptation to get back into bed.

Can these dry bones live?

A boy's thoughts turn to the end of his life. Would anybody miss him if he were gone? The anguish inside him seems so great that death appears to be the only relief. He perseverates on the way it might happen.

Can these dry bones live?

Her husband sits in front of the television for hour after hour. They have not spoken more than a few words to one another in days. She remembers when they were dating; they could spend hours at a coffee shop, discussing big ideas. Now, he rarely has an expression on his face. His eyes have been drained of joy, and he stares blankly at the screen.

Can these dry bones live?

For people who live with depression . . . for people who love people with depression . . . these scenes are all too easy to imagine. But God called the prophet Ezekiel to prophesy to the dry bones, and promised that by God's healing power, flesh would appear and those dry bones would live again.

PRAYER: On this day, hear my prayer for those who suffer from depression, whose bones seem dry and lifeless. Be also with their loved ones, the doctors, the therapists, the researchers, the scientists, and the healers, so that once again those bones might live. Grant us understanding of the complexities of the human mind, because God, we trust that you do know how to make dry bones live again, and that you want this healing to be available for all your children. Amen.

THINGS ARE NOT AS THEY SEEM

Ron Buford

Some take pride in chariots, and some in horses, but our pride is in the name of the LORD our God. From Psalm 20

IF THE BIBLE TEACHES US ANYTHING, it is that might and power do not always win the day—even if they seem to for a while. Moses led the children of Israel across the dry ground of the parted Red Sea with chariots and soldiers in pursuit—soldiers who, when the waters began to suddenly flow back, drowned under the sheer weight of their armament. Using a mere slingshot and a smooth stone, the small shepherd boy David assuaged the trembling and paralyzing fears of the Israelites, slaying the giant Goliath, who had long terrorized the Israelites with booming voice, size, and armor. Jesus, a poor peasant carpenter, ultimately disestablished the powerful Roman and Jewish authorities, who thought they could end his influence and power by executing him. But God resurrected Jesus and made him a force more powerful than his enemies or followers could ever have imagined.

Is there some situation or power causing you anxiety or grief today? Know that it is subservient to the power of God and your ability to overcome your own fear of its power in your life. Embrace God's love for you, God's willingness to get involved on your behalf—even if you've made mistakes. Expect results.

PRAYER: Gracious God, I am afraid in this situation. Help me to put my trust in you. Help me do everything in my power to change things in positive ways. Help me act, not out of powerlessness, immobility, anger, fear, gossip, or retribution. Instead, O God, help me to plan and live for victory and success. Oh, and until it comes, please give me the strength to wait for it. In the name of Jesus, the resurrected One by whom and in whom we are all continually resurrected. Amen.

Our Papa in Heaven

Martin B. Copenhaver

When we cry, "Abba, Father!" it is that very Spirit bearing witness with our spirit that we are children of God. From Romans 8:12–17

MARTIN LUTHER MUSED that Joseph must have been a wonderful father, for Jesus to have chosen to address God as Father. (Luther also said that his relationship with his own father was so difficult that he couldn't address God as Father without shuddering.) But the term Jesus actually used is even more remarkable—"Abba," which is an intimate term of endearment, more like "Papa," or "Daddy." The word comes from the gurgling sounds that an infant makes before she has learned to talk.

It is the first "word" an infant utters (and typical of a father to assume that the word refers to him: "She's talking to me!"). When Jesus addresses God as Abba it reflects the intimacy of his relationship with God, like an infant's close and trusting relationship with a nurturing parent. When Jesus calls God "Abba" it also makes clear that even before we have the right words—or any words at all—we have enough with which to approach God. Even our wordless gurgles or sighs too deep for words can be enough.

That someone could have such a close relationship with God is remarkable. But the Apostle Paul goes on to affirm a still more remarkable truth: through Jesus, we are invited to have that kind of relationship with God as well. Not only is Jesus the Son of God but, through him, we are God's daughters and sons, and God is our Abba, too.

PRAYER: Abba, I thank you that, although you are mighty and mysterious, you also seek an intimate relationship with me, like that of a child and a nurturing parent. Amen.

Awesome

Quinn G. Caldwell

Because you arose, Deborah, arose as a mother in Israel . . . . From Judges 5:1–12

THOSE WHO HAVE TROUBLE with women's leadership in religious institutions (or political ones, for that matter) could use a little time spent with Deborah. She's awesome: the most powerful prophet of her day (read: she knew what God was saying), she was also its judge (read: everybody did what she said). They called her the mother of the nation. She was such a force that Barak, the best general in Israel, would refuse to go into battle without her by his side. The story says that through her leadership, God gave the Israelites victory over their enemies, and peace for forty years. All this in what was definitely a man's world. Like I said, awesome.

Today's passage is part of a song of victory that Deborah and Barak sing together; the excerpt is from a part that Barak sings to the people about Deborah's greatness.

What particular gifts of leadership do the women in your church bring? Who are the judges, the generals, the mothers, and the prophetesses that shape your congregation's life? When was the last time you sang a song—public or otherwise—of their greatness?

PRAYER: Gracious and loving God, we give thanks for all the gifts of women's leadership in our churches, in all their forms. Grant us the grace to see and celebrate and be blessed by these gifts wherever you have given them, for your sake and for ours. Amen.

The Cat Who Walked by Faith

Lillian Daniel

So we are always confident; even though we know that while we are at home in the body we are away from the Lord—for we walk by faith, not by sight. From 2 Corinthians 5:6–17

A CONTAINER OF KENTUCKY FRIED CHICKEN appeared to be dancing in the middle of the dark street, with a life of its own, so we stopped to investigate.

Out of the chicken box crawled a terribly skinny kitten with long black fur and four bright white paws. She had been making that box dance, as she tried to lick out the last crumb for nourishment. Now, she purred, leaning into me with her whole body. We adopted that little stray and named her "Little Boots."

Little Boots thrived with cat food, a trip to the vet, and lots of love. But she remained very small, and displayed the silliest behavior. She would sneak up on our other cats, as if to attack them, but she would be right in front of them, in plain sight. By the time she pounced, the cats had moved away. She couldn't figure out how they knew she was coming.

It was only when we found her walking on a second story porch rail, precariously sticking her paw out into the air feeling for her next step, that we realized the obvious. Little Boots was blind. From then on, that cat became my hero. Nothing stopped her. When she ran into a wall, she turned back and ran the other way. When she walked into a piece of furniture, she remembered where it was the next time. She didn't sit still. Her little white paws were always out in the air in front of her, testing, to find her next foothold.

She was tiny and the world was dangerous.

But Little Boots seemed to walk by faith, not sight.

PRAYER: Wonderful Creator, you have populated your world with so many creatures, and we human beings are but one example of your handiwork. Help us to see your majesty in all your animals, from the roaring lion to the courageous kitten. Amen.

No Fool

Quinn G. Caldwell

Fools say in their hearts, "There is no God." From Psalm 53

So IF YOU'RE READING THIS DEVOTIONAL, I assume you are more or less in the "there is a God" camp. You're no fool.

On the other hand, neither are those who say in their hearts, "There is no God." Not really.

Sometimes, atheists' disbelief has its roots in science or philosophy. More often, it stems from unpleasant interactions with believers, either in lived experience, or in story or history. You know the list: the Inquisition, so-called witch trials, pogroms, the Crusades, discrimination of all kinds, threats of hell. A recent study of nonchurchgoers ages sixteen to twenty-nine found that 87 percent think that Christians are judgmental.

Since God seems to have decided to not show up in person much anymore, but instead to rely on her people to be her representatives, you can hardly blame atheists if, having met only these kinds of reps, they decide that God isn't worth their time. In fact, that's a decidedly unfoolish response under the circumstances.

What God needs, then, is a different kind of representative, one that won't convert people away from God, but will invite them to love. A representative that lives a life of grace and welcome and invitation and love and service, one who lives a life of adventure and tenderness.

God needs representatives who are not fools. Representatives like you.

PRAYER: God, let all of my life be a witness to your love, and an invitation to life with you. Amen.

WHAT A MIRACLE FEELS LIKE

Christina Villa

When he saw that they were straining at the oars against an adverse wind, he came towards them early in the morning, walking on the sea. From Mark 6:45–56

THIS SENTENCE FROM MARK is just one example of the peculiar way the Bible often has of describing extraordinary events. Jesus walking on water is surely one of the major astounding things in the entire New Testament. And yet here it's related almost as an afterthought, a minor detail, as in "she stepped off the curb, into a puddle."

You'd think there might be a little more build-up to a spectacle like this, some mention of the urgency Jesus felt to get out to the boat full of disciples by the most direct route. But no, he sees them in trouble and goes over to help, "walking on the sea." No drama at all, just a flat statement.

This does often seem to be the way longed-for good news or desperately needed help arrives in our lives. Without fanfare or advance notice, often after you've stopped waiting and wishing for it—there it simply is, like your lost dog sitting on the back steps. The job offer from an interview last year. The college acceptance letter amid a pile of rejections. The positive pregnancy test after years of infertility. You can't believe it, you thank God, you look twice to make sure it's really true.

When you're straining at the oars against an adverse wind, remember that at any moment you might look up and see salvation walking toward you, even if that seems as impossible as walking on water.

PRAYER: Thank you for life-changing miracles. Amen.

SOMEBODY OUGHT TO SAY SOMETHING

Kenneth L. Samuel

O give thanks to the LORD, for [God] is good; for [God's] steadfast love endures forever. Let the redeemed of the LORD say so, those [God] redeemed from trouble and gathered in from the lands, from the east and the west, from the north and the south. From Psalm 107

HOW MANY TIMES in any given day are we assaulted by bad news? Seems like we can barely recover from one depressing declaration before we are confronted by another. If it's not a headache, it's a heartache. If it's not a problem finding a job, it's a problem keeping a job. If it's not a mortgage meltdown, it's another financial bail-out. If it's not hell at the workplace, it's hell in your home life.

But in the midst of this, the psalmist declares that there is good news, which every believer in God ought to be talking about. And this good news is not illusory; it does not deny the fact that we live in perilous times, and it does not attempt to shift our focus to an other-worldly utopia.

It is the good news that despite all of the troubles, trials, and traumas we face, love endures. The love of God is steadfast, and it endures forever! Ain't that good news?

It is the good news that all of our suffering is redemptive—which is to say that God uses our pains to produce greater stamina, greater integrity, and greater maturity in us. In God's processes of redemption, bad is exchanged for good. Ain't that good news?

It is the good news that, despite all that has transpired to tear us apart, God has gathered us together—"from the lands," east and west, north and south. And it is our togetherness that gives us strength to face the challenges ahead. Ain't that good news?

Somebody ought to say so!

PRAYER: Gracious God, please do not allow our recitations of bad news interrupt our declarations of your good news! Give us hearts to believe, eyes to see, and courage to speak! Amen.

AGAIN AND AGAIN AND AGAIN

Quinn G. Caldwell

Crowds again gathered around him; and, as was his custom, he again taught them. From Mark 10:1–12

A FAITHFUL CHURCHGOER WAS TALKING with a skeptical friend about why he bothered going to church. The friend asked him what his favorite part of the service was. "Oh, I love most of it: the songs, the Doxology, Communion. The pastoral prayer can be pretty boring sometimes, but I even get something out of that. Overall, though, I guess I would say I get the most out of the sermon."

"How many sermons do you think you've sat through in your life?" the friend asked.

The man said, "Oh, I don't know. Couple thousand?"

"And do you remember them all?"

"Of course not!"

"Then why bother? What's the point?"

The man thought about it for a moment, then asked, "Do you remember every meal you've ever eaten?"

"No."

"Neither do I," replied the man. "But I sure am glad I ate them."

PRAYER: God, I wish I didn't have to feed my spirit so much. I wish I could hear about you just once and then be yours forever. But it looks like I'm going to need to hear it again and again. So send me the discipline to come often to the table of your Word, and send me preachers good enough to keep me fed. Amen.

HOW GOD USES CRISIS

Anthony B. Robinson

Now when these things begin to take place, stand up and raise your heads, because your redemption is drawing near. From Luke 21:25–28

WE'RE LIVING IN AN APOCALYPTIC TIME. Apocalyptic times are times when everything is shaking and everyone is getting shaken up. Jesus spoke of such times, when there would be "signs in the sun and moon . . . and on earth distress among the nations." At such times, he said, "People will faint from fear and foreboding." But then Jesus said a weird, challenging, and true thing: in such times, don't hunker down—stand up. Don't crawl in a hole—lift up your head and stand tall, because redemption is near.

In times of crisis, we are tempted to hunker down, to hold on, and to hide out. But God, Jesus tells us, can use crisis to bring redemption, to make a new world and a better world. God can use crisis to make a new church or a new you. Think about it. At least sometimes, when your world has seemed to break apart, it has been the opening to a new and a better day. It wasn't death but birth that was happening. God can use the present crisis and times of shaking to do a new thing. But if we're going to be a part of it, we can't let fear make us faint. We can't allow foreboding to paralyze us. It's time, when everything is shaking, to "Stand up, raise your heads, because your redemption is drawing near."

PRAYER: Come Holy Spirit, break us open and make us new. And when things seem to be breaking up and open all around us, give us eyes and hearts to see the new thing you are doing. Amen.

The After-Tax Blessing

Lillian Daniel

For, as I can testify, they voluntarily gave according to their means, and even beyond their means. From 2 Corinthians 8:1–7

EARLY IN MY WORKING LIFE, I met with a financial planner. It seemed absurd since we were deeply in debt. We had nothing to save, let alone invest. But a wise friend had said this was just the time for such advice.

He reviewed our budget. We had been making progress with our credit card debt but there was more to shovel out from under. We had also recently become tithers, giving 10 percent of our income to the church. The two felt connected in my mind. We had made progress on the debt while growing in generosity. But I was embarrassed to tell that to a financial planner. I knew he was going to tell us to give less away, and to pay off the debt as soon as possible.

So when we got to the subject of charitable giving, I told him we were tithers. "Tithers, huh?" he said. "Is that 10 percent of after-tax income or pre-tax income?"

"After tax, of course," I said. After all, we were tithers, not fanatics.

After a long awkward pause, I asked, "So what do you think of that?"

"It's fine," he said, "if all you want is an after-tax blessing!"

Then he laughed heartily and joyfully. Turns out, he was a member of a UCC church himself. His philosophy of financial planning had extreme generosity at its core. God had clearly sent a prophet our way, and he had issued us a challenge.

PRAYER: Generous God, please take my worries about money and put them on your shoulders, so that I do not carry them alone. Grant me a generous spirit, and the means to give beyond my means. Amen.

HOPE

Kenneth L. Samuel

*It is of the L*ORD*'s mercies that we are not consumed, because [God's] compassions fail not. They are new every morning: great is thy faithfulness.* From Lamentations 3:20–23 KJV

HOPE IS NOT JUST A VISION OF THE FUTURE. Hope is also a mandate for the present. Hope has a way of ordering our present in such a way that our present becomes congruent and consistent with our promise.

As a boy, I was always getting into trouble for one thing or another. One hot summer afternoon, while being reprimanded for one of my many misdeeds by my mother, the telephone rang. I was greatly relieved by the phone call, because I thought it would surely shift my mother's attention away from her upbraiding of me. To my dismay, however, my mother continued her tongue-lashing of me to the person on the phone. After several humiliating moments, my mother abruptly handed me the telephone receiver. On the line was my Aunt Naomi. Aunt Naomi was renowned among me and my siblings for giving the best Christmas gifts. At Christmas, she gave each of us no shirts, no ties, no pajamas, and no books. At Christmas time, Aunt Naomi gave each of us two crisp twenty dollar bills—to spend as we liked. (This was quite a discretionary sum for a poor boy growing up in the sixties.)

On the phone, Aunt Naomi said to me simply and succinctly: "Boy, you better straighten up! Christmas is coming." That's all it took for me to get my act together. The hope of what Christmas would bring me in December made me change my attitude and my behavior in August.

Hope is as real today as it will be in days to come. Hope in God puts the present in perspective as we prepare ourselves to receive the promises ahead. And do I need to inform you that God gives greater gifts than my Aunt Naomi?

PRAYER: Sovereign God, we thank you for the hope that renews us day by day and keeps us moving forward in faith. Amen.

FALLING IN LOVE

Anthony B. Robinson

I love you, O LORD, my strength. From Psalm 18

WHAT IS IT LIKE TO COME TO FAITH, to believe that God has come in Jesus, and that he is the way, the truth, and the life?

I'll tell you what I think it isn't like. It's not like being convinced by carefully presented and rational arguments so that it all makes total sense and no one will think you are foolish. Nor is it like having proof or conclusive evidence that allows you to say, "Here's the evidence; now you can believe." It's not like any of the things that often seem so powerful and self-evident in this world, things of which we say, "It's rational" or "It's scientific." Coming to faith is more like falling in love. We can't help ourselves. And we can't whittle it down to an explanation. It's more like being swept up or away by something beautiful. Not everything that is true or real makes sense.

I think that for a long time I doubted my faith because I felt I needed to have evidence sufficient to convince super skeptics. I needed to be able to make a case to people who thought that something couldn't be true unless it was rational. I no longer think that.

"I love you, O Lord," wrote the psalmist. Coming to faith is more like falling in love. We don't make sense of Jesus, or figure God out. It's the other way around. Given half a chance, Jesus can make sense out of our lives. "I love you, O Lord, my strength."

PRAYER: Thank you, God, for the gift of faith. When some discount or despise faith, help me not to be defensive but to keep on loving. Amen.

CAN I LIVE HERE?

Kenneth L. Samuel

LORD, *who may dwell in your sanctuary? Who may live on your holy hill? Those whose walk is blameless and who do what is righteous, who speak the truth from their hearts and have no slander on their tongues, who do their neighbor no wrong . . .* From Psalm 15 NIV

I HAVE TRAVELED across counties, countries, and continents to visit shrines and cathedrals. I've been blessed to visit the sacred sites of the Holy Land in Israel. I've toured the Vatican and stood in St. Peter's square before the grand basilica in Rome. I've stood at the Acropolis in Athens where philosophers expounded and the Apostle Paul preached. I've sailed the Aegean Sea to the Island of Patmos, where the Apostle from John received the book of Revelation.

Yet, despite all these visits to sacred places, Psalm 15 reminds me that the essence of sacredness is not in a location but in a lifestyle. Sacred sites are preserved and revered because they help us to feel closer to God, and yet the psalmist informs us that we can be no closer to God than the values we uphold in our everyday lives. As inspiring as they are, visits to holy places (including church on Sunday morning) do not constitute real holiness or sacredness.

Real holiness is determined by the honesty of our relationships, by the justice we promote in our communities, by the respect we express for others, and by using our financial blessings to help those in need. The sacred is not really about special places, but good values that should be lived out in every place.

And when we live our faith in the love we share, in the service we give, and in the justice we promote, we never leave the holy place, because we personify it.

What? Didn't you know that you are the temple of the most high God? Let's become the church that we invite others to attend.

PRAYER: God, let me be a sanctuary—in love, in service, in justice—so that I never leave your holy place. Amen.

I Just Don't Get It

Christina Villa

Then the LORD spoke to the fish, and it spewed Jonah out upon the dry land.
From Jonah 2:1–10

JONAH IN THE BELLY OF THE WHALE is one of the top Bible stories non-religious people bring up as an example of the absurdity of the Bible. In their view, you have two choices with the Bible. You either believe it is literal truth or you think it's all a fairy tale. And if you think the belly of the whale is actually a metaphor for something else, you aren't really religious anyway, you're an English major.

I like the metaphor way of understanding the Bible, because I was an English major. But sometimes I feel trapped in that understanding, just as I would feel trapped by a requirement to take it literally. Thinking of the Bible as mainly metaphor can make it seem like a big book of coded stories whose meanings need to be deciphered with the decoder ring of education.

Once my father, then in his sixties, told me that he regretted never having been able to "understand" classical music the way he "understood" Dizzy Gillespie and Count Basie. Years later, in his eighties, he called me up to say he'd just been to Border's where they had a fantastic sale on classical CDs—just $3 each! Incredible! So he bought three of them and listened to one in the car—and loved it.

Maybe it was the $3 deal that made him think classical music wasn't so intimidating after all, but for whatever reason, he stopped worrying about how to understand it and just let the music come out of the dashboard at him.

This would be a great way to take in the Bible, it seems to me. Don't get trapped in the maze of having to account for every absurdity, on the one hand, or come up with a metaphorical meaning for everything on the other. Don't worry that you don't "understand" it. Just let it come out of the dashboard at you.

PRAYER: Dear God, you who invented Count Basie, thank you for bringing Mozart to my Dad. Let us not be intimidated. Amen.

AUGUST 31

WET FEET

Anthony B. Robinson

When the soles of the feet of the priests who bear the ark of the LORD, the LORD of all the earth, rest in the waters of the Jordan, the waters of the Jordan flowing from above shall be cut off; they shall stand in a single heap. From Joshua 3:1–7

THERE'S AN INTERESTING THING about this story of Israel crossing the Jordan here in the Book of Joshua. God says, "You've got to get your feet wet."

This is, of course, their second time to pass through the waters on their Exodus journey. The first time, entering into the wilderness, was at the Red Sea. This one exiting the wilderness, at the Jordan, is the second. And there's a difference between the two.

At the Red Sea the people had only to wait until dry land appeared, and they could cross over. They didn't have to do a blessed thing but wait for God to act. Here, on the other side of the wilderness, it's different. The people have to put their feet in the water before God will act, before God will "cut off" the waters of the Jordan, so that the people are able to pass over to the new land and life.

At the Red Sea, God made the first move. God held back the waters. God does that sometimes. God takes the initiative, makes the first move, surprises us. But other times it's different. Here at the Jordan, for instance, God asked the people to make the first move. They had to get their feet wet before God would hold back the waters.

Sometimes when we are waiting on God, I wonder if God is waiting on us? I wonder if God is waiting for us to get our feet wet? Possibly the key to a breakthrough is wet feet? Maybe today you need to get your feet wet?

PRAYER: Help me to discern, God, whether it's time to wait for you to make the first move or time to go on in and get my feet wet. When it's the latter, grant me courage to take the first step and then the next, trusting that you will lead me. Amen.

SEPTEMBER

A GRADE OF "INCOMPLETE"

Lillian Daniel

Now may the God of peace . . . make you complete in everything good so that you may do God's will. From Hebrews 13:20–21

LITTLE CHILDREN IN SCHOOL are taught the importance of completing their assignments. In college, if you don't write your final paper, you get a grade of "Incomplete," which seems to imply that when you finally write that paper, you will be complete.

But then we become grownups, and we discover that most of our important jobs are never complete. We may finish up one aspect of a project at work, but that leads to another one. A student may complete a homework assignment, but the teacher has a job that is never complete. Many of us have jobs that are never complete.

Take parenting. Parents of small children will look at the parents of teenagers and say, "Tell me it gets easier!" But parents of teenagers will tell you that it just gets more complicated. Parents of adult children tell me that the job of parenting is really never done. Kids move out, and then in many cases, they move back in. But even if they live in their own place, it's not as if our children ever graduate from needing parents.

You don't one day suddenly complete the job of parenting. It continues even after your children have children, and are doing that job themselves, with those same incomplete results.

In life, we don't get a gold star for getting the big jobs done. Rather, I think God gives us a gold star for hanging in there, still working, in the incompleteness of life.

For in the end, people are not complete until God completes us. One day we will meet the alpha and the omega, the beginning and the end. We will see God face to face, and finally be complete.

But until then . . . there's nothing wrong with taking the occasional incomplete.

PRAYER: Gracious and patient God, stick close by me in the incompleteness of life's work. Give my efforts purpose and meaning, if not completion. Amen.

HOLY GROUND

Donna Schaper

Then the LORD said to him, "Take off the sandals from your feet, for the place where you are standing is holy ground." From Acts 7:17–40

I HAVE NEVER LIKED THE IDEA that some ground is more holy than other ground. I appreciate the reminder to notice how holy the ground is, but I am not willing to elevate one ground over another. Nor can I pick out one great time and lift it above another. Or take a Sabbath only on Sundays. Monday can be very holy itself. I like the phrase one of my parishioners uses: remember the future. Now is then. Then is now. I might argue that we should keep our sandals off all the time, in all spaces.

Yesterday we carried two weeks of frozen compost to the local community garden and placed it in the offering plate. The offering plate was a white drum with a handle you can turn. Our egg shells, onion skins, coffee grounds, apple cores, grapefruit peels, squished limes, and garlic casings were on their way to resurrection as next year's Swiss chard. Or red leaf lettuce. Perhaps even a sweet pea will rise from these offerings. Remembering the future is the only way to have a future. You have to build now for later. As the very successful head of Amazon says, over and over, we need to be three steps ahead of our last three steps, which steps will shift each time we take them.

OK, OK, OK. I know we're supposed to *carpe diem,* seize the day, live in the moment, and all that. Still, the truth of every moment is the way it treated yesterday. It has a past as last year's compost, a present as this year's onion, and a future as next year's chard. Now is later, later is now, and soil needs eternal, not temporal, attention. Forgetting that taking out the garbage involves holy time and holy ground is a mistake. Maybe sandals have a use . . . but spiritually we need them on less than we think.

PRAYER: O God, keep our sandals in our hands and our minds aware of how sacred time and space—here and now, then and later—are. Amen.

CARNIVORES AND VEGETARIANS

Lillian Daniel

Therefore do not let anyone condemn you in matters of food and drink or of observing festivals, new moons, or Sabbaths . . . These have indeed an appearance of wisdom in promoting self-imposed piety, humility, and severe treatment of the body, but they are of no value in checking self-indulgence. From Colossians 2:16–23

IN MY HOUSEHOLD, my daughter and I are vegetarians, while my husband and son are carnivores. But when I say my daughter is a vegetarian, do not confuse her with a person who actually eats vegetables. Her brother says she would be more accurately described as a "starch-itarian." I think he, with the typical diet of a fifteen-year-old, would most accurately be described as a "cheeto-tarian."

Planning menus at my house would be good preparation for heading up the United Nations. When it comes to food, everybody has an opinion, and everybody speaks a different language. Since I am the cook, this delicate diplomatic responsibility falls to me. So I have no trouble imagining what it would be like to live at the time Paul wrote this letter to the early church, when members of the various religious sects condemned one another for their food choices and festival preferences. As a parent of teenagers, my life is no less complicated.

What Paul tells all these people is something we still need to hear. You can make different food choices, based on ethics or tradition. You can celebrate different festivals, and worship in different ways. But don't think any of this makes you better than the other person. In fact, beware that in your efforts to live well, you do not fall into self-indulgence. Live and eat intentionally, but don't become obsessed with yourself.

PRAYER: Lord Christ, you have promised us an eternal heavenly banquet where all of us, in our uniqueness, will be fed. I thank you, God, that at that time I will not have to do the cooking. Amen.

SEPTEMBER 4

DEEDS THAT OPEN DOORS

Kenneth L. Samuel

He distinctly saw an angel of God who came to him and said, "Cornelius!" Cornelius stared at him in fear. "What is it, Lord?" he asked. The angel answered, "Your prayers and gifts to the poor have come up as a memorial offering before God. Now send men to Joppa to bring back a man named Simon who is called Peter." From Acts 10:1–8 NIV

CORNELIUS ENTERS THE NARRATIVE of the Acts of the Apostles not because of his status, culture, or class. The door of the narrative is open to

Cornelius because of his deeds. It is Cornelius' deeds of prayers and gifts to the poor that open the door to an epiphany in his life. An angel informs him that God has taken note of what he has done to help those whom Christ called "the least of these." And it is his deeds of prayers and gifts to the poor that open the door to his cross-cultural relationship with the Apostle Paul and his pivotal role in helping to spread the gospel to people of all nations.

As Christians, we are often duped into thinking that what makes us distinctive from other people is our doctrinal creeds and our unique liturgies. But beyond faith statements and religious resolutions, God still takes special note of what we do to help relieve the suffering of those who are poor in spirit, poor in health, and poor in resources. Deeds of service to the poor still open doors to greater communion with God and to greater community among people of different cultures and creeds.

Christ has opened the door of acceptance and salvation to all of us. Our creeds may help us to see that this door is open, but it will take Christ-like deeds to get us in.

PRAYER: God, help us to be doers of your Word, not just hearers. Let our sacrifices of love, our acts of kindness, and our expressions of compassion announce to the world that we are your disciples, indeed! Amen.

SEPTEMBER 5

DOMINION AND DOXOLOGY

Anthony B. Robinson

When I look at your heavens, the work of your fingers . . . . What are human beings that you are mindful of them . . . ? Yet you have made them a little lower than God . . . . You have given them dominion over the works of your hands; you have put all things under their feet. From Psalm 8

ISN'T THIS A WONDERFUL PSALM FOR SUMMER! "O LORD, our Sovereign, how majestic is your name in all the earth! When I look at your heavens, the work of your fingers, the moon and stars that you have established, what are human beings that you are mindful of them?" I hope that you get to lie under the night sky next summer and look up at starry heavens. What's really wonderful about this psalm is the way it holds together our human calling to exercise care and stewardship over God's earth and its creatures with a sense of wonder and awe.

Dominion—"you have put all things under our feet, all sheep and oxen, and the beasts of the field,"—is not license to use creation for our human purposes alone or selfishly. No, this trust and task is enfolded in doxology. The psalm begins and ends with doxology: "O LORD, our Sovereign, how majestic is your name in all the earth." Our power and responsibility can only be rightly understood and exercised in context, in doxological context. Praising God, first, last, and always, we come to see our role and responsibility right. Dominion requires doxology.

PRAYER: Holy One, may the wonder of your creation renew us and recall us. Renew our sense of awe and gratitude so that we may be recalled to exercise our stewardship for the earth and its creatures with passion and humility. Amen!

ASKING FOR HELP

William C. Green

Remember the ministry to me . . . From Philippians 2:25–30 TM

IT'S BETTER TO GIVE THAN RECEIVE but the best givers are good receivers. Otherwise giving is one-sided and leads to resentment. We act as though others need us more than we need them and miss what they have to give.

My father, generous in his own gifts to the family at Christmas, loved to hand them all out before opening any of his own presents. When he got to the gifts given him, he found it hard to express appreciation, as though whatever he received was of less interest than what he had to give. Generously giving, he diminished the happiness of the rest of us. It can be much easier to give than to receive.

Why? Are we afraid of being dependent on others and looking "needy"? Do we really think we're not? What can our help to others mean if we hide an equal need for theirs? Does withholding our need get others off the hook—or us?

Paul was a great giver. He was also a great receiver. Amid adversity in Rome, he did not hide behind his strong faith as though neediness was faithlessness. He knew that but for the help he received from God through others he would have had little to give. He welcomed the "minister to my need," (Phil. 2:25 NRSV) Epaphroditus, sent by a congregation in Greece, before finally sending him home, praising the support he had received.

PRAYER: Keep me from acting as though I'm not needy, too, God. Amen.

A SHARED WITNESS

Kenneth L. Samuel

And when this letter has been read among you, have it read also in the church of the Laodiceans; and see that you read also the letter from Laoodicea. From Colossians 4:7–17

NEWS FLASH: The letters of the Apostle Paul, sent to churches throughout the region of Asia Minor in the first century, were not e-mailed, faxed, or texted to individual church members. They were sent to corporate bodies of believers and they were always read aloud in the collective settings of Christians, gathered together. The letters of Paul were never intended to be read by individuals in isolation. They always evoked a shared witness, and a shared hearing and shared reflection.

Our culture is in grave danger of losing the value of shared experiences and shared expressions. Individual iPods, personal computers, and headphones that block out the rest of the world keep us contained within the confines of our individual interests. The lack of comprehensive standards in education means that, as a nation of people, we share very little in terms of common references. Our collective consciousness is eroding and our sense of shared values is in serious jeopardy.

Much of our technology has been used to build a global network of isolated individuals. Why don't we take off the earphones and just spend a few days talking and listening to the special people in our lives? Or how about buying copies of the same book for a group of friends and planning to read and discuss it together? Or why not watch the same movie with your family followed by dinner at the same table while you engage in shared discussion? Or . . . maybe we could all go to church together and share a common experience with God.

PRAYER: Dear God, help us this day not to experience life in isolation. May we connect with you through the people around us. Amen.

SCOFF

Quinn G. Caldwell

Happy are those who do not follow the advice of the wicked, or take the path that sinners tread, or sit in the seat of scoffers. From Psalm 1

IS ANYBODY ELSE OUT THERE tired of sarcasm? Am I the only one sick of his own smug superiority, of earning cheap laughs while desperately trying to appear sophisticated or something?

I do try to avoid it, but it's just so darn easy! You don't actually have to know much to make yourself seem superior to somebody else (especially somebody else who's both in earnest and not present: sitting ducks!). All you have to do is make it seem like you know more than the other guy. Simple, fun(ny), and, apparently, addictive. I find myself doing it all the time without even realizing it. Some might blame this on my generation, who grew up bathing in irony and sarcasm, but since the psalmist commented on scoffers a zillion years ago, I suspect it might be an older and a deeper sin than just one generation could turn out.

Here's where I would usually give you guys advice. But since I still haven't found what works, this time I'm just going to tell you the next thing I plan to try: today, I'm going to go one whole day without sarcasm. Should I find myself getting my snark on, or glance in the mirror and notice even a hint of a sneer, I will stop and pray the Lord's Prayer, slowly and intentionally. I will mean it.

I have no idea if this will work; I suppose the test will be whether I make fun of myself tomorrow for my earnestness today.

PRAYER: Dear God: Help. Amen.

DOES IT REALLY MATTER?

Kenneth L. Samuel

As he taught, Jesus said, "Watch out for the teachers of the law. They like to walk around in flowing robes and be greeted in market places, and have the most important seats in the synagogues and the places of honor at banquets. They devour widows' houses and for a show make lengthy prayers. Such men will be punished most severely." From Mark 12:35–40 NIV

HOW SAD BUT TRUE that most religious debates emphasize principles of doctrine instead of relationships with people. In Jesus' day, teachers of the law insisting on a doctrine concerning whose son was the Messiah were the same religious teachers who confiscated the homes of poor widows. Doctrinal orthodoxy was more important to them than human compassion and relationships.

But what does religious doctrine really matter when religious doctrinaires are denying and neglecting human life?

One of my professors in seminary told the story of attending a conference conducted by a noted Christian theologian. My professor had read many of the noted theologian's books and had found his Christology (doctrine of Christ) questionable. So he prepared five pages of discussion points to bring to the conference. But after lecturing, the theologian announced that he would be unable to take questions because he was on his way to a mission trip to the poorest regions of the Sudan, where he planned to deliver food and help build housing.

My professor said that as he assessed his own commitment to Christian service, he tore up his pages of doctrinal inquiry. "I just couldn't bring myself to interrupt the work of Christ with questions about church dogma," he said. Class dismissed.

PRAYER: Sovereign God, we pray that what we believe about you will find its fullest expression not in church doctrine, but in the love and care we give to others. Amen.

THE C STUDENT

Christina Villa

Consider your own call, brothers and sisters: not many of you were wise by human standards, not many were powerful, not many were of noble birth.
From 1 Corinthians 1:26–31

IN A RECENT ISSUE of my college's alumni magazine, the president's letter was about the admissions committee's agonizing over the great many qualified applicants for limited places in the incoming class. So impressive was the applicant pool this year that even "the acclaimed oboist who also started an animal shelter in her community" and "the budding actress who rock climbs and is fluent in three languages" were not admitted.

The spell cast by the hyper-competitive college admissions process is not easy to opt out of. When one of my sons was eleven or twelve, he was getting a haircut and the barber asked him how he was doing in school. "Oh, I get mostly C's," my son said. The barber, Charlie, stopped snipping and looked my son straight in the eye in the mirror and said, "That's just right, that's just where you want to be." Then he resumed clipping and said, "You're the guy they'll want to hire when you grow up because they know you'll try really hard."

Oh great, I thought. Charlie had cut my son's hair since he was little. No matter how busy the shop was, we always had to wait for Charlie. Sometimes it was a very long wait. But Charlie, soft-spoken and polite, had patiently demonstrated the clippers for my son when he was four years old and suspicious of haircuts. My son trusted him and was loyal to him. And now Charlie was telling him that it was OK to be a C student.

Maybe I should have hustled the kid into the car and said something about how you can't listen to everything your barber tells you. But I didn't say anything. The world needs only so many trilingual, rock-climbing oboists, after all. But it always needs more trust, more loyalty, and more people like Charlie.

PRAYER: O God, release the high school seniors and their parents from the clutches of college anxiety, and restore the sight of those blinded by the accomplishments of others. Amen.

SEPTEMBER 11

DO NOT NEGLECT YOUR GIFTS

Donna Schaper

Do not neglect the gift that is in you, which was given to you through prophecy with the laying on of hands by the council of elders. 1 Timothy 4:14

WHOEVER WROTE THE LETTER to Timothy was pretty smart. Flattery will get you everywhere—and the idea that we have a gift in us makes us feel good. Unfortunately, the good feeling is a lot like bubble gum. The sweet goes out after a few chews. What is your gift? Is the emphasis on "your?" Or "gift"? If I could tell you what my groove or gift was, in any given situation, you need not fear that I would neglect it. I'd be much more likely to overdo it, which is to say give it over and over again, long after it had worn out its usefulness or gumption.

What is a gift? It is a groove or rut of person and moment that, neglected, impoverishes history. Some people know how to never miss missing an opportunity. Others have better timing. Some people know how to be selfish at just the wrong moment so that their self-centeredness takes on the sinking water of tragedy over time. Others know how to be quiet equally aptly and nurse a wound in private. Still others nurse way too much in private and would endow their families (and congregations) with greatness if they would just speak up. Thank you, ancient scripture, for alerting us to pay attention to our grooves and our ruts and our gifts.

SEPTEMBER 12

WHAT WOULD YOU DO IF YOU WERE NOT AFRAID?

Lillian Daniel

"I tell you the truth," Jesus said to them, "no one who has left home or wife or brothers or parents or children for the sake of the kingdom of God will fail to receive many times as much in this age and, in the age to come, eternal life." From Luke 18:18–30 NIV

WHAT WOULD YOU DO if you were not afraid? What would you do if you had no chance of failing? Spend some time in prayer with those two questions and see where God leads you.

Sometimes it is our family members who get in the way. They want the best for us, but they are scared we will get hurt or will fail. So they steer us toward the safe course rather than toward the risky one. Could you follow your heart's desire anyway?

Sadly, sometimes our family members do not want the best for us. A husband brings home a box of doughnuts for his wife who is trying to lose weight. He pretends to be generous but he is sabotaging her. He doesn't want the status quo, or the balance of power, to change. Can she make a healthy change anyway?

Sometimes we have to walk away from our family members in order to follow Jesus. Sometimes we have to shut out their comments in order to hear God's calling more clearly. Sometimes we have to do something they don't want us to do. And Jesus says, sometimes you have to do it anyway.

PRAYER: Dear God, what would I do if I weren't afraid? What if it separates me from my family? If it is your will for me to step away from my family, walk with me anyway. Amen.

MOVING THE HEART OF GOD

Kenneth L. Samuel

The LORD said, "I will blot out from the earth the human beings I have created —people together with animals and creeping things and birds of the air, for I am sorry that I have made them." But Noah found favor in the sight of the LORD. From Genesis 6:6–8

I CAN'T SPEAK FOR EVERYONE, but for most of my life I believed that the providential will of God was settled and fixed for eternity. I believed that there is absolutely nothing I could ever do to change or to move the heart of God. I believed that the immutable or unchangeable nature of God rendered any attempts to alter God's plan futile and sacrilegious.

I'd never really reflected much on a God who creates humanity and then repents over that creation. A God who has second thoughts about what God has created, and then decides to wipe it out. Completely. Could there be any stronger resolve from God than that found in Genesis 6:7? "I will blot out from the earth the human beings I have created—people together with animals and creeping things and birds of the air, for I am sorry that I made them." This providential plan meant death and destruction for all of us. This divine intention spelled annihilation for the whole

275

human family. Had this divine plan been executed, none of us would be here today.

What altered this providential plan? What was it that unsealed our predestination toward destruction? What moved the heart of God? One person, called Noah, found favor in the sight of God. Favor, not because of human merit, but because of divine mercy. God's favor and mercy toward one opened an avenue of renewal and reconciliation for all. And God, who had repented because God made humanity, repented again, and decided to redeem humanity.

My concept of God's immutability has changed. My prayer life is a continuous attempt to move the heart of God away from the judgment we deserve toward the favor we receive by grace. I am confident that the heart of God can be moved, and that whenever God's heart moves, it moves toward mercy.

PRAYER: Creator and Redeemer God, I know that the wages of my sins call for death, but today I appeal to your unmerited favor and your immutable mercy. Please open the door to new life for me, and for all others, in your name. Amen.

"Listen to Your Life"

William C. Green

I've found my lost sheep . . . . I found my lost coin. From Luke 15:1–10 TM

GOD IS NOT ABSENT. We are. We are when we lose direction, get lost going our own way, but keep on going anyway until we reach a point where we want to give up.

With such times in mind, Frederick Buechner writes: "Listen to your life. Listen to what happens to you, because it is through what happens to you that God speaks . . . . It's in a language not always easy to decipher, but it's there, powerfully, memorably, unforgettably."

Listening for this voice, we gradually find the direction we need and regain the hope we lost. Our attention is now on God's promise of guidance and strength. At first it's hard to get. It's hard to believe that God is speaking in what happens to us, especially in difficult circumstances that can also be plain wrong. "I don't deserve this!" "It's not right; it's not fair!" "How can a loving God let this happen?"

We can't always decipher God's promises by ourselves. That's why we've been given the church, or others to think and hopefully pray along with us. Maybe it's time to get out of the corners we paint ourselves into and seek out others we've disregarded before.

It's not all bad to feel helpless. Maybe that's God's way of getting our attention.

PRAYER: God, you're not away somewhere, you're not lost. I'm grateful that I don't have to be lost either. Amen.

FALLING

Donna Schaper

But as for me, my foot had almost slipped, I had lost my foothold. From Psalm 73 NIV

LOTS OF PEOPLE ARE AFRAID OF FALLING—and they aren't all old or frail. A wise physical therapist told me that we should be less afraid of falling than we are of not being able to catch ourselves when we fall. I have watched my eighty-five-year-old mother climb stairs. She knows how to catch herself—and she catches herself so well that she doesn't fall. Catching has to do with muscles and alertness and practice and foresight, as in scanning the whole route ahead of you before you step.

Falling is a serious physical matter, attending to human fragility, muscle development, and that wonderful word "balance." It is also a spiritual matter, something that concerns the young as well as the old. It is way too easy for a kid to fall in with the wrong crowd.

Spiritual balance involves attention to the communities who might catch us if we start to fall. It has to do with having friends or parents who will notify you when you are off the path or in a dangerous pattern. It has to do with strengthening our core muscles of nation, congregation, and family in such a way that we keep an eye out for each other—and don't relegate the frail to social insecurity. And it has to do with catching each other, lest, when we trip, nobody is there to break our fall.

PRAYER: O God, stumblers and bumblers we are, each and all. Hold us when we fall. Amen.

BEHEMOTH AND LEVIATHAN

Quinn G. Caldwell

Gird up your loins like a man; I will question you, and you declare to me. . . . Look at Behemoth. . . . Can you draw out Leviathan with a fishhook? From Job 40–42

I LOVE THIS PART OF JOB. Up till this point, I'm always with Job, demanding from God an explanation for terrible things. But here, where God's all, "You better check yourself before you wreck yourself," I come around to cheering God on.

Basically, God says the annoying thing that parents everywhere say: "Because I said so." It's an unsatisfactory answer, but the poetry God uses to establish her dominion is magnificent. It's completely about the natural world. "You want to know why I get to make the decisions, Job? Look around. Can *you* make a huge animal? Can *you* make a huge sea monster?" God describes them in glorious detail, and the reader cannot help but be seduced by the proof.

Christians have long argued about whether the natural world can tell us all we need to know about God, or whether we need special revelations as well. All I know is, the Book of Job says if you want to know about the glory of God, look at a living thing. It doesn't have to be an elephant; a spider weaving a web is just as magnificent. Your cat in your lap or a bird out on the porch are just as astounding.

Today, spend some time really looking at a living thing. Unless you're able to make one of those yourself, then praise the one who can.

PRAYER: God, thank you for revealing yourself to me through and in your creations. Grant that I might remember to stop—often—to notice your world and praise your name. Amen.

TRIAL SEPARATION

Lillian Daniel

For I am convinced that neither death nor life, neither angels nor demons, neither the present nor the future, nor any powers, neither height nor depth, nor anything else in all creation, will be able to separate us from the love of God that is in Christ Jesus our Lord. From Romans 8:31–39 NIV

WHEN I WAS TEN, my parents sat me down in our formal living room to explain that my dad would be moving out for a while. "Are you getting a divorce?" I asked. "No," they said, "This is just a trial separation."

My ten-year-old emotional barometer had gauged the tension between them. My young ears had heard the arguments. My little heart had beat to the rhythm of their anger. Perhaps a separation might be worth trying. At least it meant our family was trying something.

I worried I would never see my dad, but I ended up seeing him more than ever. He took me to the new James Bond movie and out to eat spaghetti. We had one-on-one conversations we had never had before. For a few months our little family tried the separation and I confess that I liked it.

And then just as suddenly, my dad moved back in, and our deep conversations and spaghetti dinners passed away. The old dynamics swept over our family like an irresistible wave, pulling us into the rip tide of rusty resentments and sorry score-keeping. Living in the same house, we were trying out separation all over again.

I love this scripture because it promises us that nothing can separate us from the love of God. We human beings are always trying out separation, but God is always and consistently practicing connection.

PRAYER: Holy Spirit—use our trial separations to teach us how to connect to you and to one another, one day, in this life or the next. Amen.

THE GREAT IN SPITE OF

Anthony B. Robinson

I will praise the LORD as long as a I live; I will sing praises to my God all my life long. From Psalm 146

I WAS A STRANGER in an unfamiliar city, attending a conference. I was far from home and, in the words of Jesus regarding Martha, I was "anxious about many things."

But it was Sunday and I went to worship in a nearby church. I was in an unfamiliar church among people I did not know. And yet, as we rose to join in the opening hymn, something happened. I was caught up in praise.

Lost, I was found. Found in the big story of God's grace and purpose. My voice was set loose in praise and a sense of wonder and gratitude was renewed in my heart.

The praise of God invites us to cease our frequent and restless preoccupation with ourselves. Praise of God challenges our natural self-centeredness and sense of accumulated grievance. Praise invites us to turn our attention to what makes life good and to the generosity we have experienced.

That Sunday, in a strange city and church, far from home, my voice was set loose in praise of God. Losing myself in praise of God, I was found.

At least sometimes, praise of God is a great "in spite of." In spite of the evidence to the contrary, our praise dares to assert God's presence, God's power, and God's faithfulness. I hope that today you will sing that great, defiant "In spite of" and live your week in that spirit of trust and hope.

PRAYER: God, the fir tree's uplifted branches are as hands raised in praise. The song of the birds this morning is a song of praise. The rushing water of the creek babbles your glory. When all creation praises you, do not let me be found mute or silent. Amen.

BE KIND

Donna Schaper

For the whole law is summed up in a single commandment, "You shall love your neighbor as yourself." From Galatians 5:2–15

CHAPTER 5 OF GALATIANS is worth a good long read. It is about the subject of Christian freedom, which the writer imagines is a kind of slavery to love. It is about the difference between the law and grace, using circumcision as an example, concluding that it matters little if we are or are not circumcised. Instead it matters a lot how we talk about the subject to each other.

Maybe you don't need to read this chapter in Galatians. You may have no issues about right and wrong, cultural customs, the right way to dress, the right foods to eat. You may never have spoken of chocolate cake as "sinful" or scoffed at someone who was obese. You probably attend church meetings and tolerate all the points of view expressed by your mutual members. If so, skip this chapter.

If, however, you find yourself coiled culturally, intolerant of difference, unkind when someone smokes in public or brings a dog to a meeting, sit down for the long read. You will learn what it means to be in love with each other. You will also be brought to attention by the warning that sometimes when we "bite and devour one another," we actually find ourselves chewed up, even consumed.

Be kind. Fall in love. Think less about circumcision, ancient or modern, and more about love.

PRAYER: O God, we pray that we can be a little yeast that leavens the entire dough of community and that when we are gone, people miss us because our kindness is lost. Amen.

SPIRITUAL BUT NOT RELIGIOUS? PLEASE STOP BORING ME.

Lillian Daniel

And I tell you, you are Peter, and on this rock I will build my church, and the gates of Hades will not overcome it. From Matthew 16:10–18

ON AIRPLANES, I dread the conversation with the person who finds out I am a minister and wants to use the flight time to explain to me that he is "spiritual but not religious." Such a person will always share this as if it is some kind of daring insight, unique to him, bold in its rebellion against the religious status quo.

Next thing you know, he's telling me that he finds God in the sunsets. These people always find God in the sunsets. And in walks on the beach. Sometimes I think these people never leave the beach or the mountains, what with all the communing with God they do on hilltops, hiking trails, and . . . did I mention the beach at sunset yet?

Like people who go to church don't see God in the sunset! Like we are these monastic little hermits who never leave the church building. How lucky we are to have these geniuses inform us that God is in nature. As if we don't hear that in the Psalms, in the creation stories, and throughout our deep tradition.

Being privately spiritual but not religious just doesn't interest me. There is nothing challenging about having deep thoughts all by oneself. What is interesting is doing this work in community, where other people might call you on stuff, or heaven forbid, disagree with you. Where life with God gets rich and provocative is when you dig deeply into a tradition that you did not invent all for yourself.

Thank you for sharing, spiritual but not religious sunset person. You are now comfortably in the norm for self-centered American culture, right smack in the bland majority of people who find ancient religions dull but find themselves uniquely fascinating. Can I switch seats now and sit next to someone who has been shaped by a mighty cloud of witnesses instead? Can I spend my time talking to someone brave enough to encounter God in a real human community? Because when this flight gets choppy, that's who I want by my side, holding my hand, saying a prayer and simply putting up with me, just like we try to do in church.

PRAYER: Dear God, thank you for creating us in your image and not the other way around. Amen.

NOSTALGIA AIN'T WHAT IT USED TO BE

Martin B. Copenhaver

No eye has seen, nor ear heard, nor the human heart conceived, what God has prepared for those who love God. From 1 Corinthians 2:6–13

THIS MORNING I PICKED THROUGH MUSTY ARTIFACTS in our basement in search of one item and I was waylaid by many others. There was the "Best Chicken Feeder" award which was given to our son in preschool, a program from our daughter's first dance recital, an article about our wedding from Karen's hometown newspaper, a note from my mother sent to me at college, the deed to our first house. I could go on, of course, and I did this morning, wading into all of those items until I was chest deep—heart deep—in nostalgia.

Nostalgia is a very natural and powerful emotion, particularly for those of us who are older. But nostalgia has its dangers. If it gives us renewed appreciation for the ways God has blessed us in the past, then it can be a wonderful occasion for thanksgiving. But nostalgia also can make us idealize the past in ways that make the present pale by comparison. So nostalgia can rob the present of delight and the future of hope.

As Christians we draw on the past in a myriad ways, of course, but our faith is always forward leaning. We are assured that the good old days, no matter how good, are nothing compared to what God has in store for us. Paul quotes from Isaiah to remind the Corinthians, but perhaps also to remind himself: "No eye has seen, nor ear heard, nor human heart conceived, what God has prepared for those who love God." So look back, yes. But lean forward.

PRAYER: God of yesterday, today, and tomorrow, help me to look back in ways that keep me leaning forward. Amen.

SEPTEMBER 22

Saints

Quinn G. Caldwell

Then Peter began to explain it to them, step by step, saying, "I was in the city of Joppa praying, and in a trance I saw a vision." From Acts 11:1–8

HERE'S WHAT IT MEANS to be a saint: it means you have direct access to God. It means that you can see the Heart that breaks for all that is broken.

Here's who is a saint: every member of the church, and that means you.

You know that throughout history the church has recognized certain people for their closeness to God, people like Peter from today's story. But in our tradition, everyone who is a member of the church is a saint, able to communicate directly with God, gifted, at least sometimes, with visions of God's heart. And when we're really getting it right, we saints then find ways to pass what we know about God on to the people around us, spreading vision and grace freely, as Saint Peter did.

Today, pick at least one saint who has already gone home to God, and at least one who is still with you. Say their names out loud and offer them up to God. Remember at least one thing that each one taught you about God. Say it out loud, and offer it up. Then sing like you mean it:

PRAYER: "For all the saints who from their labors rest, who through the years their steadfast faith confessed, your name, O Jesus, be forever blessed. Alleluia, alleluia! Still may your people faithful, true, and bold, live as the saints who nobly fought of old, and win with them a glorious crown of gold. Alleluia, alleluia!*" Amen.

*"For All the Saints," words by William W. How, 1864 (adapted).

SEPTEMBER 23

PERSECUTION HURTS

Lillian Daniel

There they strengthened the souls of the disciples and encouraged them to continue in the faith, saying, "It is through many persecutions that we must enter the kingdom of God." From Acts 14:21–28

PAUL AND BARNABAS, and many of the characters you have met in the book of Acts, knew plenty about persecution. They were well received by a few, and abused by many. They had to make sense of what was happening to them, so they said that persecution was part of entering the kingdom, or realm of God.

But here's the thing I worry about. I don't want us to sit back and accept persecution, or to think that it's any kind of gift from God. It's awful to be treated badly, as an individual or as a group, and I can't believe God takes any delight in angry mobs, in bullying, or in any kind of abuse.

I think that life contains many persecutions, and that it is through real life that we enter the realm of God. But persecution is not good for us. It's not something to put up with, and it's certainly not something to seek out.

God created human beings for flourishing. And so when you feel like you are not flourishing, know that God is with you, not as one who leads you into persecution, but as the One who leads you out of it.

It is in the journey away from persecution that we enter God's realm. And let's just admit that the journey through it is still very, very hard.

PRAYER: God, is there someone in my life who is being persecuted? Is there anything I can do about it? Are there people in the world whose suffering I have stopped paying attention to? Am I being persecuted myself? Inspire me to stand up against persecution, wherever it may be, even in my own heart. Amen.

DEATH IS NOT THE END

Christina Villa

Let the saints be joyful in glory. From Psalm 149 KJV

EVERY YEAR ON NOVEMBER 1, All Saints Day, I remember Sacred Heart Cemetery in the town where I grew up. It was a huge Polish cemetery situated on a long sloping hill next to a busy intersection. Starting at dusk on November 1, the eve of the Catholic All Souls Day, the entire cemetery would be lit up with thousands of red votive candles, one on nearly every grave. It looked like the dead were getting ready to have a party and had turned on all the lights in the house.

It sounds weird to say that the cemetery looked festive, but that's exactly how it looked. Lit up like Times Square, it looked more like life than death. It confused the categories of living and dead. It made the dead seem less separated from us, and not so different from us. When I was a child, those candles burning all night on all those graves used to make me think that it must make the dead people happy.

Of course that's a childish belief with no theological depth, but now I wonder: why not? If death is not the end, then it's not the end of celebration or joy. And not just the theoretical, pie-in-the-sky kind of celebration and joy, either. The real thing, the exact same happiness we know now, the kind that makes us light Advent candles and put up Christmas lights. The kind of happiness that makes us wish it could last forever. And possibly, it does.

PRAYER: Here's hoping perpetual light means lasting joy. Amen.

THE DANGERS OF TALKING TO YOURSELF

Anthony B. Robinson

The farm of a certain rich man produced a terrific crop. He talked to himself: "What can I do? My barn isn't big enough for this harvest." Then he said, "Here's what I'll do: I'll tear down my barns and build bigger ones. Then I'll gather in all my grain and goods, and I'll say to myself, Self, you've done well!"
From Luke 12:16–19

WHAT'S REALLY STRIKING about this parable of a wealthy man who built huge barns to store his great harvest is to whom he talks. He talks to himself; no one else.

In the four verses of the parable he spoke to himself three times. He never heard from anyone else until, suddenly, in the final verse: "But God said to him, 'You fool! This very night your life is being demanded of you.'"

Whom do you consult when you make important decisions? Who is part of the ongoing conversation of your life? When and how do you get outside your own head?

On Sunday I hope that you will be part of a worship service. Part of what happens when we worship is we widen our conversational circle. We are including God, as well as other people, in our conversation. We are listening for God's word in scripture and sermon. We are talking with God in prayer. We are talking with others in the congregation who also seek to have their conversation enlarged, and corrected, by God's word.

I've often heard people express appreciation for worship by saying, "Worship changes my perspective." Or, "Worship gives me a different way of seeing things." That happens when we widen the conversation and listen to voices besides our own, voices that are quite possibly wiser and deeper than our own.

PRAYER: As I worship today, God, speak your word into my life and give me a fresh and hopeful perspective. Amen.

LET IT GO BEFORE SUNDOWN

Martin B. Copenhaver

Be angry but do not sin; do not let the sun go down on your anger. From Ephesians 4:20–26

ONE IMPLICATION OF THE AFFIRMATION in this verse, "Be angry but do not sin," is that not all anger is sinful. There is such a thing as righteous anger. Anger is an appropriate response to injustice. In fact, all important social change is, in some way, fueled by anger.

Just as surely, not all anger is righteous or just. Thomas Aquinas, writing in the fourteenth century, singled out three ways in which anger can be sinful: when we get angry too easily, when we get angrier than we should, and when we hold onto our anger longer than we should.

It is because of our tendency to hold onto anger longer than we should that the author of Ephesians also counsels, "Do not let the sun go down on your anger." That may sound a bit like comedienne Phyllis Diller's advice, "Never go to bed mad. Stay up and fight," but it is more helpful, reminding us that there are dangers in holding onto our anger. Sometimes we can relish the experience of feeling wronged. Anger, which can be righteous, can easily turn self-righteous as well. So beware anger that you hold onto too long. As writer Anne Lamott observed, hanging onto resentments is like drinking rat poison and then waiting for the rat to die.

Is there some anger that you need to let go of before the sun goes down today?

PRAYER: God, let me confess that it is a temptation to hold onto my anger. Anger can help me feel righteous and superior. So help me let go of my anger before the sun goes down—for the sake of others, and for my own sake, as well. Amen.

HYPOCRITE

Quinn G. Caldwell

The LORD said, "Because these people draw near with their mouths and honor me with their lips, while their hearts are far from me, and their worship of me is a human commandment learned by rote; so I will again do amazing things with this people, shocking and amazing." Isaiah 29:13–14a

I OFTEN HEAR FROM WORSHIPERS who are unsure whether they should say or sing something in worship. One guy can't get his head around the Trinity and wonders whether he should be singing the Doxology with the rest of us. A woman doesn't think she should pass the peace because she rarely feels particularly peaceful herself.

They're worried about being the kind of hypocrite from Isaiah describes. I love that about them.

Here's what I tell them: If you don't believe something, and don't want to believe it, and are not open to new insight on that point, then don't say it.

But if you're simply not sure you believe something, or if you don't believe it now but would like to believe it, or if you're willing to be changed, then go for it. If we were all expected to believe everything about the faith before we even walk in the door, then the whole place—including the pulpit—would be empty. Instead, we're all in the process of talking and living ourselves into belief.

I tell them to think of the words like beautiful hand-me-down clothes that may not fit now, but which they just might grow into. I tell them go ahead, say the words bold and proud, and see whether you aren't convinced in the saying.

Which is not hypocrisy, but hope.

PRAYER: God, don't let me be a hypocrite, but don't let me pass up on truth just because I don't get it the first time, either. Amen.

A Mere Tip of the Hat

Martin B. Copenhaver

The kingdom of heaven is like a mustard seed that someone took and sowed in his field; it is the smallest of all the seeds, but when it has grown it is the greatest of shrubs and becomes a tree, so that the birds of the air come and make nests in its branches. Matthew 13:31–32

IN HIS MEMOIRS Oscar Wilde recalled the experience of being brought from the prison, where he was held after being declared—in the strange manner of his day—"guilty" of homosexuality. He writes: "When I was brought down from my prison between two policemen, a man I know waited in the long dreary corridor so that, before the whole crowd, whom an action so sweet and simple hushed into silence, he might gravely raise his hat to me as, handcuffed and with bowed head, I passed him by. Men have gone to heaven for smaller things than that."

After Episcopal Archbishop Desmond Tutu won a Nobel Peace Prize for his nonviolent struggle against apartheid in South Africa, he was asked to recall the formative experiences of his life. He replied, "One incident comes to mind immediately. When I was a young child I saw a man tip his hat to a black woman. Please understand that such a gesture is completely unheard of in my country. The white man was an Episcopal bishop and the black woman was my mother."

These two stories remind me that even a small, fragile gesture can take on grand dimensions when it is offered in love. Our own efforts may be small, but through them the largest of all realities—the love of God—can be communicated. A mere tip of the hat can offer hope and change a life.

PRAYER: God, remind me not to neglect the small acts of compassion so that you, in turn, might fill them with your great love. Amen.

Bunch Ball

Anthony B. Robinson

Indeed, the body does not consist of one member but of many. From 1 Corinthians 12:12–20

When I coached six- and seven-year-olds in soccer, I noticed their default style of play was "bunch ball." Everyone ran to the ball, forming a swirling scrum where shins were kicked, kids wailed, and the ball went nowhere. When the ball did squirt out of the pack, there was no one there to get it.

My mantra as a soccer coach became, "Play your position," which is not as easy as it sounds. It means you have to know what your role is and you have to trust your teammates to know their position and play it. That means not rushing into someone else's part of the field just because the ball goes there. When kids on a soccer team got this, it had the quality of a revelation.

In many congregations we also play bunch ball. We seem to think that everyone needs to be in on every decision and everyone has to have the chance to express his or her opinion on every matter, often second-guessing those to whom a task or decision has been assigned. We sanction our congregational bunch ball with words like "participatory," "congregational," and "inclusive."

Paul spoke of the church as a body, the body of Christ, and suggested that the different parts (people) had different roles. When we forget that, the body gets sick. He urged people to play their part and respect others, allowing them to play theirs.

I know I'm mixing my metaphors (team and body), but the idea is the same. Play your position. Avoid congregational bunch ball. Trust others to play their part. Because, after all, when we're caught in the congregational scrum, we tend to lose sight of the goal: being part of God's mission of saving lives and repairing a broken world.

PRAYER: When I am tempted to rush into someone else's part of the field and take over, help me play my position, my part in the body of Christ, that your mission may be served and that you, Jesus, may be glorified. Amen.

The Young and the Old

Donna Schaper

Then Pharisees and scribes came to Jesus from Jerusalem and said, "Why do your disciples break the tradition of the elders? For they do not wash their hands before they eat." From Matthew 15:1–9

I REMEMBER WHEN MY PARENTS first saw me wearing blue jeans. They were horrified. Daily I meet people who don't approve of Facebook or don't like baseball caps worn backwards. Have they really forgotten how they broke their own parents' hearts, right in front of the neighbors?

Generational warfare is universal and maybe even harmless. People seem to need to justify themselves. One of the ways we do it is by wearing what our parents didn't. The disciples had bad manners and some people thought that needed comment. Jesus didn't.

In the name of Jesus, we keep an eye on the lame, the blind, the feeble, and the old—and the young. Elders deserve respect because they are elders. Youth lose when they forget to respect the old, just as the old lose if they don't try to find out what younger people are thinking under their baseball caps. The best thing we have learned in my congregation, which is getting younger, is not to mention age very much. That way we treat each other as people, which is what matters. Customs don't. People do.

Thomas Jefferson argued that in matters of custom, we swim with the flow, and in matters of principle, we make like a rock. My hope for younger people and older people is that they know what it means to love a person like Jesus did—and learn to avoid the shallow self-promoting sneers.

PRAYER: O God, let us forget about the young and old for a while and grant humanity to all. Amen.

OCTOBER

MERCY

Quinn G. Caldwell

For judgment will be without mercy to anyone who has shown no mercy; mercy triumphs over judgment. From James 2:1–13

MERCY ALWAYS SOUNDS TO ME like a word for bigger-deal people than I am. If I were the king, I could be merciful. If I held a loan that someone was having trouble paying off, I could be merciful. If I were holding a sword and standing over a fallen foe, I could show mercy then, too. It's hard to imagine little old me being in any position to show mercy in day-to-day life, though.

James thinks differently. He thinks it's a day-to-day kind of thing.

Maybe I didn't have to have such a big sigh when my partner forgot to bring home milk, even though he totally said he'd do it, and then totally didn't.

Maybe I didn't have to lay on my horn quite so harshly when that lady cut me off on the way to work this morning, even though she was obviously in the wrong.

Maybe mercy is about self-control, about choosing not to use power to convict someone (even tiny power, like a disappointed sigh or an angry horn blast), choosing not to vent one's spleen just because it feels good.

So today, I will try to be self-controlled. I will focus more on relationships than being right, more on building others up than pointing out the ways they've wronged me. Today, I will try to show the world the mercy I hope to one day receive when I find myself kneeling before the One with all the power.

PRAYER: God, please be merciful. And let me be, too. Amen.

OCTOBER 2

THE POWER IN BLESSING

Martin B. Copenhaver

May the LORD bless you and take good care of you. May the LORD smile on you and be gracious to you. From Numbers 6:22–27 (paraphrased)

THERE IS GREAT POWER in the act of blessing. So why we don't offer more blessings for one another?

We may assume the people we care about don't need a blessing. We think our children need advice. We see that our parents need support. A friend needs a listening ear. A spouse needs a kind word. Someone who has annoyed me needs a piece of my mind. We may not consider that what someone may need more than anything else—what that person may be hungry for, in some cases dying of hunger for—is a blessing.

Or we may have concluded that someone doesn't deserve a blessing. There is an old Gaelic blessing: "May those who love us, love us. And those who don't, turn their hearts; and those who don't turn their hearts, may they turn their ankles, so we'll know them by their limping."

Doesn't that capture the kind of blessings we are sometimes tempted to offer? It's more like a curse—which, of course, is the opposite of a blessing. Sometimes the good words stick on our tongues.

So it's important to remember that words of blessing are borrowed words. We are asking God to bless because we may not have any good words of our own to offer. To say, "May God bless you," is to borrow the power of God to offer good words when that seems beyond us. It is asking God to take the lead.

PRAYER: God bless those I would like to bless, and those I am unable to bless on my own. Amen.

DOUBLE-DIPPED

Quinn G. Caldwell

Peter said to them, "Repent, and be baptized every one of you in the name of Jesus Christ so that your sins may be forgiven; and you will receive the gift of the Holy Spirit. For the promise is for you, for your children, and for all who are far away, everyone whom the Lord our God calls to him." . . . So those who welcomed his message were baptized. From Acts 2:37–42

MY PARENTS WANTED us to make our own decisions about whether to be baptized. As a young adult, I took the plunge. Years later, my grandmother made a confession. It turns out that she, convinced that my parents were putting her grandchildren's wee souls in danger of perdition by not baptizing us as babies, had baptized each one of us over her kitchen sink a few days after our births.

I was full of chagrin at all the rules that had been broken. One: I was baptized not just in private, away from a congregation, but in secret. Two: It happened without the consent or knowledge of those responsible for me. Three: it was done based on a belief that neither my parents nor I hold. Four: Worst of all, I've been double-dipped.

Looked at this way, it could not have gone more wrong. Looked at another way, though, it really couldn't have been more right. One: My parents thought carefully about their children's baptism, and made a decision that had integrity. Two: My grandmother did what she did for love of grandchildren she believed to be *in extremis*. Three: Knowing my grandmother, I guarantee you that no font has ever witnessed a baptism sweeter (or crazier) than the ones witnessed by Grandma Stell's kitchen sink. Four: In the fullness of time, having been loved and raised by these people who took baptism so seriously, I came to ask for it on my own, which means that something worked.

So, yeah, I've been baptized all wrong and way too much. But I've learned that God cares way less about rules than I do, and that there can never be too much love poured out on the world.

PRAYER: God, pour your love into the world and let it overwhelm us all! Amen.

OCTOBER 4

WHO WAS YOUR FAVORITE TEACHER?

Christina Villa

The LORD God has given me the tongue of a teacher, that I may know how to sustain the weary with a word. From Isaiah 50:4–9a

A LOT OF PEOPLE seem to hold a grudge against public school teachers, especially during budget controversies. I have a theory about why people are so ready to jump all over teachers for being "glorified baby-sitters" who work "part-time" (out at 2:30!) and "take summers off."

Ironically, teachers may be singled out this way because they are not just glorified baby-sitters but instead crucially important figures in our lives. Everyone reading this, no matter how old, can probably name a teacher they have never forgotten, one who opened up some new world to them, took them seriously, or just plain looked out for them. Many of us are lucky and can name several.

But you don't turn into a saint just because you go into teaching, and there are also some bad teachers out there. With all the influence and power they have over the young, a bad teacher can do some serious human damage. My theory is that a lot of the antiteacher people in the budget debates aren't ready to forgive the really bad teacher who humiliated them or singled them out for abuse or turned them off to learning altogether. And now they're getting their revenge.

It's too bad, because by some weird physics of education, one really good teacher can go a long way toward counteracting the effects of several bad ones. A great teacher really does "sustain the weary with a word." They are never boring, always enlivening, even in such subjects as, say, geometry or biology (thank you Mr. Beardsley and Mr. Nelson). They stand up there and talk—it appears that's all they do—but, oh, what a lifelong difference it makes if it's the right person standing up there talking.

PRAYER: Bless all teachers, guide those who shouldn't be in the classroom to another profession, and give my regards to Mr. Beardsley and Mr. Nelson. Amen.

OCTOBER 5

SING

Quinn G. Caldwell

With gratitude in your hearts sing psalms, hymns, and spiritual songs to God.
From Colossians 3:12–17

THERE ARE ABOUT 5,400 ANIMAL SPECIES that make complex, intentional, repeatable, musical vocalizations. That is, there are about 5,400 species that sing. The majority live in the trees, a few live in the oceans, a very few live underground, but there is one—only one—singing species that lives on the ground: us.

Another thing: humans are the only singing species with a precise and shared sense of rhythm, which is what allows us to sing together. Two birds might sing the same song, but they cannot sing it together.

Another thing: if a roomful of people sings at the same time, they start to breathe at the same time as well. Some studies suggest that if the drumbeat or bass line is strong enough, their hearts will begin to beat together, too. And if we're singing together and breathing together and our hearts are beating together, then it's like we're one body. And you know whose body it is.

Another thing: all the other species stop singing when danger approaches. But humans sing louder the closer the danger gets. We sing together, and we become large, and we do not back down.

So come racism, and "We Shall Overcome" you. Come fear, for "It Is Well with My Soul." Come war, for tonight is your "Silent Night." Come death, for "Jesus Christ Is Risen Today." Come, all ye faithful, and sing.

PRAYER: Lord, I can't read music and I can't carry a tune in a bucket. But I'm-a sing your praises anyway. Amen.

OCTOBER 6

SEE AND SPEAK

Donna Schaper

And their eyes were opened. From Matthew 9:27–34

A SIGHTED PASTOR ON LONG ISLAND preached this text with a companion, who was physically blind. His sermon addressed the kind of blindness that Jesus healed and the kind of blindness that we choose. The second can't be healed until we choose against it.

We keep so much to ourselves in a kind of blindness to the need we have to know what others think of us.

I have a friend who clearly has been taught another way. She always says what she sees. I have never met her without her acknowledging something about me. "You look good in purple." "You seem tired." "Your walk has more bounce in it today. What's up?" Clearly she has trained herself to see. She has trained herself not to be blind to the enormous appreciation deficit disorder of our days.

Knowing how Jesus loved to open eyes, I am thinking of imitating my friend. I am thinking of saying out loud what I see. I am going to notice what I think I have already seen, which is what some insist is the goal of all travel. I am going to avoid what Anne Lamott calls the "malignant Advent calendar" in which we see a door but refuse to open it. She claims to have been taught an agreement as a child. She would not see what she did see. She would not open doors. Secrets were behind them. As an adult, she learned to open doors and not only to see what she saw but also to speak it, out loud.

I'd like my eyes to be open. And if genuine macular degeneration comes my way, I imagine I will still rely on Jesus to keep me open.

PRAYER: O God, open our eyes and then open our mouths. Keep us from being a part of closed-door living. Give us a key to unlock sight and sound. Amen.

OCTOBER 7

"OUR FATHER"

Kenneth L. Samuel

This then, is how you should pray: "Our Father in heaven . . . ." From Matthew 6:7–15 NIV

IN ALL MY LIFE, I have seen my mother visibly shaken and upset on just a couple of occasions. One of those occasions occurred a few years ago. My sister, my two brothers, and I were at my mother's apartment in New York discussing some family business. The discussion got heated and exploded into a fireball of disagreement among the four of us. Out of anger and frustration, things were said that should have been tempered, or not said at all. That's when I saw my mother visibly shaken; deeply disturbed. She didn't calm down until she'd extracted a promise from me and each of my siblings that nothing else would be said until each of us got over the anger and remembered that we were family.

Days later I asked my mother why she had become so upset. None of our angry expressions were directed at her. "We go at one another all the time," I said to her. "It's no big deal." She looked at me squarely and with a solemn tone said, "Perhaps you do . . . but not in my presence."

If prayer is an acknowledgement of the presence of God, our Divine Parent, then we can never pray without remembering that each of us is a part of God's human family. We cannot really go to God in prayer without taking with us the quality of our relationships with one another. Prayer can be personal, but it can never be private. It always exposes our relationships with our brothers and sisters. Prayer reminds us that without human community there can be no divine communion. Prayer lifts each of us out of the secluded silos of our own self-centeredness and ushers us into the communal consciousness of "Our Father" / "Our Mother" / "Our Creator" / "Our Redeemer" / "Our God." And there is nothing that displeases "Our God" more than our disrespect and disregard for one another.

PRAYER: Dear God, today, as we acknowledge your presence we also acknowledge our need to reconcile and be reconciled to our brothers and sisters. In your presence, help us to find better ways to love one another. Amen.

BORN AGAIN

Anthony B. Robinson

But to all who received him, who believed in his name, he gave power to become children of God, who were born, not of blood or will of the flesh or of the will of man, but of God. From John 1:10–18

EARLY IN MY MINISTRY a group of angry church members confronted me. They demanded to know if I had been "born again." They weren't bad people, but they were frightened. They were asking if I was in their camp and one of them. "Born again" sounded like a slogan or a code, a way of saying who was in and who was not.

Twenty years ago the Berlin Wall came down. A thirteen-year-old girl from the eastern side somehow made her way to a Christian community in West Berlin and found shelter there. Several years before, this child had been sold into prostitution by her mother.

One day in that Christian community there was a baptism. The pastor poured water into the font and as he did so he spoke of being "born again from above." Sitting near the back, the thirteen-year-old girl listened to his words.

After the service, she went to the pastor who stood near the font. Shyly she asked, "Can I be born again?" For her, the words were not a formula or a slogan. They were not code words. They were truth and life. The answer was, "Yes."

Because of the first experience, the words "born again" were pretty much lost on me until a friend told me the story of the second, the thirteen-year-old German girl. Her naïve question to the pastor somehow seems so much closer to the truth of the invitation and powerful promise found in these early verses of John. "To all who receive him . . . he gives power to become children of God, born not of will of man, but of God."

PRAYER: I'm your child, God, while I run this race. And I don't want to run this race in vain. I'm your child, God, while I run this race. Amen.

BE QUICK ABOUT IT

Martin B. Copenhaver

You must understand this, my beloved: let everyone be quick to listen, slow to speak, slow to anger. From James 1:17–27

JAMES REMINDS US that there are some things we should be quick to do, like listen, and other things we should be slow to do, like talk and express anger.

We might want to expand the lists. Here are some things I want to be slow to do: presume that I really understand what is going on in another person's life; be convinced that I am right; walk away from a friendship; assume that someone meant to hurt me; say something that may wound another; conclude that there is nothing I can do to help; think that what someone else most needs is my advice. It's not that it is always inappropriate to do any of these things, but often it is, which is reason enough to slow down and reflect.

And here are some things that I want to be quick to do: express appreciation; extend forgiveness; offer encouragement; apologize when I know I have messed up; stand up for the oppressed; offer words of confession; remember the promises of God; praise God in all circumstances; keep quiet when I cannot improve upon the silence. All of these things may sound good in the abstract, but the point is to do them now and not delay.

As Henri Amiel affirmed, "Life is short, and there is little time to gladden the hearts of those who journey with us . . . so be quick to love and make haste to be kind."

PRAYER: O God, help me to be slow to do those things that may do harm and quick to do those things that I should do right now. Amen.

A MOTHER'S IMAGINATION

Lillian Daniel

Jesus and his disciples had also been invited to the wedding. When the wine gave out, the mother of Jesus said to him, "They have no wine." And Jesus said to her, "Woman, what concern is that to you and to me? My hour has not yet come." His mother said to the servants, "Do whatever he tells you." From John 2:1–11

YOU KNOW, MY MOTHER THOUGHT I could do anything, too. She was always exaggerating my gifts.

When it was time to apply to college she told me I should go to Harvard. When I explained that my grade point average was not represented anywhere in that school's statistics, she would say, "Oh, nonsense, just apply."

Once I started working, she was always giving me a promotion, telling people I was doing the work of my boss. When I tried to correct her, she would just keep talking. My churches were tripled in size; my first articles turned into books and a seat on the association's committee on ministry made me a bishop—all through the power of a mother's imagination.

Listening to my mother, you would have thought I was some kind of miracle worker, but I knew better, and so did Harvard.

So I have always delighted that the first miracle Jesus performs is the result of his mother's imagination. His mother tells him that they have run out of wine, and he says, 'Woman, what concern is that to you and to me?" He's as annoyed as anyone when his mother puts her enormous vision for him out there.

But Jesus actually was a miracle worker. And someone had to get him started.

Sometimes a mother's imagination is a miracle in itself.

PRAYER: Dear God, this day, I pray for those who nag and those who brag. I pray for all the people who see possibilities in me long before I do. And I pray not to be annoyed by those people. You have put them here for a reason. Amen.

NO WORRIES

Christina Villa

[Josiah] broke down . . . the carved and the cast images; he made dust of them and scattered it over the graves of those who had sacrificed to them. He also burned the bones of the priests on their altars. From 2 Chronicles 34:1–7

JOSIAH'S ZEALOUS DESTRUCTION OF EVERY PAGAN IMAGE he could find seems a little over the top—especially that idea to burn the bones of the priests on their own altars. He doesn't stop until he has "demolished all the incense altars throughout all the land of Israel."

I know all this zealous destruction of false gods and pagan images is supposed to make Josiah one of the good guys in the Bible. But his approach to things reminds me of how easily and often we overrespond to perceived threats. We seem to like doing that. There are germs and the gallons of hand sanitizer we keep buying; a few years ago there were the faulty brakes on everyone's Toyotas; winter weather advisories turn every snowfall into a killer blizzard; and let's not even get started on the hazards that lurk in food, not to mention the people who might secretly be terrorists.

There's always something to be afraid of. And as a world-class worrier myself, I can see the appeal of Josiah's method. How great would it be if you could just wipe out every trace of whatever is out there that threatens you? The trouble is that no sooner is one worry eliminated, one false god demolished, than another one springs up to take its place. After a while, it's pretty clear that some of us need something, anything, to be afraid of.

Do our serial worries really function as false gods? Do we find our only comfort in eliminating or destroying them? Only to find ourselves fixated on yet another one? Do we really want to spend our lives worshiping what we fear—with a break on Sunday to distract us?

PRAYER: Let every day have at least a little Sunday in it. Amen.

ENOUGH ALREADY

Martin B. Copenhaver

[A rich farmer] thought to himself, "What should I do, for I have no place to store my crops?" Then he said, "I will do this: I will pull down my barns and build larger ones, and there I will store all my grain and my goods." . . . But God said to him, "You fool! This very night your soul is being demanded of you. And the things you have prepared, whose will they be?" From Luke 12:13–21

WHEN WAS IT EXACTLY that we began to need such big closets?

When my family lived in Phoenix, we had a comfortable home that was built in the early 1980s and, like most homes built in recent decades, it had very large closets—not large enough for Imelda Marcos' shoe collection, mind you, but plenty large for all the stuff we had.

When we moved to Massachusetts, we bought a house built in 1931. And, like most homes built in that era, it has small closets. This made unpacking a particular challenge. We simply did not have storage space for all of our stuff.

How did we end up with all this stuff, anyway? And is that why so many houses are so large these days? After all, as the comedian George Carlin put it, what is a house but a large box to keep all of our stuff, with a lid on it? And we have a lot of stuff these days. So now the average American house is twice as big as it was fifty years ago, while in the same time period family units became smaller.

How much stuff is enough? And how much space is enough to store it all?

For most of us, "enough" is defined as something more than what we have, a shifting standard that can be, and often is, adjusted upward.

I've never been to a dog track, but I'm pretty sure about one thing. I think I know the name of that wooden rabbit that keeps the panting pack running around the track. That rabbit's name is "Enough." And, whether it is a dog race or a rat race, no one ever seems to catch it.

PRAYER: God, your creation is infused with your generosity. You take care of our every need. Quiet our hearts—and rebuke us—when we fear that there is not enough. Amen.

OCTOBER 13

QUIBBLING AND QUOTING

Lillian Daniel

When the Sabbath arrived, Jesus lost no time in getting to the meeting place. He spent the day there teaching. They were surprised at his teaching—so forthright, so confident—not quibbling and quoting like the religion scholars. From Mark 1:21–22 TM

"SO WHAT DOES YOUR CHURCH BELIEVE?" If someone asked you that question, what would you say?

In the spirit of confession, let's acknowledge that many of us might respond by telling the person what our church does not believe. We might say, "We're not closed-minded, but open to all ideas. We welcome everybody, unlike some other churches. We're not like the fundamentalists who take scripture literally. And we're not like the churches who won't ordain women."

"OK," says the patient inquirer. "So what do you believe?"

We might continue, "Well, we believe that people can be free to believe many different things, so that's a tricky question to answer."

"OK, then," says the inquirer, now less patient. "Then what do you believe?"

"Well, I'm on a journey. It's a private matter. Here are the authors who have meant something to me and can say it so much better than I could . . . Blah, blah, blah."

309

Oh, just stop it.

We are told that one of the things that impressed Jesus' listeners was that he spoke plainly, "not quibbling and quoting like the religious scholars." He just put his beliefs and teachings out there and was ready to withstand some debate.

You can be open-minded and still know what you think. You can be accepting of other people's ideas but still willing to articulate your own. You can rejoice in the many diverse paths to God and still invite your neighbor to church.

Just say it.

PRAYER: God, you have already given me the words to express how I know and love you. Help me get over the quibbling and quoting, and just say it. Otherwise, how will they know? Amen.

OCTOBER 14

TOUCH

Donna Schaper

God did extraordinary miracles through Paul, so that when the handkerchiefs or aprons that had touched his skin were brought to the sick, their diseases left them and the evil spirits came out of them. Acts 19:11–12

GRUELING GARDENING CAN BECOME JOYFUL GARDENING with the arrival of a cool cloth for a hot forehead. Discouragement can turn to encouragement if the right person at the right time in the right way gives us a pat on the back. Caressing a child's chin after the tricycle spill can stop the tears and put the kid back on the bike. Hasn't someone told you many times about the importance of a strong handshake? Touch is tremendously important to human beings. It can change the cycle and change the momentum. Ask those who are lonely, they know. Ask those who have been touched in a way they should not have been touched, they also know.

Paul apparently had the divine touch. He knew how to fill his aprons and his handkerchiefs with the spirit of God. We can too. The ordinary moves to the extraordinary when we channel the touch of God with our own hands and clothing. Such holy touch has to be careful not to get conceited or formulaic or fraught with its own power or need. Healing happens from the open heart, not the self-aggrandizing one. As long as our touches are small, even domestic, as domestic as the laundry, we too can provide extraordinary miracles.

PRAYER: O God, open our hearts so that, when we use our hands, we open our hands, we touch with healing grace. Amen.

OCTOBER 15

WISDOM BITES

Anthony B. Robinson

Wisdom begins with the fear of the LORD, *but fools despise wisdom and instruction.* From Proverbs 1:7–33 CEB

WHEN I THINK OF WISDOM I think of my grandmother, Victoria Moon Robinson. Orphaned as a child, she was raised by a kind family in Ohio. As a young woman she became a licensed pharmacist, not all that common for women in the World War I era. She also played the organ at church and for services at my other grandparents' funeral home there in the remote but beautiful town in northeastern Oregon where they all lived.

In her later years, she was crippled by arthritis. Nevertheless, she presided, with love and wisdom, from a large chair in her living room.

One day, I was probably about twenty at the time, I must have said something that struck my grandmother as arrogant or callow or too full of myself—perhaps all of the above. She fixed me with a stern look and said, "Mister, don't you ever think that you are any better than anyone else."

Her words had a bite to them, which, in my experience, real wisdom often does. In the Book of Proverbs, what separates the wise from the foolish is not that the wise have no need of correction, but that when they get it they listen and pay attention, even if it bites. The foolish, on the other hand, neither listen nor pay heed. The foolish can't handle correction.

Part of what made me pay attention when my grandmother spoke sharply to me was that I knew, beyond the shadow of a doubt, that she loved me. I knew she was and always would be in my corner. But she loved me enough to challenge me. We're blessed when we have such people in our lives. Is there someone like that in your life?

And we're blessed when we listen and pay attention, even when wisdom bites.

PRAYER: Holy One, grant me the grace to hear and heed your wisdom, even, or perhaps especially, when it bites a little. Amen.

APPOINTED AND AUTHORIZED

Donna Schaper

And he appointed twelve, whom he also named apostles . . . to have authority to cast out demons. From Mark 3:13–19a

APPOINTMENT AND AUTHORIZATION ARE WORDS USUALLY ASSOCIATED with a new job or job description. We get our credentials, we get our keys, and we get our security pass. We are sent. Jesus appointed and authorized twelve whom he then called by name to go out and speak his message and cast out demons. They mostly had on-the-job training for a very new job, called being "apostles."

We, too, are called to be disciples who become apostles. We, too, are sent out to do things we don't know how to do. We are appointed and authorized in the same way the original untutored and uneducated disciples were turned into apostles. You only have to remember the word "apostate" to understand the word "apostle."

An apostate is one who gets it all wrong. An apostle is one who gets it kind of right. Imagine the trust of Jesus in his people, which is to say us. He imagines we can get it right. He imagines we can do things we don't know how to do. He imagines we can de-demonize the world. He imagines we can find the clumsy words to speak his gorgeous message. We are appointed and authorized. Our names have been called.

PRAYER: May the courage of the original apostles be ours. May we accept the appointment to speak of Jesus with all we have and whatever we have. Amen.

OCTOBER 17

HANDS

Quinn G. Caldwell

Then they brought the tabernacle to Moses, the tent and all its utensils, its hooks, its frames, its bars, its pillars, and its bases; the covering of tanned rams' skins and the covering of fine leather, and the curtain for the screen; the ark of the covenant with its poles and the mercy seat; the table with all its utensils, and the bread of the Presence; the pure lampstand with its lamps set on it and all its utensils, and the oil for the light; the golden altar, the anointing oil and

the fragrant incense, and the screen for the entrance of the tent. . . . The Israelites had done all of the work just as the LORD had commanded Moses.
From Exodus 39:32–43

HERE'S THE THING ABOUT HANDS. The same pair can be used to build a bomb and to stroke a child's face; to smack your spouse around and to paint a masterpiece; to flip somebody off and to remove a cancer from an ailing body. It's all about who's in control.

The Israelites had just blown it big time: they had cast themselves a golden calf to worship. The story glosses over the actual process of making the calf, but it must have taken a lot of work, some of it quite skilled, to produce such a thing. A lot of work, a lot of craftsmanship, a lot of time, a lot of loving care . . . all to produce one of the worst abominations God seems able to imagine.

Now here are those same people, offering the Tabernacle. The hands that created an abomination have now woven, and dyed, and cast, and sewn, and built a great portable cathedral in the desert. Those same sinning hands have now produced tools to dispense forgiveness, and furniture for righteousness, and containers for covenant, and a seat for mercy, and a great thing of beauty rising in the starkest of surroundings.

When left to their own devices, the best the people could come up with were a cow and a party. With God in control, they crafted mercy, and forgiveness, and beauty.

Who's going to control your hands today?

PRAYER: God, I know whose playground idle hands are. So grant me tasks to do with mine that will be gentle, beautiful, creative, and just. Amen.

APPLAUSE IN CHURCH

Anthony B. Robinson

Praise God in [God's] sanctuary! . . . Praise God with the blast of a ram's horn!
. . . Praise God with drum and dance! . . . Let every living thing praise the
LORD! From Psalm 150 CEB

I WAS RECENTLY IN A CONGREGATION where everything was greeted with applause. Well, okay, not quite everything. People applauded the choir's anthem, the children's song, all the announcements, and even the prayers of a lay leader. But no one, as I recalled, applauded the offering.

Is applause in church okay or not? Is it okay sometimes but not other times? I've been in some churches where thunderous applause seemed like another form of praise of God and just right. And I've been in churches where applause made it seem that worship was a performance and the congregation an audience and just wrong.

What I mostly noticed in the church where everything but the offering was responded to with applause is that the open and empty spaces in which God might move and get to us were all filled up. They were filled in and filled up with applause. No silence was allowed.

That church seemed long on friendly, but short on mystery.

While I have experienced times when applause in worship was spontaneous, joyful, and somehow right, when applause becomes a norm or expectation it does turn worship into something it isn't, namely, a performance. Worse, it fills up the spaces, the silent spaces following a powerful solo or anthem or sharing or testimony where God's presence is palpable, or might be.

Another way to put this reservation about applause is to say that applause tends to move us out of our hearts and into our heads. We ask, "Did I like that?" "Should I applaud?" "Will it make him/her/them feel good and appreciated?"

One thing that gifted worship leaders do, in my observation, is—they don't do too much. They lead with a light touch. They leave room for God. They hold the space. And only very rarely do they invite applause.

PRAYER: Thank you God, for worship. It's a different and special time. Thank you for worship leaders who lead lightly and don't need applause because they know it's not about them. Amen.

JESUS' FRIENDS IN TROUBLE

Martin B. Copenhaver

That day a severe persecution began against the church in Jerusalem. From Acts 8:1b–8

SOMETIMES WHEN I READ Jesus' warnings that his followers will be hated or when I read about the way the early church was persecuted, I wonder what I am doing wrong. After all, I have not been hated for being a follower of Jesus and no one has persecuted me. Instead, I live a rather comfortable life and the church I serve is on the cover of our town's phone book. People seem to be glad we're here. What has changed? Has the culture really come around to the point that it embraces the gospel? Alas, there is another possibility. Perhaps we as Christians no longer represent a clear alternative to the ways of the surrounding culture. Perhaps we just don't seem worth persecuting anymore.

And yet, Jesus still knows how to get his friends into trouble. I am thinking of the woman who is grilled at a cocktail party because her church is opening its doors to homeless people and "ruining the neighborhood." There is the young financial advisor who is passed over for promotion because he resisted pressure from his boss to push financial products that were not suitable for his clients. There is the attorney who defended someone on death row for sixteen years. When he went to the execution he had to move through a crowd of shouting people holding signs that damn both the condemned prisoner and his lawyer to the fires of hell. There is the fourteen-year-old at a boys' camp who stands up to his cabin mates and says, "I don't think it is right to call someone 'gay' as a put-down. There is nothing wrong with being gay."

Those examples all come from my congregation. Yes—Praise God!—Jesus still knows how to get his friends into trouble.

PRAYER: Dear God, in the words of the old hymn,* "Grant us wisdom, grant us courage, for the living of these days." Amen.

*"God of Grace and God of Glory," words by Harry Emerson Fosdick, 1930.

OCTOBER 20

GOD TALK

Quinn G. Caldwell

Whoever speaks must do so as one speaking the very words of God. From 1 Peter 4:7–11

WHEN I READ THIS LINE, I frantically flipped through the book, looking for the part that said Peter was talking only about how to act in worship.

Turns out Peter was talking about all the time. He says it's our job to try to have everything that comes out of our mouths be something that God would say. Every. Thing.

How would your day be different if when you called customer service and got someone in another country, you treated him as God would?

What would happen if when gossiping in the break room, you only said things about your colleagues that might proceed from the mouth of the God?

What would it be like if when your kids are at their most difficult, you only said things to them that a loving creator would say?

Frankly, I doubt I could handle doing that for a whole morning, never mind a whole lifetime. So let's start small: pick an hour and spend it trying to say only what God would. At the end of that hour, ask yourself if it went better or worse that most of your hours go. If it's the latter, drop it. But if it's the former, well, then, you know what to do.

(P.S. And since I totally know how your mind works: no, you don't get to demand that the people around you worship you even though that *is* the kind of thing God would say.

Or was nobody else thinking that? Just me? OK then, never mind.)

PRAYER: God, may the words of my lips be acceptable in your sight. Amen.

SING ONE ANOTHER'S SONGS

Martin B. Copenhaver

And with gratitude in your hearts sing psalms, hymns, and spiritual songs to God. From Colossians 3:12–17

IN PAUL'S LETTER TO THE COLOSSIANS, in the midst of a demanding list of commands to live a righteous life, it is startling to come upon the command to sing: "and with gratitude in your hearts sing psalms, hymns, and spiritual songs to God." Why did they need to be commanded to sing? Isn't singing a great joy?

Well, perhaps the Colossians couldn't agree on what kind of songs to sing. It is amazing how controversial music can be. A while back the Methodists were planning to publish a new hymnal. They started with a survey in which they asked which hymns their members would most like to see included. "Rock of Ages" topped the list. They also asked which hymns they would least like to see included. The number one choice? "Rock of Ages."

It is telling that, in his command to sing, Paul refers to three different kinds of music: "psalms" (that is, songs from the Bible), "hymns" (songs of praise not from the Bible), and "spiritual songs," which could mean just about anything. Sing psalms, hymns, and spiritual songs. So Paul was saying, "Sing different songs. Even in a style you don't like, because it may be speaking from the heart, or to the heart, of someone else in your community of faith."

That may be why Paul had to command the people of Colossae to sing. To sing together—out of our different cultures, languages, backgrounds, and, yes, musical tastes—can be a radical act. It would be wonderful if it could be said of each of our congregations: "It is the kind of place where they joyfully sing one another's songs."

PRAYER: God, tune my heart for praise so that I might sing joyfully and, in singing, be drawn together with all who worship you. Amen.

ACTS OF GOD

Christina Villa

The voice of the LORD is powerful; the voice of the LORD is full of majesty. . . .
The voice of the LORD causes the oaks to whirl, and strips the forest bare; and
in [the LORD'S] temple all say, "Glory!" From Psalm 29

WHILE WATCHING ONE OF THOSE STORM SHOWS on the Weather Channel,
I was struck by pictures of trees with their bark stripped off by the wind.
I didn't know that could happen. I couldn't begin to imagine a wind powerful enough. For a few unpleasant seconds, I thought about how fragile
and vulnerable we all are here on earth. Then I successfully put that idea
out of my mind.

This scripture passage reads like a tornado report from biblical times.
Trees whirl and snap, the forest is stripped bare. The psalm is clear that all
this is caused by "the voice of the LORD." To which the people say, "Glory!"
Apparently, that's the kind of thing they said when they saw evidence of
something more powerful than they could imagine. They didn't rush to
forget about it.

None of us are very likely to give God glory for being powerful. We
tend to think of power negatively, dwelling on all the ways it can destroy
and be abused. When was the last time you heard a prayer begin,
"Almighty God"? Sometimes I hear "Gracious God," and "Merciful God,"
and "Loving God" so often that I wonder if God isn't feeling a little pres-
sured to exhibit only these qualities.

People abuse power; God doesn't. What good, I wonder, are God's
mercy and grace if they are powerless?

PRAYER: Holy, holy, holy LORD, God of power and might, heaven and earth are full of
your glory. Amen.

TRAIN

Quinn G. Caldwell

Now, discipline always seems painful rather than pleasant at the time, but later it yields the peaceful fruit of righteousness to those who have been trained by it. Therefore lift your drooping hands and strengthen your weak knees, and make straight paths for your feet, so that what is lame may not be put out of joint, but rather be healed. From Hebrews 12:7–13

I'M NOT MUCH OF A FAN of sports metaphors in the life of faith, mostly because they tend to be used to get cheap laughs at the front end of sermons. I suspect it also probably has something to do with my not playing any sports myself. But I've recently become something of a runner, and the more I've done it, the more convinced I've become that the running metaphors one finds all over the New Testament actually work quite well.

Herewith, the top ten ways I think the life of faith is like running:

1. Most of the time, it feels like work.
2. Every once in a while, it feels like flying.
3. You can do it alone, but you'll do it faster and better with other people.
4. If your knees aren't at least a little bit sore at least a little bit of the time, you're not doing it hard enough.
5. Somebody will try to tell you that certain clothes are required to do it well; they're wrong.
6. When people who don't do it see you doing it, they wonder why the hell you would bother.
7. But they're also just a little bit impressed, especially if you look like it's not coming easy to you.
8. It's hard to start and easy to quit.
9. The longer you do it, the harder it is to quit.
10. If the only time you ever do it is when you're being chased, you're totally going to get caught.

PRAYER: Holy God, may I run and not grow weary, walk and not faint. Amen.

WHAT ARE YOU HUNGRY FOR?

Martin B. Copenhaver

As a deer longs for flowing streams, so my soul longs for you, O God. From Psalm 42

YOU PAD INTO THE KITCHEN, go directly to the refrigerator, open the door and peer inside. You are vaguely hungry, but you can't tell exactly what you are hungry for. You survey the options: Cold sausage pizza? No, that's not it. Leftover salad? That's not quite it. You take a bite of strawberry yogurt, but put it back on the shelf. The refrigerator is full enough, and your stomach is empty enough, but nothing seems exactly right.

Suddenly, it's as if you hear the voice of your mother reminding you, "Don't leave the refrigerator door open." So you close the door and wait for the voice to fade. Then you open the refrigerator again, lean on the door and stare blankly at the options, hoping that one will finally beckon.

It seems to me that many of us spend our lives like that, with indistinct longings that we are not sure how to satisfy. We yearn for something and know not what. We may try a bit of this and that for a time, perhaps only in our imaginations, but nothing is quite right or enough to satisfy. Someone described the people of our age as "those who don't know what they want from life and don't get it."

The psalmist cries, "As a deer longs for flowing streams, so my soul longs for you, O God." Could it be that all of us long to have a relationship with God, but that much of the time we don't recognize that that is what we were hungry for all along?

PRAYER: "Spirit of the Living God, fall afresh on me. Melt me, mold me, fill me, use me."* Amen.

*"Spirit of the Living God," words by Daniel Iverson, 1926.

OCTOBER 25

ELIJAH

Quinn G. Caldwell

For thus says the LORD, the God of Israel.... From 1 Kings 17:8–16

WHAT WOULD IT TAKE FOR YOU TO BELIEVE in somebody else's god? What would it take for you to at least listen to what the person has to say?

Elijah heads to foreign territory, where they worship a different god. There he meets up with a widow and tells her about his god. She doesn't end up converting to his religion, but does recognize that Elijah has said some true things about the world and about God.

You already know that interfaith dialogue can teach you true things, right? Well, hanging out with the Muslim or Wiccan next door is one thing, but I think it's a lot harder to talk with people who are part of my religion but who think about it very differently than I do. I'm not talking about Presbyterians or Methodists here; I mean Pentecostals, I mean fundamentalists, I mean conservative Evangelicals, I mean whatever it is that you would define as the opposite of you. In many ways, it's easier to talk with people who are very different than it is to talk with ones who are sort of similar—but that doesn't mean they can't have something true to teach you about God.

I'm not saying you need to convert or anything (the widow didn't); I'm just saying that God sends Elijahs to tell us about God all the time, and that sometimes they come from the unlikeliest of places.

PRAYER: God, when you send a messenger to teach me about you, give me the grace to listen, regardless of whether she's one of us or one of them. Amen.

OCTOBER 26

PERFECTION . . . BUT!

Kenneth L. Samuel

Now Naaman was commander of the army of the king of Aram. He was a great man in the sight of his master and highly regarded, because through him the LORD had given victory to Aram. He was a valiant soldier, but he had leprosy. From 2 Kings 5:1–14 NIV

WE COULD ALL CLAIM PERFECTION in life if it were not for just a few critical "buts" that interrupt our positive personas and disclose our deeply embedded flaws. We like to think that our positive attributes far outweigh our negatives, and often we are tempted to deny or ignore our negatives altogether.

Naaman, a man who lived in the ninth century BCE, was a great man of high distinction. He was the commander general of the Syrian army—the super power of the Middle East at the time. Naaman was a powerful man among powerful people such as the king of Syria. Naaman also had power with God, for it was through Naaman that God had given victory to Syria, one of Israel's enemies. In addition to his position, his highly respected bearing, and his divine connections, Naaman was also noted to be a man of great valor. We're tempted to wonder what else could be added to such a sterling list of attributes and accomplishments. And then, at the very end of Naaman's most impressive résumé, there comes the critical "but" . . . "but he had leprosy." And if it were not for that one critical flaw, the life of Naaman would never have been opened to total encounter with others and to total transformation with the Divine.

We are often preoccupied with the pageantry of our professional achievements, our personal accomplishments, and our public accolades until a critical "but," a hidden flaw, an almost forgotten weakness discloses our deepest needs. On the other side of those critical "buts," however, there is the invitation to redemption.

PRAYER: Dear God, help us not to inhale the hype about ourselves. Remind us that new life begins after we acknowledge the critical "buts" of our well-concealed flaws. Amen.

OCTOBER 27

WE ARE NOT CLIMBING JACOB'S LADDER

Anthony B. Robinson

And he dreamed that there was a ladder set up on the earth, the top of it reaching to heaven; and the angels of God were ascending and descending on it. From Genesis 28:10–19

I LOVE THE SONG, "We are climbing Jacob's ladder, we are climbing Jacob's ladder . . . every rung goes higher, higher, every rung goes higher, higher."

But on reading the actual story in Genesis, I noticed something. We human beings aren't the ones climbing the ladder. It is angels, messengers of God, who are ascending and descending the ladder from heaven to earth. So what?

We can get the idea that it is all about us climbing ladders, whether worldly or spiritual. Getting to the right neighborhood, the right job or school. Becoming more spiritual can be another ladder to climb. We can get the idea that by our resolute and steady climbing, we shall attain some God place.

Except our story says something different. It says that God comes down to this place, to our place, wherever that place may be. And then we, with Jacob, stammer in astonished surprise, "Surely God is in this place and I did not know it."

The popular author Karen Armstrong, in a recent book, urges that true religion is our human search for an ultimately unknowable God. Reading this, I thought, the gospel says something different. It says that God has come in search of us. In Jesus, God comes down the ladder to find us, even when we aren't very "spiritual," even when we are lost and on the run.

PRAYER: I thank thee, O God, that the good news is not about my upward climb, but about your downward descent; that faith begins when we, though like Jacob lost and on the run, are found by you. Amen.

OCTOBER 28

TUNNEL VISION

William C. Green

Happy are those . . . who do not turn to idols or join those who worship false gods. From Psalm 40:1–11 GNT

IDOLATRY IS TRUSTING what ends up breaking our hearts. In our day the culprit is often said to be the love of money, success, pleasure, or, perhaps, a partner thought to offer as much. But these are not the real heartbreakers.

What shatters us is more subtle. It can sneak up without our knowing it. It sounds less dramatic than the havoc it wreaks. It's called tunnel vision.

Tunnel vision fixates on part of what we face. I see what I want to be true about a friend, a partner, or a job—or I see what's dead wrong—and it's as though that's the gavel. Court adjourned. This way of reacting can acquire a godlike grip on us. This is idolatry. Devoted to our own moods and reactions we come to a dead end. It's heartbreaking.

When we're finally disillusioned, what can we do? We know we're missing something. It isn't found where we've looked before. But maybe then, like a beginning swimmer learning to trust the water, we can quit clutching our own feelings and look less anxiously at what's before us. Maybe we will learn that we're held up by something broader and deeper than we've taken into account. Faith gives that a name. The grace of God.

PRAYER: You hold me up in the palm of your hand, God. Your love is what I've been looking for. I see what I've been missing. Amen.

OCTOBER 29

JUST A SMIDGEN

Ron Buford

[Jesus] said, "With what can we compare the kingdom of God, or what parable will we use for it? It is like a mustard seed, which, when sown upon the ground, is the smallest of all the seeds on earth; yet when it is sown it grows up and becomes the greatest of all shrubs, and puts forth large branches, so that the birds of the air can make nests in its shade." Mark 4:30–32

HAVE YOU EVER WORKED with a great cook who did not use teaspoons, tablespoons, or cup measures? They might say, "Use just a smidgen of this or that—it's my secret ingredient."

"How much is a smidgen anyway?" the student asks.

She'd say, "Oh, about this much," grabbing "a smidgen" between her thumb and forefinger.

The cooking lesson is nearly complete when the meal is served and the delicate balance of spices and ingredients is experienced, and understood. The student must then be able to replicate the recipe, connecting ingredients, technique, timing, and presentation.

It will take several tries for the chef in training to get it just right, replicating and perhaps even enhancing the original experience.

Jesus, the master teacher, teaches us that mixing prayer, Bible study, fellowship, work for justice, forgiveness, with just a "smidgen" of hopeful expectation, persistence, and love brings forth the realm of God into our lives. With it, God transforms our weaknesses, failures, loneliness, disappointment, battles with illness, addiction, and grief that seem too hard to bear . . . into life's greatest masterpieces.

From tiny seeds of hope, patience, persistence, love, and faith come great trees that, when fully grown, serve as a perch for others to come, sit, observe, and find the lessons they also need to thrive—and all because of "just a smidgen."

PRAYER: Gracious God, I'm trying this recipe and it's not feeling like a masterpiece yet. Help me to keep cooking until my life is a masterpiece from your perspective. Even if I cannot see it yet . . . I believe . . . a smidgen. May that smidgen make something of a masterpiece in my life today. Thank you. Amen.

NAMELESS HEROES

Kenneth L. Samuel

The next morning the Jews formed a conspiracy and bound themselves with an oath not to eat or drink until they had killed Paul. More than forty men were involved in this plot. They went to the chief priests and elders and said, "We have taken a solemn oath not to eat anything until we have killed Paul. . . ." But when the son of Paul's sister heard of this plot, he went into the barracks and told Paul. Then Paul called one of the centurions and said, "Take this young man to the commander; he has something to tell him." So he took him to the commander. Acts 23:12–18a

THE APOSTLE PAUL PLAYED a leading role in the spreading of the gospel and in the establishment of the first-century church. Indeed most of the narrative of the book of Acts is a vivid chronicle of the life, witness, and ministry of Paul. But behind every major character, there is always a host of supporting characters.

These are the foot soldiers who work inconspicuously and almost invisibly in the background. They are seldom noted, easily overlooked, and almost never remembered. Their names are often forgotten or never mentioned. They are like the nameless young man of Acts 23. Barely noticed. Yet this nondistinct, nameless young man is the agent God used to intercept a plot to murder Paul and stifle the spread of the gospel among the Gentiles.

To how many nameless heroes and heroines do we owe our success? How many forgotten souls have sacrificed and selflessly intervened on our behalf to save us from pending doom? How many times has God used minor characters to deliver major victories for us? We could so easily forget them and believe that we have made it by our own abilities. But the truth is that without their pivotal contributions, we would not be. A full appreciation of Paul's life and ministry must also include an appreciation for the life and ministry of the nameless one.

PRAYER: Dear God, for the countless, nameless persons whom you have used throughout my life to save my life, I give you thanks. Amen.

BONE

Quinn G. Caldwell

The hand of the LORD came upon me, and he brought me out by the spirit of the LORD and set me down in the middle of a valley; it was full of bones. . . . I prophesied as he commanded me, and the breath came into them, and they lived, and stood on their feet, a vast multitude. From Ezekiel 37:1–14

HERE'S WHAT THE STORY SAYS: dry bones are not the final state of things. Death will not win. Here's what it says: life wins.

Here's what it doesn't say: that they were human bones. Or that those bones went back together in their original order. Or that the bodies at the end were the same as the bodies in the beginning.

We tell this story as if it's only about humans, as if we're the only species God loves enough to waste the energy on. But this is the God that notes the fall of every sparrow, right? Surely God noted the fall of every pterodactyl. Surely, God noticed the fate of the hominid *Australopithecus afarensis* just as fully as he does that of the hominid *Homo sapiens*.

Ninety-nine percent of all the different species that once lived are now extinct. And yet, the place is full of life. Why? Because God does not let extinction win. The dinosaurs go down to bones and molecules, and the mammals rise up to take their place. *Homo habilis* goes extinct, and up rises *Homo sapiens*. One very particular *Homo sapiens* goes down to dust, and rises up the King of Heaven.

Death happens, but so does resurrection. Extinction happens, but so does evolution. And if our bones fit together differently when we walk out of the valley than when we walked in, maybe that's not so bad.

PRAYER: For evolution, thank you. For resurrection, thank you. For not giving me a protruding brow ridge and shallow brain pan, thank you, thank you, thank you. Amen.

NOVEMBER

I Was a Teenage Werewolf

Lillian Daniel

And not only that, but we also boast in our sufferings, knowing that suffering produces endurance, and endurance produces character, and character produces hope, and hope does not disappoint us, because God's love has been poured into our hearts through the Holy Spirit that has been given to us. Romans 5:3–5

SOMETIMES PARENTING IS A JOB that is so hard, you couldn't pay me to do it. And sometimes it's a job I do so poorly, you wouldn't pay me to do it.

And sometimes motherhood is not a job at all, but a calling that feels like a beautiful blessing I did nothing to deserve. But most of the time, mothering is hard work.

I know that mothering is hard work not so much because I have done it, but because I put another good woman through it. When I look back on some of the things I said to my mother during my high school years, I now understand why she occasionally referred to me as "Lillian, the Teenage Werewolf."

She had been shaped by the 1957 movie, "I Was a Teenage Werewolf," whose absurd plot would only make sense to someone in the doldrums of parenting of teenager. "A troubled teenager seeks help through hypnotherapy, but his evil doctor uses him for regression experiments that transform him into a rampaging werewolf." Oh, now I get it! Who knew there was such a simple explanation?

Today's scripture promises us that, while there often is not a simple answer, there is meaning to the hardest times in life. It says that suffering produces endurance, and endurance produces character, and character produces hope. I think that parenting produces all those things too.

Parents think they are working for all those qualities in their children. But perhaps in all those parenting struggles, God is working for those qualities in the grown-ups too.

I pray that God is still working on me. Especially now that my own teenagers are more than capable of howling at the moon.

PRAYER: Thank you, God, for endurance, character, and the hope that does not disappoint us. Amen.

NOVEMBER 2

FAVORITES

Donna Schaper

God shows no partiality. From Acts 10:30–35

LISTEN TO A LITANY of that slave master, the self. Only you can prevent narcissism. It is all up to you. You are number one. If you don't take care of yourself, who will?

These are all active justifications for the nearly universal excessive regard most of us have for ourselves. There are passive ones as well. If you have ever really tried to get outside of your own head, or your own origin, or your own race or sexual orientation, you have come to know an exquisite form of failure. We are in traps. They could be called homes as well, especially as we learn to think of ourselves as spokes and not wheels.

"God shows no partiality" is good news for humanity and bad news for the self-consciousness of the narcissist. I know how hard I competed with my brother and sister to be my parents' favorite. I also know that my three kids loved the game of "favorites." It goes like this. All three grab me around the knees. (They were short then.) One says, I'm your favorite, right? I say yes, with enthusiasm. The second does the same. I repeat my yes, with enthusiasm. The third does the same, and again I lie. The game ends, eyeball to eyeball with three short people, one at a time: "You are my favorite and you are my favorite and you are my favorite." Everyone laughs and the game of partiality is over.

God couldn't be God and have favorites. Get over it. God can only be God and be impartial. The morally immature don't get it and assign superiority to their selves or their class or their national origin. Grown-ups don't.

PRAYER: Thank you, God for the gift of impartiality, which requires that we grow up. Amen.

NOVEMBER 3

WATER

Quinn G. Caldwell

And the people complained against Moses, saying, "What shall we drink?" He cried out to the LORD, and the Lord showed him a piece of wood; he threw it into the water, and the water became sweet. From Exodus 15:22–27

HAVE YOU NOTICED how many of the stories in the Bible revolve around water? Seas, wells, floods, rivers, bitter water, holy water, living water. The biblical storytellers had water on the brain because they needed to think about it pretty much all the time just to survive. In their mostly arid home-lands, they had to haul their water when at home and search for water when abroad. Once they found it, they had to make sure it was drinkable, or they could be in big trouble.

My guess is the average reader of these devotionals can't relate. Most of us are never thirsty for longer than it takes to walk to the faucet, and we don't think twice about whether our water's safe, unless we know of a specific threat nearby.

But most of the people in the world are more like the biblical authors. They spend their days searching for and carrying and purifying water.

Much of the world would give anything for a magic stick that provided them with sweet water.

Here's what our God does: pours water out in the desert. Here's what our God does: takes the water that's undrinkable, and turns it into the sweet water of life. Here's what our God does: sends her people out to do the same.

PRAYER: God, grant me a draught of your living water, and so fill me up that I overflow into your world. Amen.

NOVEMBER 4

THE ROUGH PLACES

Christina Villa

Every valley shall be exalted, and every mountain and hill shall be made low: and the crooked shall be made straight, and the rough places plain. From Isaiah 40 KJV

WHILE LOOKING THROUGH A CATALOG of luxury bedding, I found myself absorbed by page after page of things you can put on top of your mattress to make it more comfortable. You can get a mattress topper made of surgical grade foam rubber, or stuffed with feathers from the world's fluffiest birds. They're supposed to help you sleep by eliminating "pressure points," the places where your body comes in contact with your mattress when you lie down on it.

The problem of sleep deprivation caused by lying down seems to me especially cruel, if such a problem actually exists. I have my doubts. After all, throughout history and around the world people have managed to sleep on things that aren't fluffy at all, like the ground. Exactly how comfortable does a person need to be?

Maybe it's because I grew up in New England, but I think there is such a thing as being too comfortable. The risk of too much comfort is not so much that you'll become decadent and immoral. The risk is that you'll become afraid. The more comfort you acquire, the more you fear life's "rough places" and begin to devote your life to smoothing them out. There's a direct line between those giant, over-stuffed reclining sofas with individual cup holders and a desire to move to a gated community.

Life is pretty full of rough places, not to mention pressure points. But we're not put here to spend our lives looking for the most ingenious padding to put between us and life's every unyielding surface. We don't hear it very often in our therapeutic culture, but sometimes the best thing to do is tough it out.

PRAYER: Let me see how comfortable I already am. Amen.

NOVEMBER 5

WHO IS THAT SINGING?

Martin B. Copenhaver

Philip ran up to [the chariot] and heard him reading the prophet Isaiah. He asked, "Do you understand what you are reading?" He replied, "How can I, unless someone guides me?" From Acts 8:26–40

ONE DAY, WHEN OUR CHILDREN WERE STILL VERY YOUNG, a Beatles song came on the radio. I grew up listening to the Beatles so, of course, I began to sing along. Then our daughter, Alanna, asked, "Who is that singing?"

For a moment, I was taken aback by her question. How could she not know who is singing? Isn't that something that is passed on in the genes?

And then I remember thinking, If she doesn't know about the Beatles, what other things have I mistakenly assumed I would not need to tell her? Obviously, we cannot assume that our children have somehow brought with them, or will pick up somewhere, the most important things we have to share, including the Christian story of God's fierce and indefatigable love for the world.

One does not learn the story by osmosis. It has to be told. After all, the Christian faith is always just one generation away from extinction.

In Acts, we read about an Ethiopian official who, after a visit to Jerusalem, was reading the prophesies of Isaiah while he was riding in a chariot (you have to really want to read something to read it in a moving chariot). Philip was inspired to approach the chariot and asked, "Do you understand what you are reading?" And here is the Ethiopian's poignant reply: "How can I, unless someone guides me?"

Exactly. No one is born knowing the story of our faith. It has to be passed on, one generation at a time.

So teach your children, or your grandchildren, or the children of your church the story that has been shared with us. And, somewhere along the line, teach them about the Beatles also.

PRAYER: God, you are here, there, and everywhere. Equip us and inspire us to tell the story that has been shared with us. Amen.

The Goodness of God in the Land of the Living

Kenneth L. Samuel

Teach me thy way, O LORD, and lead me in a plain path, because of mine enemies. Deliver me not over unto the will of mine enemies: for false witnesses are risen up against me, and such as breathe out cruelty. I had fainted, unless I had believed to see the goodness of the LORD in the land of the living. Wait on the LORD: be of good courage; and he shall strengthen thine heart: wait, I say, on the LORD. From Psalm 27:11–14

SOMETIMES RELIGION CAN BE A MEANS of escape from the urgent realities of now. Gradualism has not been a friend to those who have for centuries been made to suffer the indignities of racism, sexism, and heterosexism. Only those who are free from the pressure of persecution can afford the luxury of prolonged, incremental change.

The psalmist possesses a faith that is not just eternal but imminent. It is a faith that does not just hope for the best; it is a faith that anticipates the realization of hope. What keeps the psalmist faithful is the anticipation of hopes and dreams that are expected to be realized in this life. No pie in the sky bye and bye when we die, but something sound on the ground while we're still around—this is the faith of the psalmist.

"I had fainted, unless I had believed to see the goodness of the LORD in the land of the living."

Faith to believe in God's ability to make dreams come true in our lifetime is what gives gay people the impetus to marry and women the impetus to seek entry into clubs for men only and a black man the impetus to run for president of the United States. Waiting on God does not put our dreams on indefinite hold. Waiting on the God places our dreams on an immediate process of unfolding.

"Wait, I say, on the LORD," and let the realization of our heart's desires begin now!

Beyond Tolerance

William C. Green

As they were going along the road, they came to some water; and the eunuch said, "Look, here is water! What is to prevent me from being baptized?" From Acts 8:26–40

THE EUNUCH WAS AN ALIEN (Ethiopian) and sexually compromised (castrated). He had somehow come upon Scripture and saw himself in a passage from Isaiah, which includes the words, "In his humiliation justice was denied him."

God is still speaking and tells Philip to join this man, for the eunuch knew he needed guidance to make further sense of what he was reading. Philip does as he's told and the man ends up baptized: welcomed into God's family just as he was.

What is to prevent anyone from being baptized and welcomed into the church? Is it having ways different from ours? Is it questionable belief? Is it sexual orientation? Is it perhaps citizenship and the possibility of illegal status? Or is it that we ourselves defy God's love by customs and habits of belief that contradict the welcome of Jesus, whoever we are, and wherever we are on life's journey?

Sometimes the worst discrimination is not overt. We believe in tolerance. So perhaps we can tolerate people becoming part of church while privately harboring doubt or resentment. Tolerance is not the same as respect. Philip respected the eunuch and concentrated on the man's own spiritual questions. He followed those questions. He did not lead by admonition or advice like, "You've got to understand that while I welcome you, many will have doubts. Keep your ways to yourself."

PRAYER: Welcoming God, lead us beyond tolerance to respect for the differences among us that make us your people. Amen.

NOVEMBER 8

BUT GOD

Anthony B. Robinson

But God raised him up, having freed him from death, because it was impossible for him to be held by its power. From Acts 2:14–24

WE SOMETIMES OVERUSE the little word, "but." We say something nice to our spouse or partner as a prelude to "but, dear . . . ." Or we express appreciation for something said by a speaker while our words are a build-up to our "but . . . ." We discard a good idea, saying, "but I can't do that." We scatter our little negations like weed seed.

Here, however, it's not our word of negation. It's not our "but." It's God's. It's God's definitive disjunction in the face of the world's violence and of death's seemingly last word and final power.

Here in Acts, Peter has told the story of Jesus. He repeats all the sad words again: "betrayed," "handed over," "crucified" and "killed," each one a nail in the coffin. The world has done its worst. But that's not the end of the story. Peter went on, "But God." But God has the last word. And that word is life. That word is resurrection. "But God raised him up, having freed him from death, because it was impossible for him to be held by its power."

Amid the terror of the Nazi years in Germany, a leader of the Confessing Church, Martin Niemoeller, preached a sermon titled "But God." He spoke of all the ways that Hitler, the Nazis, and their brutality and mendacity seemed to have utterly triumphed. Then Niemoeller went on. Then he said, "But God." "But God raised him up because it was impossible for him to be held by death's power." But God. God will have the last word.

When it seems the end has come, "but God." When you see no way forward or out, "but God." When death has done its work and it seems all hope is gone, "but God." Because of these two little words, because of the defiant divine disjunction, everything is different now.

PRAYER: O God, we give thanks that you have both the first word and the last one. Trusting this, may the words we speak and the lives we lead between be faithful to your Word. Amen.

OH GOD, WHAT WERE YOU THINKING?

Lillian Daniel

O the depth of the riches and wisdom and knowledge of God! How unsearchable are God's judgments and how inscrutable God's ways! From Romans 11:33–36

"WHY DID GOD LET THOSE PEOPLE GET HIT BY A HURRICANE?" "Why is God letting her suffer when she has lived such a good life?" "Why does God let a jerk like that get away with what he's done?"

People ask me questions like this periodically. Implicit in the question is that I, as a pastor, would have an answer. But of course I do not. And quite frankly, I would be suspicious of anyone who claims to have one.

Only God knows God's mind. The rest of us can only seek. But the life and witness of Jesus tell me this much. God does not torture us, or hurt one person only to spare another. In Jesus, the man of sorrows, I see that even God suffered agony and death; and on the cross, even Jesus wondered, for a moment, about the point of it all.

I believe that one day all of our questions will be answered. I believe that at the moment we enter eternal life, Jesus will be there to greet us, and not just with open arms. I believe that when we die in Christ, our minds will be opened, no secrets will be hidden, and our eternity will be spent in understanding.

Until then, our job is to live life and live it abundantly.

PRAYER: Holy Spirit, in the time between confusion and complete understanding, use the world around me, the people around me, your church, and your holy word to bring me closer in wisdom to you and your ways. Amen.

TREMBLE

Quinn G. Caldwell

Work out your own salvation with fear and trembling; for it is God who is at work in you. From Philippians 2:12–18

SOMETIMES YOU TREMBLE because you're scared, or cold. Sometimes it's because of neurological or muscular issues. Sometimes you just overdid it at the coffee shop.

But actually, you're trembling all the time. Everything is. A physicist will tell you that there's not a thing anywhere that's not constantly vibrating, at the atomic level, with the Energy that created and drives the universe.

When the Bible speaks of trembling in the presence of God, most people assume it's talking about trembling in fear.

Maybe, but I think it's more like this: the closer you get to the sun, the hotter you feel. The closer you get to one of those big metal balls in science class, the more your hair stands up. And the closer you get to the Source of all the creation's energy, the more you vibrate. The trembling that's always there anyway, trace of the Hand that created you, suddenly intensifies. The life of the cosmos courses through you and you begin to hum, to sing like a plucked string. Suddenly, you're all potential energy.

And the only thing to do then is to go kinetic.

PRAYER: In the beginning was you, God. All things came into being through you, and without you not one thing came into being. What has come into being in you was life, and the life was the energy of all the cosmos. Fill me up with that power until I tremble, and then send me out full of it to do your work. Amen.

A "GROWN FOLKS' CONVERSATION"

Kenneth L. Samuel

You must love the LORD your God and obey all God's . . . commands. Listen! I am not talking now to your children who have never experienced the discipline of the LORD your God or seen his greatness and awesome power. . . . They didn't see how the LORD cared for you time and again through all the years you were wandering in the wilderness until you arrived here. . . . But you have seen all the LORD's mighty acts with your own eyes! From Deuteronomy 11:1–8 NLT

AS A YOUNG BOY, I would often watch my mother conversing with friends and relatives. Every now and then, she would turn to me and say: "This is a grown folks' conversation." That was my directive to leave the room. Usually, I couldn't care less what was being discussed, but whenever my mother said that the conversation was for grown folks only, it always made me wonder what secrets the adults were hiding from us kids. Were they talking about doing something that they had told us was wrong? Was there something good that only grown folks could enjoy and talk about?

The eleventh chapter of Deuteronomy is a grown folks' conversation. It is addressed to those who had lived through Israel's forty-year Exodus out of Egypt and entrance into the promised land, when the children of Israel had seen God do many great things. They had witnessed the super power of Egypt thwarted and the emergence of their own people as a great nation. They had worshiped on Mount Sinai, witnessed miracles in the desert, and been sustained and satisfied in dry, barren places. Deuteronomy 11 is a conversation directed to the grown folks who had seen God's power to save and deliver firsthand.

Yet it was a conversation that could not be limited to grown folks only. For if Israel was going to remember God's deliverance and keep God's commandments as directed, the grown folks of Israel would certainly have to open up and share with the young folks of Israel. All of the agony and ecstasy, all of the joys and pains, all of the misery and miracles of their sojourn would have to be recalled and recounted over and over again if those who were not there and had not seen were going to honor and perpetuate the faith of their ancestors.

What conversations about life, love, and freedom are we keeping from young people today? What firsthand testimonies are we reluctant or afraid to share? The life of our faith and the life of our nation are dependent upon "grown folks' conversations" that must not be limited to grown folks.

PRAYER: Gracious God, we thank you for all that we know, by our own experience, of your love and power. Now enable us to share with those who may not understand, simply because they have never been told. Amen.

DIVINE GENTLENESS

Donna Schaper

But the wisdom from above is . . . gentle. From James 3:17–18

WE HEAR A LOT OF TALK about lost tenderness, increasing toughness; lost softness, increasing hardness. The writer of James suggests the divine origin of gentleness. That origin may matter more than we think.

Gentleness turns the tide of a conversation, when we respond with a smile to a person headed straight to the land of rude. It changes the tone of meetings, when we insert a joke onto the table where everyone else has decided to take matters too seriously. It changes what we say about recessions, when we insert a fact, quietly, about how white families have a dollar for every dime black families have in accumulated wealth.

How do we say something like that with gentleness? We say it quietly, softly, and slowly. We acknowledge every time we complain about how the recession is hitting us that it has hit others longer and harder. What is gentle about such truth? It takes the long view. It depersonalizes. Gentleness is wisdom from on high. We are allowed to bring it down to earth.

PRAYER: Spirit of Gentleness, tenderness, and grace, grant us a divine tone to our speech. Let it be gentle, wise, and real. Amen.

GOD'S OSTRICH

Christina Villa

Yet it has no fear; because God has made it forget wisdom, and given it no share in understanding. When it spreads its plumes aloft, it laughs at the horse and its rider. From Job 39:13–25

GOD IS TALKING TO JOB here about the ostrich, of all things, pointing out that it's careless with its eggs—dropping them just anywhere on the ground—but unafraid that they'll be trampled. Why is the ostrich so unconcerned? Because God has "given it no share of understanding." It has no fear because it has no "wisdom." God makes this sound like an advantage for the ostrich.

Blissfully ignorant, the ostrich, which can't fly, is the fastest two-legged animal on earth—able to outrun a horse. It seems cruel of God to mention the carefree ostrich, blasting past horses and laughing, to the overburdened Job, who isn't going anywhere and certainly not laughing.

When an ostrich is threatened but unable to run away, it will fall to the ground and stretch out its neck in an attempt to be less visible. It doesn't actually bury its head in the sand, but close enough. So it appears that the ostrich's main strategies for getting through its life are to run away, and if that doesn't work, bury its head in the sand.

This might work for the ostrich, but bearing in mind the words of Joe Louis—"You can run, but you can't hide"—it won't work for you or me.

For better or worse, with Job, we carry the burdens of wisdom and understanding—as far as they take us.

PRAYER: The next time I'm tempted to run away, or look the other way, or in any other way dull my consciousness, let me remember I am thankfully not an ostrich. Amen.

GOING DEEPER

Anthony B. Robinson

He said to Simon, "Put out into the deep water and let down your nets for a catch." From Luke 5:1–11

SIMON PETER AND HIS BUDDIES had been fishing all night, but had nothing to show for it. Nothing! Nothing but aching muscles and chilled bodies. "Master," Simon Peter said to Jesus, "we have worked all night long but have caught nothing."

Have you been there? I have. You've worked hard and long and yet it feels as if you have nothing at all to show for it. Your nets have come up empty. You're bone-tired and soul-weary. And yet, it is at just this point that Jesus commands Simon Peter to put out into deeper water and let down his nets for a catch. When he does, the nets are full to bursting.

Sometimes when our own notions of success come up empty or our own ideas of how things are supposed to be are completely spent and exhausted, it gives God a chance to show us another way, a different idea of success and a new vision of ourselves. Sometimes when we're at the end of our rope, there's a reason we're there.

PRAYER: God, grant me grace to die to my own definitions of success and be raised up to a new life trusting your call, your power, and your grace. Amen.

WE ARE NOT OUR OWN

Kenneth L. Samuel

What? Know ye not that your body is the temple of the Holy Ghost which is in you, which ye have of God, and ye are not your own? For ye are bought with a price: therefore glorify God in your body, and in your spirit, which are God's.
1 Corinthians 6:19–20 KJV

IN THIS PASSAGE, the Apostle Paul would have us know that the sovereignty of God is not limited to the spiritual dimensions of life, but to the body and flesh dimensions as well. Paul says that even what we do with our bodies is subject to the will of God, for we belong not to ourselves, but to God. This is the divine precept behind the directives given us to eschew prostitution, promiscuity, and all forms of addiction to toxic drugs. Anything that we do to debase or destroy our bodies is an affront to God, who created us to embody God's spirit. And this divine precept of God's claim to our bodies is also the reason we should be careful not to do damage or claim ownership to any other person's body as well. Social slavery and political torture must as surely be violations of God's ownership of the human body as personal sexual improprieties.

PRAYER: Sovereign God, help us to honor you as ruler of our bodies in all that we do sexually. And let your sovereignty also be reflected in how we politically and socially respect the bodies of other people. Amen.

GETTING LITTLE

Anthony B. Robinson

Truly I tell you, whoever does not receive the kingdom of God as a little child will never enter it. From Luke 18:15–17

WE SPEND A FAIR AMOUNT OF TIME, money, and energy trying to get big and important. We strive to be significant, to compile an impressive résumé, to let people know we're righteous and on the right side. We want to be big people, independent people, people who are in charge of our lives and in control.

Along comes Jesus and says, "Want to be with me? You'll have to get little, to become smaller." Really? How does that add up?

God's way of perceiving is different than our own, different than the world's. Sometimes what the world counts as big and important, God doesn't; and what the world sees as insignificant and inconsequential may be in God's sight grand and glorious. Getting small, little, dependent: it's less about us. Less about us, and more about God. To God be the glory!

PRAYER: Dear God, right-size me. Make me little enough to enter your strange realm and participate in your unexpected reign. Amen.

REMEMBER YOUR BAPTISM

Martin B. Copenhaver

After this Jesus and his disciples went into the Judean countryside, and he spent some time there with them and baptized. From John 3:22–36

MARTIN LUTHER, THE GREAT REFORMER, was clearly a genius and a person of great faith, but he was also something of a tormented soul. Among other maladies, he suffered from what would be called clinical depression today. Out of those depths, he affirmed that there is no greater comfort than baptism. In dark times, he would remind himself: "I am baptized. And through my baptism the God who cannot lie has bound himself to me." Particularly when he did not feel worthy of another person's love, he clung to the tangible expression of God's love in baptism.

Someone confided about the experience of growing up as a teenager with a terrible case of acne. When she looked into the mirror each morning, she would recoil from what she saw. But then she would splash water on her face and, in the words spoken at Jesus' baptism and echoed in her own baptism, she would say, "I am beloved." In the soapy water of her sink she was able to seek comfort and strength in the recollection of the promise of her baptism.

What do you see when you look in the mirror? Do you see lines of anxiety or anger or blemishes of some kind? Do you like what you see? If you are not entirely pleased with the one who looks back at you in the mirror, remember your baptism. In that act, the God who cannot lie has called you beloved.

PRAYER: Ever-loving, never-lying God, thank you for the promise of my baptism and for calling me beloved, even when I feel unlovable. Amen.

CHASTE

Quinn G. Caldwell

I mean, brothers and sisters, the appointed time has grown short; from now on, let even those who have wives be as though they had none, and those who mourn as though they were not mourning. From 1 Corinthians 7:29–31

PAUL THOUGHT THE WORLD WAS ENDING . . . soon. Like, next week. And since there wasn't much time left, he thought people ought to use it to focus on the next world. He thought they should withdraw totally from all the things that tied them to this world: sex, mourning, joy, possessions, business, politics. He wanted them to be chaste.

It's true: the world might end next week. But it probably won't. And after a while of the kind of chaste living that Paul recommended, he and his followers began to realize that, too. After a while, they realized that while they did need to hold themselves in readiness for the end, they were going to need to figure out how to live in this life until we got there.

So they started living as humans again, doing all the things that humans do (and that Paul had first warned against). But they were living as Christian humans now: they still found ways to be chaste. Sometimes we think that chastity means abstinence from sex. What it actually means is living and loving morally: treating the creation as if it belonged to God, treating each person as a beloved child of God, doing what Jesus did.

It's true: God is transforming this world even as you read. By living chaste lives engaged with the world rather than withdrawn from it, we as Christians become part of the transformation.

PRAYER: God, grant that I might be chaste in all I do, from sex to politics, and grant that through my chastity you might transform the world. Amen.

NOT ANOTHER MOVING DAY

Lillian Daniel

Now the LORD said to Abram, "Go from your country and your kindred and your father's house to the land that I will show you. I will make of you a great nation, and I will bless you, and make your name great, so that you will be a blessing." From Genesis 12:1–9

BY THE TIME I WAS IN HIGH SCHOOL, I had attended nine schools in seven different countries. As the daughter of a journalist, we moved constantly and had many adventures, with most of my childhood spent in Asia, and three years in London. My mother used to say that I was like a cat: whichever way you threw me, I would land on my feet.

But as a parent, I have chosen not to raise my own children like cats. I want a little more stability for them. When we moved from Connecticut to Illinois to follow new callings, it was a heart-wrenching decision, and one I do not want to repeat anytime soon.

The Bible is full of stories of people who move. Usually, they are not choosing to move. They are compelled to move, to flee for their lives, or to follow a divine calling. This is still why most people move. They flee political oppression, or they long to improve their lives. Immigrants are daring people. They do not play it safe.

In my own life, all that chaos had within it one steady stream, and that was the church. While we couldn't always attend the same church, wherever we moved, we found a spiritual home. Church was my one constant in a changing world.

I didn't get to live in my own country until I was in the ninth grade, and I arrived like a foreigner, with an English accent and funny clothes. But I never doubted that God was with me in my latest home and that together, we were on a great adventure.

PRAYER: Welcoming Lord Christ, use our congregations to warm the heart of the outsider. Open my heart to someone new in town. Let the stranger be my friend. Amen.

The Next Generation

Anthony B. Robinson

But charge Joshua, and encourage and strengthen him, because it is he who shall cross over at the head of this people and who shall secure their possession of the land you will see. From Deuteronomy 3:23–29

As we grow older, what's our job? Do we have something important still to do? These words of God to Moses may have something to say to us on this score. Moses is to turn his attention to the next generation, to his successor, to Joshua. "Charge Joshua, and encourage and strengthen him."

Sometimes in the world of generational cohorts, taking care of number one, and AARP interest group lobbying, we may forget that the job of those who are mature isn't just to watch out for themselves, it's to prepare the next generation, to encourage and strengthen a new generation. Who's your Joshua? Who's your Lydia (from Acts 19)? Whose gifts and leadership are you called to summon, encourage, and strengthen? And in our congregations, how are we who have held the reins of power doing at letting go and empowering others? Which next generation person can I pray for, encourage, and strengthen today?

PRAYER: We do not live to ourselves alone, O God. We are part of a people, of your people. Help us to do our part to call forth the next generation, to encourage and strengthen them. Amen.

REVERENCE IS THE FOUNDATION

Kenneth L. Samuel

The fear of the LORD *is the beginning of wisdom; all who follow his precepts have good understanding. To him belongs eternal praise.* From Psalm 111 NIV

WHAT SOME BIBLICAL TRANSLATIONS CALL "the fear of the Lord" is better translated, "reverence for God." According to the psalmist, this reverence, this awesome respect for the Lord, is the foundation of all wisdom.

All of our wisdom and understanding about life and the world rests upon an awesome reverence for God. Quests for knowledge, scientific inquiries, and philosophical postulations that are not grounded in a reverence for God may lead us to more information but cannot give us the wisdom and the understanding to properly interpret and apply the information.

In the words of Dr. Joseph Lowery, "we have the knowledge of how to build smart bombs, but we send smart bombs on dumb missions." Knowledge derived from information can give us data about life; but only the wisdom derived from God can give us understanding about how to protect and preserve life. We should never forget that every world war and every holocaust has been started and sustained by persons of impressive knowledge who nonetheless needed wisdom derived from divine reverence.

PRAYER: God, we thank you for being our foundation and our future. Grant that all of our educational and scientific endeavors be grounded in our awesome reverence for you. Amen.

NOVEMBER 22

CONVERSION

Quinn G. Caldwell

And now why do you delay? Get up, be baptized, and have your sins washed away, calling on [God's] name. From Acts 22:2–16

SHANNON BEGAN COMING TO OUR CHURCH some time ago. She was raised in a vaguely Christian, but not churchgoing, family. She is gorgeous, hip, kind, thoughtful, and plays a mean jazz piano. She quickly became an ornament and pillar of our church.

It hardly seemed possible when she told me she hadn't been baptized. But it made perfect sense when she said she wanted to be, for God had clearly been steering her life for some time.

When the day arrived, the church gathered around the font. As I began to speak the old, old words, Shannon began to cry. I asked the ritual questions; the congregation laid hands on her; we all blessed the water together. Through it all, she wept and wept, so that by the time I touched the baptismal water to her forehead, the Holy Spirit had already baptized Shannon with her own tears. Before we were done, most of us in the congregation were weeping as well.

Shannon took her baptism so seriously that we could not help but be reminded that there is nothing—nothing—we do in the church that is more important than this. It's a reminder we can all use from time to time. So go find some water now; any water will do. Touch it. Ask God to remind you of your own baptism, and know you are beloved.

And if you're reading this but haven't been baptized yet, just what are you waiting for?

PRAYER: God, thank you for water, and for people around me, and for your sweet Spirit. Amen.

NOVEMBER 23

WHAT IS YOUR TESTIMONY?

Ron Buford

I myself have seen and have testified that this is the Son of God. From John 1:29–34

THE GOSPEL NARRATIVES, Matthew, Mark, Luke, and John, are compelling testimonies to a life-changing, mysteriously powerful spiritual presence wrapped in human form—Jesus. The gospel writers' reflections on Jesus' greatness and on people's reactions in his day still inspire people across continents and centuries.

You, too, have holy moments to share. Do you recognize and capture these moments or toss them away? Reclaim them.

John received a holy impression that a miraculous presence in human form would seek him out, asking to be baptized. John testifies to his impression being confirmed on the unforgettable day Jesus came to be baptized.

God is still speaking to you in holy impressions. Do you miss God, thinking you are not worthy? Stop belittling yourself. You are one of God's windows into the world.

Whether age nine or 109, you are still having holy moments. Was it the first time you saw the twinkle in the eye of someone you love? Was it at an altar of prayer or communion? Was it was when you first held your newborn child? Was it the time some new idea flowed through you? Was it during the look you exchanged with someone and knew it would be your last? Take time, despise the fear, set your story free among those you love. It is not too late, even if it involves someone dead; imagine him or her sitting across from you. Verbalize or write your testimony to a divine moment—it is God's presence present to the world. Unleash it!

PRAYER: Gracious God, help me to recognize all the places I see you and give me the courage to write or verbalize a testimony to my encounter with you. Amen.

Christians are Joyful Sinners

Martin B. Copenhaver

Woe is me! I am lost, for I am a man of unclean lips, and I live among people of unclean lips; yet my eyes have seen the King, the LORD of hosts! From Isaiah 6:1–5

DOES WORSHIP IN YOUR CHURCH include a prayer of confession? If so, it is probably near the beginning of the service. One reason for this placement is that God's presence reveals things to us. In God's clarifying presence we see things about our lives that we might not see otherwise. So when Isaiah had a dramatic encounter with God in the temple, his first response was confession. And it can be the same for us in our worship.

Some congregations no longer include a prayer of confession in their worship because the practice is considered too "negative." They contend that people have enough difficulties in their lives without the church adding to the burden. But confession is not about adding a burden. Quite the opposite. It is about being unburdened. Ultimately, there is no joy in denial. But there can be great joy in receiving forgiveness.

As Christians we don't need to traffic in denial. We can afford to be realists. We are free to face the truth about ourselves: good and bad are inextricably intertwined within us. Sometimes we act nobly, but even then our motivations can be mixed. This is not a hopeless admission. We are free to be realists because our hope is in God. In confession, we rely not on our own goodness, but on God's forgiveness. The God in whose presence we see our lives with jarring clarity at the same time shows us that we are loved, nonetheless.

PRAYER: Dear God, when given a chance, I mess up. Sometimes, when not given a chance, I mess up anyway. So I am grateful that I do not have to rely on my own goodness, but rather on your forgiveness. Amen.

WHAT ARE YOU LOOKING FOR?

William C. Green

He was in the world, and the world came into being through him; yet the world did not know him. . . . But to all who received him, who believed in his name, he gave power to become children of God. From John 1:10–18

IT'S OFTEN SAID, "I've got to see it to believe it." When I can see how much someone cares about me, I'll believe it. When I can see the success I want at home, at work, or in the church, I'll believe it. When I can see the difference it makes when I do something worthwhile, I'll believe it.

Today's reading turns that thinking on its head. The message is, "I've got to believe it to see it." At heart, we find what we're looking for—and when we don't, we conclude that something's wrong. We're easily given to self-fulfilling prophecy. Scientists and philosophers, grown wise in this multicultural era, remind us that we all look out at the world, not on the basis of fact, but through the lens of our own biases and beliefs.

Given all that is wrong in so many ways, it's hard to find the assuring spirit of Christ. Habits of doubt can color our personality and shape our whole outlook on life.

The empowering love of God is present working through us to bring about the best. That's been true since the beginning of time, and is so evermore. That's the bias of faith. It makes us want to look for and live out this truth. Believe it and you'll see it, however imperfectly.

PRAYER: Help us to believe you so we can find you, God. So may we receive your power and guidance in all we care about and love. Amen.

THE PEACEABLE KINGDOM

Anthony B. Robinson

"The wolf shall live with the lamb, the leopard shall lie down with the kid, the calf and the lion and the fatling together, and a little child shall lead them."
From Isaiah 11:1–9

"THE PEACEABLE KINGDOM" of Isaiah is depicted in Edward Hicks's famous painting of that name. The images sometimes show up on Christmas cards, too. Wolf and lamb dwelling, improbably, together while a small child plays over the head of a deadly viper. Realists dismiss these images of predator and prey reconciled as the sheerest sort of seasonal sentimentality.

But if we back up a few verses and read all of Isaiah 11:1–9, we see that the first part describes the kind of leaders God seeks, and the kind of ruler the Messiah shall be. God's chosen do not judge by appearances, rather they "shall judge the poor with justice and defend the humble in the land with equity." In other words, a biblical standard for leadership is that a leader shall work to make the world, or a part of it, safer for the vulnerable, for the lambs and calves, for the poor and the children.

Today hold in your heart Isaiah's vision of God's Messiah, Jesus, and Isaiah's powerful vision for all leaders: protection of the vulnerable, making the world safer for the least powerful, taming the lions so that the lambs have a chance to live.

PRAYER: God, I pray for all those leaders who do seek to make the world a safer and brighter place for the vulnerable, for the sick and the weak, for the small and the suffering. Sustain, uphold, and encourage them. Amen.

COMPLAINING AT THE COFFEE SHOP

Lillian Daniel

And I said: "Woe is me! I am lost, for I am a man of unclean lips, and I live among a people of unclean lips." From Isaiah 6:1–5

THE OTHER DAY I WAS AT MY LOCAL COFFEE SHOP, where you are not allowed to say "small, medium, or large," but must instead order your coffee size in a foreign language, all in the name of good taste and high prices.

I stood in line behind a group of women with very high standards. I could tell they had high standards because nobody they talked about met them.

They griped about the coach who doesn't get the practice schedule out on time, the teacher who gives too much or too little homework, the roadwork that never seems to get done. You name it. Nothing in our little village met their standards.

But we live in a pretty nice little village, from those volunteer coaches who miss work for the kids, to the hardworking teachers in basically well-equipped schools. At least there's someone repairing the cracks in the road, when all over the world there are communities without roads, without schools, and without the luxuries of e-mailed sports schedules and soymilk, decaf, pumpkin lattes.

I hated listening to the women in line ahead of me, not because I was any better than them, but because I have been there myself. Sometimes, when listening to other people complain, I get swept up in their drama. I pile my complaint on top of theirs until, by the end, we've all convinced each other that our situation is intolerable.

Whenever I take part in those conversations, I leave feeling like I am a person of unclean lips, living among a people of unclean lips.

PRAYER: Let the words of my mouth and the meditation of my heart be pleasing unto you, O God. And let my lips produce more thanksgiving than complaint. Amen.

BETTER TOGETHER

Ron Buford

The people were filled with expectation. From Luke 3:15–17, 1–22

WHEN I WAS IN HIGH SCHOOL, Ralph Waldo Emerson blew into my life and took my breath away. His essay on self-reliance says a lot more about my life values than I'd care to admit. And yet, there are things we simply cannot do alone; that is what church is all about. It's not about obligation, pleasing some temperamental deity, or the inspiring sermons, music, and liturgy.

It's about something we often take for granted . . . the miracle that happens when God's diverse children gather, filled with expectation that God might show up to trouble the waters of our hearts and minds, filling our bellies with the unquenchable fire we need to get through another week, inspiring new ideas and action, gently descending upon us like an unexpected dove.

Beneath the collective and secret longings of people pretending that everything is OK lie the real and hidden hopes of longing people. God, like a knowing lover, gently turns the doorknob of our longing hearts, awakening them to quiver within us.

Many leave worship thinking and feeling nothing happened. But the open and expectant left with new power and courage to do things they never thought possible.

Amid the ascending hopes of people and the descending power of God, we publicly baptize our sons and daughters just as Jesus was baptized—among neighbors and friends, into community. In the presence of God, the living and the dead, saints past, present, and future, we claim their lives and reclaim our own for hope, sealed with our unbreakable promise to love them and to be loved . . . no matter what.

PRAYER: Gracious God, we remember and thank you for our baptism and our congregations. We give thanks that we belong to you, body and soul, in life and in death, and that we also belong to a great community that has claimed us for hope, no matter who we are or where we are on life's journey. Help us to live and love together as people who remember your love and our promises. Amen.

COMMUNICATION

Lillian Daniel

I do not want to seem as though I am trying to frighten you with my letters. For they say, "His letters are weighty and strong, but his bodily presence is weak, and his speech contemptible." From 2 Corinthians 10:1–11

WHAT IS YOUR FAVORITE FORM OF COMMUNICATION? Would you rather deal with a sticky situation in an e-mail, in a letter, on the telephone, or face to face? There is no one right answer to this question. But most of us have a preference for one type of communication over another.

After reading an e-mail, we might complain, "Why didn't you come talk to me about that in person?"

Or after a difficult conversation, someone else might wish that the whole thing had taken place in writing, to give all involved time to think about their words and the consequences.

There is no one right way to communicate. God has given us many ways to get our point across, and to listen to others.

Paul, the great leader of the early church, had his critics. In this letter, he admits that there are people who think he is a loser, unimpressive physically and a poor speaker, and that some people think even his letters are downright scary. But his letters sure packed a punch, and that's why we are still reading them two thousand years later. He found his way to communicate. He didn't have to be good at them all.

Sometimes, I get impatient with people whose communication preference is different from mine. I want them to adapt to my way, so that I can understand them better. But what I really should pray for is the wisdom to understand them in their own words.

After all, I already know what I think. I'm here to learn from others.

PRAYER: Let me, like Paul, aspire to live out what I communicate. Holy Spirit, open my ears, my mind, and my heart. Amen.

THE VALUE OF A GOOD NAME

Kenneth L. Samuel

Yet [God] saved them for [God's] name's sake, to make [God's] mighty power known. [God] rebuked the Red Sea, and it dried up; [God] led them through the depths as through a desert. . . . The waters covered their adversaries; not one of them survived. Then they believed [God's] promises and sang [God's] praise.
Psalm 106:8–12 NIV

I'M OLD ENOUGH TO REMEMBER when a person's good name meant something. My mother would send me to the corner store in our neighborhood with a list of things that she needed, but with no money. The grocer would fill the bag with the items on my mother's list and give the bag to me to take home. No payment was required at the time, simply because of my mother's good name and her reputation for paying her debts. My mother's good name alone put food on our table many nights.

A good name is still worth protecting and preserving. Promises are only as good as the people who make them. The many names of God are celebrated and revered around the globe today because those names bring the loving, sustaining, forgiving, delivering character of God before us. And whether we call God Wonderful Counselor, Prince of Peace, Ground of Being, Love Incarnate, Way Maker, Awesome Wonder, or Constant Friend, God's character is always consistent with God's name.

The children of Israel had fallen into sin, idolatry, and disobedience. But God, being true to the names of mercy and forgiveness, saved them from their self-destruction and from their menacing detractors. The salvation of Israel was not due to Israel's righteousness, but to the commitment of God to protect and preserve the integrity of God's own name.

The name of God still has the power to lift us despite our downfalls and to redeem us despite our unworthiness.

PRAYER: Gracious God, we thank you for the love, the mercy, and the salvation that we have in your name. Thank you for being all that we call you, and more. Amen.

DECEMBER

POSTPONING LIFE

Martin B. Copenhaver

Then [the rich man] said, . . . "I will pull down my barns and build larger ones, and there I will store all of my grain and my goods. And I will say to my soul, Soul, you have ample goods laid up for many years; relax, eat, drink, be merry." But God said to him, "You fool! This very night your life is being demanded of you." From Luke 12:16–21

IN THE LAST DECADE of my father's life he developed an interest in wine. There is more to this hobby than you might imagine. My father would read about the many varieties and vintages and vineyards. When a wine was purchased, it was carefully stored and catalogued. Occasionally he would even drink the stuff. That was always an elaborate ceremony, beginning with uncorking the bottle, then tasting the wine to make sure it was suitable to serve, accompanied by florid comments about bouquet and body, descriptions that no one else understood fully or, frankly, cared much about.

When friends learned of my father's interest in wine, they would sometimes give him a special gift of a rare and costly bottle. I never remember those wines being served. He always said he was waiting for a special occasion. The occasion never came. When my father died—"This very night your life is being demanded of you"—those bottles remained unopened. I believe he intended to drink them and, oh, how he would have enjoyed the ceremony of it all. But special occasions, like tomorrow, seem never to arrive. As Ben Hecht put it, "Time is a circus that is always packing up and moving away."

Of course, the point is not that we should eat, drink, and be merry while we have a chance, even as that is not the point of Jesus' parable. Rather, the point is that if we postpone little pleasures at our peril, how much more perilous is our tendency to put off doing what is truly important in life.

PRAYER: Dear God, don't let me use the future as the repository of all that is good and worthy. That is, help me to live fully in the only day in which I can live—today. Amen.

HIDDEN TREASURE

Ron Buford

Jesus answered, "Can you make the guests of the bridegroom fast while he is with them?" From Luke 5:33–39 NIV

MY MOM HAD ALZHEIMER'S DISEASE and spent her final days in a facility that cared for people so afflicted. It had been months since momma recognized me, but one morning, I went out to visit her really early in the morning before going to work. She looked at me and knew me. I cancelled my other plans for that morning, knowing two things: This moment might never come again . . . and it didn't. I also knew that no one ever again might be that happy to see me. I still remember those moments as if they happened yesterday. On bad days, they help get me through.

Similarly, Jesus tells John's disciples, a group of good and faithful people, to pause, recognize, and celebrate the good times right here, right now, amid challenge or spiritual devotion. Seeing God's gifts of life is a spiritual discipline.

Jesus also knew that days of scarcity and mourning would come to these disciples when they would live in terror as both he and John would be taken from them. So this was practical advice. They would need good memories to get them through the tough times ahead.

Make up your mind today to not only savor the good times for yourself, but to give such moments away to someone you love . . . today. Make them know how much you love them. Don't hold back. When tough times come, it may be the one thing to which they cling.

PRAYER: Gracious God, help us not be too busy, even doing good, to find and savor the treasures in life that you wrap and present . . . just to us. O Lord Jesus, please help us also remember to wrap and present such treasures to others. Amen.

FILLER

Quinn G. Caldwell

Let the words of my mouth and the meditations of all our hearts be acceptable to you, O Lord, my rock and my redeemer. From Psalm 19

I START EVERY SUNDAY MORNING SERMON that I preach with these words from Psalm 19; I'm sure you've heard other preachers do the same.

Of course it's a classic way to start, but that's not why I do it. The real, secret reason I always pray this prayer is this: I have a terror of the blank page. I hate sitting down to start a sermon and seeing that little blinking cursor on that big blank page; freaks me right out. The anxiety used to drive me to waste hours surfing the Web or playing solitaire on the computer while I searched for a way to start writing.

Then I discovered that if I just sit down and type those words first thing, I feel significantly better. I haven't really written any of the sermon at that point, but it turns out that a mostly blank page is way less scary than a blank one. I think of it as a sort of holy filler, a trick to calm me down enough to write.

Which is really not a bad way to think of it: Don't know what to do? Ask God for help. Got no words of your own? Use the psalmist's; that's what they're for. Paralyzed by the situation and don't know how to start? Pray. It is, I promise, a way better way to get started than surfing the Web.

PRAYER: God, grant that my every endeavor, the ones I know how to start and the ones I don't, might begin with you. Amen.

DECEMBER 4

KILL THE PREACHER

Anthony B. Robinson

And he rolled up the scroll, gave it back to the attendant, and sat down. The eyes of all in the synagogue were fixed on him. Then he began to say to them, "Today this scripture has been fulfilled in your hearing." From Luke 4:14–21

EARLY IN HIS MINISTRY Jesus went to his hometown synagogue in Nazareth. Since he'd been away for a while, they invited him to read the scripture and say a few words. Maybe it was Youth Saturday? Hey, let's invite this nice young man in to take part. We can all feel good about it, proud that he's one of us.

For a few minutes that how it goes. People nudge their neighbor. "Listen, he reads well." "Attractive young man, don't you think?"

But then, something happens. He preaches. And what he has to say doesn't flatter his hearers. He cites several other texts, stories from the Bible. What's his point? The point seems to be that God often finds it easier to do God's work among outsiders, people living in far-off lands, and with odd and unexpected people than it is to work with those who are supposed to be in the know or think they are in the know.

Pleasure and pride give way to pique and passion. Jesus wasn't flattering the hometown crowd with a feel-good sermon. He was saying that God's own people were so busy telling themselves how special they were that they had forgotten to be God's people, a people called to be a blessing to others. Somehow they had come to believe that being "God's people" meant that they were special in the sense of "better than" other people. They had forgotten that it meant they were called, called to be active instruments of God's purposes of healing and grace for all people. So they tried to kill him.

Not our best Youth Sunday, I mean Saturday. Or was it? Being God's people doesn't mean privilege. It isn't about entitlement. It means a calling, a responsibility, and a challenge. Do we want to hear that challenge? Whether we do or not, God keeps sending people to challenge us, and sometimes they are our own young people.

PRAYER: Renew your church, Sovereign God. Restore its ministries. Make us once again salt to the earth and light to the world. Amen.

DECEMBER 5

WHEN CRITICISM WORKS

Lillian Daniel

For godly grief produces a repentance that leads to salvation and brings no regret, but worldly grief produces death. From 2 Corinthians 7:2–12

HAVE YOU EVER RECEIVED a harsh criticism that later you considered to be a gift? At the time, you may have argued against the criticism. Perhaps you even lashed out at the one delivering the bad news. But later, after you had time to think about it, you realized you had been told something you needed to hear.

In a previous letter, Paul had said what needed to be said to the Corinthians. Once he named it, they realized they had done something wrong and they felt bad about it. That's godly grief. It's a temporary sadness that leads to better behavior in the future.

Some people don't want to feel any pain. They shut down all criticism and "protect" themselves. But what exactly are they protecting themselves from? By refusing to feel any godly grief, they shut out the possibility of forgiveness and new life.

Other people sit around criticizing themselves, day in and day out. Every little thing becomes a cause for anxiety. They worry constantly that they are not measuring up, competing against imaginary enemies and impossible standards. This strikes me as the worldly grief Paul talks about, which leads only to the death of our hope and happiness.

Sometimes we have to go through a little godly grief to arrive at God's calling for us.

And sometimes we have to shake loose from the worldly grief that takes us nowhere.

PRAYER: God, help me to know the difference. Amen.

DECEMBER 6

HEALING AND HELPING

Kenneth L. Samuel

After leaving the synagogue he entered Simon's house. Now Simon's mother-in-law was suffering from a high fever, and they asked him about her. Then he stood over her and rebuked the fever, and it left her. Immediately she got up and began to serve them. From Luke 4:38–44

THE ACCOUNT OF JESUS' HEALING of Simon Peter's mother-in-law kind of makes you wonder about Simon's mother-in-law. What kind of person gets up from a sick bed and goes immediately back to work? After being healed, Simon's mother-in-law takes no time to lie in bed and take advantage of an opportunity to be catered to a bit longer. Immediately after her healing she is back on the job, helping and serving others. Was she waiting on healing for herself, or was she waiting on God to grant her another opportunity to help others?

Most of our petitions for healing and help begin and end with ourselves. Healing, for many of us, is not a means to an end, but the end itself. When was the last time we looked past our request for a blessing to see how our blessing could bless others? When was the last time we received a gift and immediately used that gift to give back?

Some church officers and I decided to give a financial blessing to a very faithful church volunteer. We thought that the money would encourage her and perhaps assist her with transportation expenses. However, when she was given the check, she confided to a church officer that the money was needed to help buy food for her family. Then, amazingly, before she left church with the check, she asked the officer how much would a tithe of the money she had received be? She then promised to give a tenth of what she had just received from the church back to the church.

Thank God that the spirit of Simon's mother-in-law lives on in the hearts of all the faithful servants who realize that their healing is actually an opportunity to help heal others.

PRAYER: Dear God, today we pray not just for our own help and healing. We pray for a compulsion to serve others; and we pray that you will give us compassion for those who serve us. Amen.

COME AND SEE

Martin B. Copenhaver

Philip found Nathanael and said to him, "We have found him about whom Moses in the law and also the prophets wrote, Jesus son of Joseph from Nazareth." Nathanael said to him, "Can anything good come out of Nazareth?" Philip said to him, "Come and see." From John 1:43–51

PHILIP TRACKED DOWN HIS FRIEND Nathanael to report that he had seen the Messiah and that he is Jesus of Nazareth. Nathanael, who had never met Jesus, did not need to hear any more to dismiss the claim out of hand. "Can anything good come out of Nazareth?" he asked. His question, of course, was drenched in sarcasm. The savior of the world comes from a Godforsaken backwater town? Preposterous.

Philip could have responded to Nathanael's dismissal by carefully marshaling all of the reasons he believed the claim to be true, or he could have offered a testimony to his own faith. Instead, he offered a simple invitation: "Come and see." In other words, "Come and see for yourself. I can tell you what I have seen, but I cannot give you faith. I may not even be able to explain fully what I see in this person. What I can do is invite you to come and see for yourself." And, sure enough, as soon as Nathanael met Jesus, he believed in him.

This is a good example of what United Church of Christ pastor Alan Johnson calls "invitational evangelism." You may get all tongue-tied when you try to explain what your faith means to you. You may feel inarticulate or shy or uncertain. That's okay. All you need to be able to say is this: "Come and see." And, by the way, when was the last time you invited someone to church?"

PRAYER: God, give me the spirit of invitation, like a beggar telling another beggar where to find bread. Amen.

POSSESSED BY POSSESSIONS

Kenneth L. Samuel

Jesus said to him, "If you wish to be perfect, go sell your possessions and give the money to the poor, and you will have treasure in heaven; then come, follow me." When the young man heard this word, he went away grieving, for he had many possessions. From Matthew 19:21–22

HAVING PROUDLY OBEYED all of the commandments of Moses, the rich young man in this passage of scripture nevertheless fails to adhere to the one critical commandment of Christ. It is the commandment to sacrifice one's own material possessions in order to serve the poor and the outcasts.

In exchange for the sacrifice of his material treasure, Jesus offers the young man more sublime treasures. But in a world where people determine their self-worth by their net worth, Jesus' offer seems unrealistic and unreasonable, and is most often rejected. Many of us who view our material possessions as the singular sign of God's blessing in our lives would never embrace the self-sacrifice of Jesus. Consequently, the young man's tragedy is our tragedy. We walk away from self-sacrifice with great self-emptiness, for with all of the things we possess in life, without sacrifice for Christ and others, we still have little or nothing to live for.

PRAYER: God, free us from being possessed by our possessions, so that we can truly attain the things of value in this life and beyond. Amen.

SO WHICH IS IT?

Anthony B. Robinson

Bear one another's burdens and in this way you will fulfill the law of Christ. . . . All must carry carry their own loads. From Galatians 6:2–5

OK, PAUL, WHICH ONE IS IT?

In verse 2 Paul says, "Bear one another's burdens." I get that. Help someone with that person's heavy load, literally or figuratively. Give someone a ride to the hospital. Take dinner to someone in crisis. Listen to another's concerns and so help him or her carry the load. Take the kids for an evening and let Mom and Dad have a break. Pack a bag of food for someone who needs it.

But three verses later, in verse 5, Paul says, "All must carry their own loads." Pick up your own bags. Deal with your own stuff. Do your own work. Learn to be responsible for yourself. Carry your own load. When someone doesn't do his or her part of the job, someone else may end up doing it. On a long-term basis, that's not a good solution for either party.

So which is it? "Bear one another's burdens" or "All must carry their own loads"? Could it be both?

I once heard a story of a man who was doing a retreat at a monastery. At dinner he enjoyed some wonderful dark, rich homemade bread. He asked one of the monastery's brothers (who had made the bread), "Did we make this bread ourselves or was it given to us?" The brother thought for a moment and said, "Yes."

At least sometimes things aren't either/or, they are both/and. We might wish everything could be either this or that. Then life would be simple. Black or white; no grey. It's justice or mercy, but not both. It's faith or works, but not both. But since life is not simple, neither is our faith. Life is complex and so, thanks be to God, is our faith.

"Bear one another's burdens" and "All must carry their own loads." Both are true. God gives us the task of discerning when it's the time and place for one or for the other — or both in right measure.

PRAYER: Praise and thanks to you, O God, for a faith that is simple but not simplistic, for a faith that is as complex and wondrous as life is and as you are. Amen.

DECEMBER 10

WHY I DON'T WEAR A WWJD BRACELET

Lillian Daniel

Therefore God exalted him to the highest place and gave him the name that is above every name, that at the name of Jesus every knee should bow, in heaven and on earth and under the earth. From Philippians 2:9–12 NIV

I HAVE NEVER BEEN A FAN of those WWJD bracelets, where the initials stand for the question, "What would Jesus do?" They seem to imply that we should answer that question at every turn and that it should then influence our actions. What would Jesus do? OK, then I will do exactly the same.

But here's a news flash. You're not Jesus. You come into contact with someone sick? What would Jesus do? He'd perform a miracle. Are you going to do that? You run out of wine at a wedding? What would Jesus do? He'd turn water into wine. Go ahead. And then try appearing in the sky with Moses and Elijah in the transfiguration, try casting out demons, try saving humanity through the resurrection. Does wearing that bracelet give you special powers? Good luck with that.

It seems to me that the WWJD bracelets are another symptom of individualistic Christianity, where it's all about me. Yes, I know that many good people wear the bracelet to remind them to be kind and compassionate, to make good choices, often around issues of personal morality. But really, when you look at what Jesus actually did do, most of it is off limits to ordinary mortals.

And when he did engage in questions of personal morality, he said nothing about sexuality, just saying no to drugs, donating to National Public Radio or other pressing causes of our day. When it comes to personal morality, Jesus seems awkwardly stuck on telling us to give our money away, and not to the sellers of "What Would Jesus Do" bracelets. But other than that, most of what he does is sort of supernatural and crazy, and off limits to you and me, culminating in his suffering on the cross yet triumphing over death. In a world that says it's all about you, WWJD is a pretty humbling thought.

PRAYER: I give thanks that there is a God and that it is not me. Amen.

EATING RIGHT

Quinn G. Caldwell

Those who eat my flesh and drink my blood abide in me, and I in them. . . .
The one who eats this bread will live forever. From John 6:54–69

TO HEAR SOME OF US super-smart, well-educated modern Protestants tell it, you'd think Jesus instituted the Lord's Supper just to give us something pleasant to contemplate, not to actually change anything about our lives. We roll our eyes when we hear tell of some benighted historical belief that the Eucharist could actually save your life. We shift uncomfortably when we discover that our next door neighbor is retrograde enough to fret about missing an opportunity to take it. "Superstition!" we scoff. "Blind faith! Foolishness!"

We then proceed to pop our multivitamins, eat our leafy green vegetables, and take our meds as—dare I say it?—religiously as the most frequent communicant. And do you do it any less superstitiously than your neighbor takes communion, really? Aren't those vitamins really just a kind of talisman against osteoporosis or scurvy or early mortality or whatever? Aren't you just taking it on blind faith that your meds contain whatever the doctor says they do, and that the active ingredient does what it's supposed to? Are you really any less benighted about the mysteries of your meds than the average peasant was about the mystery of the Mass?

I'm not arguing for superstition here. I'm just saying that a better Expert than your doctor has recommended frequent communion as good for what ails you, so you ought to be taking it at least as religiously as your heart pills.

PRAYER: God, whether by Holy Communion or by Flintstones vitamins, save me. Amen.

THE USES AND ABUSES OF ANGER

Martin B. Copenhaver

Be angry, but do not sin; do not let the sun go down on your anger. From Ephesians 4:25–32

OF ALL THE DEADLY SINS, only anger is so precariously perched on the border of good and evil. We never speak of "righteous gluttony," or, "just lust." But sometimes we speak of "righteous anger" or "just anger." Much of the great good in the world is achieved through anger.

Martin Luther extolled righteous anger as the engine that drove him on to some of his very best work. He wrote, "I never work better than when I am inspired by anger; for when I am angry I can write, pray, and preach well, for then my whole temperature is quickened, my understanding sharpened, and all mundane vexations and temptations depart."

But anger does not always enlarge our worldview and sharpen our insights. When anger takes over, our vision can become dangerously narrowed. Anger can be the source of so much that is good and of so much that is evil. So how are we to make distinctions between the two? Thomas Aquinas, writing in the fourteenth century, singled out three disordered expressions of anger, three ways in which anger can be sinful:

First, when we get angry too easily. We all know people whose sense of justice has been twisted to the extent that they see injustice everywhere. They have an almost endless list of grievances.

Second, we can get angrier than we should. Some anger is simply disproportionate, out of scale with what prompts it.

Third, we can be angry for too long. We can hold onto our anger until it decays into a wretched mass of resentment and bitterness. Novelist Ann Lamott, says that hanging onto resentments is like drinking rat poison and then waiting for the rat to die.

Paul's advice is even more succinct: "Do not let the sun go down on your anger."

PRAYER: God, help me to make the tricky distinctions between righteous and self-righteous anger, between anger that serves and anger that is self-serving. Amen.

DECEMBER 13

O LORD, HOW LONG?

Christina Villa

O LORD—how long? From Psalm 6

THIS IS ONE OF MY FAVORITE SCRIPTURES. It is easy to memorize, and it comes in handy on occasions when you think you just can't stand another minute of whatever is going on, but you have no choice. You've got to endure until whatever it is ends. And you don't know when that will be.

So you ask: "O Lord—how long?" Because you trust that God knows how long it will go on. And bringing God into the situation reminds you that nothing in life is eternal. Nothing goes on forever—a tremendous blessing God provided with the creation of time. The flip side of grief and loss is the gratitude you feel when some nightmare experience finally comes to an end.

"O Lord—how long?" is a prayer for patience. It's helpful in situations of crushing boredom: the endless sermon, the pointless meeting, the witless lecture. It's a good prayer for the airport or the department of motor vehicles, or any other place that reliably offers maddening frustration.

But in Psalm 6, "O Lord—how long?" is a prayer of pain and fear: "My bones are shaking with terror. My soul also is struck with terror, while you, O Lord—how long?" This prayer doesn't ask for the boredom, the frustration, the pain, or the fear to end. It just asks: "How long?" The reassurance comes from knowing that it's not a matter of if—only when. You just have to hang on. And repeat the prayer: "O Lord—how long?"

PRAYER: O Lord, I don't think I can take another second of riding on this bus, waiting for the painkiller to kick in, listening to that baby cry, having this argument, lying in this hospital bed, sitting next to this hospital bed, waiting for the results, missing the dead and departed. So I ask you: How long? Amen.

HAVING IMPACT

Anthony B. Robinson

Jesus said to them, "My time has not yet come, but your time is always here. The world cannot hate you, but it hates me because I testify against it that its works are evil." From John 7:1–9

IN JOHN 7 WE FIND JESUS TALKING WITH HIS BROTHERS. They are after him to leave rinky-dink, nothing-ever-happens-here Galilee and head for the big city. Get on up to the big, public festival in Jerusalem if you want to make a difference, they tell him. Want to have an impact? You'd better work on your visibility. Get yourself where you'll be noticed by more people, noticed by the right people.

Jesus responds to their strategy suggestions as follows: "My time has not yet come, but your time is always here. The world cannot hate you, but it hates me because I testify against it that its works are evil." Tough words. What in the world do they mean?

Jesus has a different strategy for making an impact. It's not about marketing or visibility or power centers, it's about being faithful to God's will.

Instead of asking, "How can I get more notice or more attention?" Jesus asks, "What does God want me to do and say?" Instead of putting a finger up to see which way the wind is blowing, Jesus opens his heart to God's will, even if it means saying things people don't want to hear.

When you wonder how you can make a difference, remember Jesus' strategy for making an impact: stay centered on God's will and way.

PRAYER: I confess, God, that too often my mind is not set on divine things, but on human things. Today help me to stay more focused on what you want and leave the outcomes up to you. Amen.

WHEN IT'S GOOD TO HAVE A CHURCH

Lillian Daniel

For we know that if the earthly tent we live in is destroyed, we have a building from God, a house not made with hands, eternal in the heavens. From 2 Corinthians 5:1–10

IN THE DAYS AFTER A DEATH, a family will gather in my church office to discuss the service. Their arms will be full of folders of notes, legal pads with "to do" lists, bags full of records and documents. They have so much to do, and now the service.

There's often a moment when they start to ask me questions about how all this works, as if they are the first people to ever plan a service, as if they must invent it all from scratch, since that's how all the other items on that overwhelming "to do" list feel. It is then that as a pastor, I get to say, "It's OK. Let your church take it from here."

Every funeral service is a last-minute affair, but we've done this before. We're here for you. We have traditions and people on hand, musicians ready to appear at a moment's notice, cooks ready to bake and make coffee, a sanctuary that is waiting to take you and your grief in. You have a church.

Church members seem to immediately get it when I say all this. There's a moment when they understand they will not be on their own here. They have a church.

But when some of those gathered do not have a church, they are harder to reassure. It's as if they can't quite trust that we've done this before. "Have you thought of this?" they ask. "Can someone take care of that?" And when I nod, it's like they don't quite believe it. They don't have that trust, that relationship, with a church.

That's why at times of grief, it means so much to have a church. There's someone to say, "We'll take it from here." And you might actually believe it.

PRAYER: May God bless the grieving, the churched and the unchurched, with peace in the sanctuary when they need it the most. Amen.

THE SACRED BLUR
BROUGHT INTO FOCUS

Martin B. Copenhaver

For the cloud of the LORD was on the tabernacle by day, and fire was in the cloud by night. From Exodus 40:34–38

IN THIS PASSAGE the presence of God is described as a cloud. That image reminds me of a parishioner's description of his concept of God as "a sacred blur." When we recognize God in Jesus, however, that sacred blur is brought into stark, startling focus. We see what God is like and how we are to live in response to God's claim on our lives.

Some Christian traditions, including our own, often seem to speak more easily of God than of Jesus. Perhaps this stems from the difficulty we have in believing all that is claimed about Jesus. But I think the opposite often is the case. Our uneasiness with Jesus may not derive from our doubt that God was in Jesus in a unique way. Rather, our uneasiness may flow from our suspicion that it may be true after all. If it is true, then we must confront God and confront ourselves more fully, and who feels entirely prepared for that?

It can be easier, and perhaps less demanding, to think of God as something blurrier, like a cloud. When God has a human face, and lives the kind of life we do, we are given an opportunity—and the challenge—to see what a life claimed by God actually looks like.

PRAYER: Sweet and precious Lord, may we see in you both something of God and something of ourselves, so that your life might shape our own. Amen.

LIGHT

Donna Schaper

And there will be no more night; they need no light of lamp or sun, for the Lord God will be their light, and they will reign forever and ever. From Revelation 22:5–10

I THINK THAT ELECTRICITY might be a blessing but I am not sure. If it weren't for the electric light, we wouldn't be so able to work at night. We would have twelve hours for work and twelve hours for rest. We would go back to being people who could have dreams and visions because we would get the kind of rest that permits visitations from the unconscious. The sleeping pill market would dry up. Alarm clocks would never ring again.

Only a fool would want to live fully in the "good old days." But even a fool could question how well-lit so many of our days are, with the worst thing that can happen to most of us being that our cell phone is uncharged. We declare this malady so eloquently: "I am out of juice." Kurt Vonnegut predicted "lights out" factories, where the robots who did the work didn't need light at all. What is a robot if not somebody afraid they are out of "juice?"

If only we had been light about the Enlightenment, perhaps the electric bulb might not have stolen so much of our humanity from us. Since we were heavy-handed about it, we find ourselves way too well-lit, with no way to just enjoy the night sky or a little twilight.

Enter Revelations to tell us that God is our light and we need not worry about night any more. If that is true, perhaps the bulb has less power than we give it.

PRAYER: You who are our light, come and relieve us of the burden of too much light. And light up our nights in a different way. Amen.

FIGHT, FLEE — OR PRAY

William C. Green

Keep praying to the LORD our God to save us. From 1 Samuel 7:3–15 GNT

THE "FIGHT-OR-FLIGHT" RESPONSE IS WIRED INTO OUR NERVOUS SYSTEM. In the earliest humans fight took the form of combative behavior, and flight was simply fleeing from danger.

Today these primal instincts persist but in a wider range of behaviors. In everyday experience, the fight response may be seen in angry, argumentative behavior, and the flight response in social withdrawal, substance abuse, or hours on the web.

"Fight or flight" are not instincts we can outgrow. Sometimes they are important to our survival and sense of self. Sometimes they need to be controlled. But they are always part of who we are, a heritage we can't disown.

Prayer offers a third response that evolved over time. Some think it began as an effort to control or appease the powers of an awesome universe. But when prayer happens in the name, or spirit, of Christ, it's not to control or appease a higher power. It's to trust that this power is good and works to help us.

Jesus asks us to pray first and not just fight, flee—or freeze. We are given his promise that God's will is our salvation. Our job is to accept the guidance and correction, the hope and confidence that no one and nothing else alone can provide.

PRAYER: You, God, are all I have, and you give me all I need; my future is in your hands. You will show me the path that leads to life; your presence fills me with joy and brings me pleasure forever. Amen.

WORK

Quinn G. Caldwell

It is time for thee, LORD, to work, for they have made void thy law. From Psalm 119:113–128 KJV

IT'S LIKE THE PSALMIST IS GOD'S MOM OR SOMETHING, and God's slept too late on the weekend again. "What are you doing still in bed?!" she yells as she comes in and rips the blankets off. "It's past eleven o'clock! Look at this place; it's a pigsty! And you promised to mow the lawn today! Get your butt out of bed, and get to work!" The psalmists are always treating God like that, threatening to take away privileges and stuff ("No worship for a whole month if you let my enemies defeat me!"). I love it.

Unfortunately, we're not actually sure that's what the verse says. The Hebrew can be translated another way: "It's time to work for the LORD." According to this reading, it's not God who's to go to work when the place is a mess and everybody's breaking the rules; it's us. One piece of Jewish midrash imagines the rooster singing these words to the world every morning. We're the ones with the pillows over our heads, groaning because the morning light's too bright.

What issue do you care about most? What's the problem that sets your blood boiling—or makes it run cold? More to the point, what problem do you believe sets God's blood boiling? Have you done anything about it lately, or have you been sleeping in? What one thing you could do to advance that cause today?

Because, you know, this room really could use a good cleaning.

PRAYER: Dear God, wake me up and put me to work. Amen.

THINGS ARE NOT ALWAYS WHAT THEY APPEAR TO BE

Anthony B. Robinson

While they were talking and discussing, Jesus himself came near them and went with them, but their eyes were kept from recognizing him. And he said to them, "What are you discussing with each other while you walk along?" . . . Then one of them, whose name was Cleopas, answered him, "Are you the only stranger in Jerusalem who does not know the things that have taken place there in these days?" He asked them, "What things?" They replied, "The things about Jesus of Nazareth, who was a prophet mighty in deed and word before God and all the people, and how our chief priests and leaders handed him over to be condemned to death and crucified him. But we had hoped that he was the one to redeem Israel." From Luke 24:13–35

"IRONIC" WOULD BE THE WORD for this little scene. Two disappointed disciples trudged back home to Emmaus talking it all over. A stranger fell in alongside them. "What are you talking about?" he asked. Incredulous and not a little irritated, they said, "You must be the only person anywhere who doesn't know what's going on!" Just a little irony there! For the stranger talking with them is the one who really does know what's going on. Strange how often I think I know for sure how things really are (and insist I am right!), and it turns out that things are not what I thought at all. Strange and wonderful, how often my thoughts are not God's thoughts. Strange, wonderful, and astonishing that God is doing something redemptive with what appears to me to be a hopeless situation.

PRAYER: My eyes are open, God, but I don't see. I have been blinded by the cataracts of my disappointment and confused by the myopia of my certainty. Gently, God, take the divine knife of grace to my eyes that I may see. Amen.

WHAT A REWARD!

Kenneth L. Samuel

(With the reward he got for his wickedness, Judas bought a field; there he fell headlong, his body burst open and all his intestines spilled out. Everyone in Jerusalem heard about this, so they called that field in their language Akeldama, that is, Field of Blood.) "For," said Peter, "it is written in the book of Psalms, 'May his place be deserted; let there be no one to dwell in it,' and, 'May another take his place of leadership.'" From Acts 1:18–20 NIV

IT HAS BEEN SAID that we are not so much punished for our sins as we are punished by our sins. As much as we love to dwell exclusively upon the infinite mercy and steadfast compassion of God, this passage in Acts reminds us that there are severe consequences for the sins of treachery and deceit. The writer of Acts does not want us to miss any of the gruesome details accompanying the death of the disciple who betrayed his love for Jesus for a reward from the ruling religious elders. A tortured spirit . . . a violent fall . . . a disemboweled body . . . a bloody field . . . a public shame . . . a missing disciple . . . a wasted life. These are among the wages of sin; these are among the rewards of deadly deception that we ignore at our own peril.

But the most tragic thing about Judas is not his death. It is his missed opportunity for new life. It is his failure to get to know Jesus better than he did. For had Judas really known Jesus, the life of Judas would never have ended in despair. Instead of falling and faltering in a field of guilt, Judas would have thrown himself into the merciful arms of his risen redeemer, where he would have found forgiveness and strength to walk through his dismal valley into a newness of life.

PRAYER: God, help us not to forget that the wages of sin is death. But help us to also remember that your gift is eternal life—that does not surrender to death, through Christ, our Savior. Amen.

Is This a Joke?

Quinn G. Caldwell

Train children in the right way, and when old, they will not stray. From Proverbs 22:1–21

WHEN READING THE BIBLE, genre matters. If you don't know what biblical prophecy's about, you might think Revelations is a prediction of future history, and end up writing a foolish and profitable series of books about the end times.

You also might think the book of Proverbs contains God's thinking, instead of humans' thinking. They say it belongs in the category "Wisdom Literature," but when I read lines like the one above, I'm fairly certain God shelves it under "Jokes and Humor." I mean, does anyone really believe that raising children is as simple as "training" them right?

I'm pretty sure God doesn't. Look at Adam and Eve. No matter what kind of parenting technique you like best, God tried it.

Love and nurture? Check. Attachment parenting? Dr. Sears would approve. Corporal punishment? Tried it. And lots more.

And just look how we turned out. Sure, some of us, the saints and others, wound up golden children . . . the rest of us, not so much.

God's learned the hard way there's just no telling how the kids will turn out in the end, even when the parents are perfect. I think if God were to rewrite that line, it would say something half as pretentious and twice as difficult:

"Love your children hard no matter what, and somehow everybody'll get there in the end."

PRAYER: Holy God, you have loved us, and loved us, and loved us no matter how we've turned out or turned away, and that has been the saving of the world. Grant that we all might do the same with the children you've entrusted to us. Amen.

TOUCHED BY GOD

William C. Green

Jesus called the twelve together . . . and he sent them out to proclaim the kingdom of God and to heal. From Luke 9:1–6

AS A POET PUT IT, "I learn by going where I have to go." We learn who Jesus is by doing what he asks us to do: preach and heal through what we say and do, whether or not we mount a pulpit or cure illness.

Three times in my life, someone has been so bold as to place their hands on my head or shoulders and pray explicitly for God's blessing. This was more than praying at a polite distance. It involved touch—unsettling for some of us. I hadn't asked for this. Sometimes we're in no position to ask for what we need. Sometimes someone seems intuitively to know that only a power higher than our own, working through them, can touch us.

We may not be cured but we can be healed. The power of what threatens us can be broken. Think of the embrace of a loved one, or, when appropriate, a good hug. Think of someone who listens well when something is troubling you. That's a healing touch, too.

All of us need more than a good prayer or a strong hug. But all of us first need power beyond our own that directly touches us with love and confidence. That's what Jesus is all about—and how he becomes real for us and, through us, for others. This is what we prepare to celebrate all over again this Advent season.

PRAYER: God of healing and hope, touch us again and make us bold enough to share that with others. Amen.

Darkness

Quinn G. Caldwell

The light shines in the darkness, and the darkness did not overcome it. From John 1:1–14

SOMETIMES ALL THE LIGHT can get to be a bit much this time of year. Blinking lights, bubble lights, icicle lights, blue-light specials. What about those of us who like the dark sometimes? You know, who like to sit outside at night, who relish sitting in a dim bar sharing a drink with a friend, who appreciate a snuggle with the lights off?

For those of us living in modern industrialized societies, where everything is spotlighted or fluoresced to within an inch of its life, dimness can be hard to come by.

God shined bright when she entered the world . . . but it couldn't have happened without the holy darkness of Mary's womb. Without the darkness behind the closed eyelids of a laboring woman. Without the darkness of the space between a baby's skin and swaddle.

The Wise Men would never have been able to see that star if they'd been standing in the parking lot of a twenty-four-hour Wal-Mart.

So tonight, in honor of the good darkness, the holy darkness, spend some time with the lights off for once. Put on some good music, or make some music of your own. Look out at the world, or just at the backs of your eyelids. Pray to be protected and nourished and formed by the God who swept over the face of the waters before there was light. Pray for the darkness to become like the Womb that bore the world. Pray for gestation. Pray for birth.

PRAYER: God, thank you for light and dark, bright and dim. Whether I am in shining or in shadow, let me show you to the world. Come, God, come. Amen.

HARK!

Martin B. Copenhaver

In that region there were shepherds living in the fields, keeping watch over their flock by night. . . . The angel said to them, "Do not be afraid; for see— I am bringing you good news of great joy for all the people: to you is born this day in the city of David a Savior, who is the Messiah, the Lord." From Luke 2:8–20

ON CHRISTMAS CARDS and in Christmas pageants the shepherds are portrayed as gentle keepers of the pastoral scene. But the reality of their lives was much harder and rougher. They were working men on the night shift, like cowboys in the Marlboro country around Bethlehem.

Shepherds were looked down upon because they could not keep the routine of hand washing and other forms of ritual cleanliness that were so much a part of Jewish law. Also, since sheep do not keep the Sabbath, neither could shepherds. So they stayed out of town, in part, because good people would not associate with them.

And yet the news of Jesus' birth is announced precisely here—not in a palace or a temple, not where things are bright and beautiful, not to good people, or to whomever might be considered the right people. As surprising as this would have been at the time, in retrospect it seems entirely fitting because Jesus is always showing up in the most unlikely places and associating with the most surprising people.

Perhaps you are enjoying a wonderful Christmas. Perhaps it is everything you planned. I certainly hope so.

But if you are far from home or feel distant from those who are very near, if there is more tension than cheer in the air, if you are exhausted, or feel a letdown, or if in any other way this feels like an unlikely place for Jesus to show up—pay particular attention. Hark! Because Jesus is always showing up in unlikely places, including perhaps the most unlikely place of all—our own lives.

PRAYER: Jesus, surprise us with your presence and your blessing this day—as only you can. Oh . . . and Happy Birthday. Amen.

Take a Hike

Anthony B. Robinson

I lift up my eyes to the mountains: where does help come from? From Psalm 121 NIV

I RECENTLY LEARNED A NEW EXPRESSION, *solvitur ambulando.* It's Latin and means, roughly, "It is solved by walking."

Facing a tough problem, a gnarly worry, a writer's (or a preacher's) block? Go for a walk. Take a hike. *Solvitur ambulando.* It may be solved in walking.

So often when I am stewing about something the answer is not to be found by thinking harder, stewing more, making lists or hitting the matter head on (again). Going for a walk, or a run, a bike ride or a swim gets the body moving and may take the mind off the spinning wheel. And then, just when I've stopped looking for it, an insight or idea or entirely different way emerges.

This, by the way, is sort of the idea of the Christian doctrine of "revelation" (small "r"). When revelation happens we are not likely to say, "I figured it out" or "I've got it." We are more likely to say something like, "It came to me," or "It occurred to me." That is, it's not so much something we get as something we are given.

For poets, this is often the way a poem begins. It is often, in my experience, where my better sermons come from. Something "comes to me." Thank you, God.

Sometimes when we take a walk or a hike or jog, it happens. *Solvitur ambulando.* It is solved by walking.

PRAYER: When my mind is struck, remind me to get my body moving. And thank you, God, that I am able to move, to walk, to hike, to run. What a blessing. Amen.

DECEMBER 27

NOTHING BUT THE TRUTH

Kenneth L. Samuel

When Joseph came to them in the morning, he saw that they were troubled. So he asked Pharaoh's officers, who were with him in custody in his master's house, "Why are your faces downcast today?" They said to him, "We have had dreams, and there is no one to interpret them." And Joseph said to them, "Do not interpretations belong to God?" Genesis 40:6–8

IN ONE OF MY FAVORITE SCENES from *The Pink Panther,* Inspector Clouseau (a fictional French police detective) interrogates a woman suspected of perjury in a previous testimony. "Madame" the inspector says, "this time I want nothing but the truth. Don't confuse me with the facts."

This rather humorous statement reminds us of something that we sometimes forget. Knowledge of the facts does not always translate into an understanding of the truth.

While serving time in an Egyptian prison, Joseph, son of the Hebrew patriarch Jacob, encounters two fellow prisoners who have facts but who lack understanding. These two former attendants of the Pharaoh have no problem recalling the facts of their dreams to Joseph. The details are all recollected and communicated. These two men knew the facts, but they didn't know how to draw meaning from the facts.

A pastor asked a group of laypersons to talk about what really motivated each of them to attend church. One young man stated: "My life is full of so many questions. I come to church because I need some answers." A woman added this: "I've got lots of questions in my life as well. But I don't necessarily come to church for answers. I know life is not that simple. I come to church to gain understanding. I can deal with the unanswered questions and the problems in my life as long as my understanding is increasing."

Sometimes we need an understanding of why it is that we don't grasp the meaning of some things in our lives. Joseph's reply to his fellow prisoners' quest for meaning was that the interpretation of the facts of life belongs to God. We may have all the facts, but God has the truth that gives our lives meaning, purpose, and value. It's enough to motivate us not only to go to church, but to seek God in all our ways.

PRAYER: Dear God, as we encounter the facts of life today, please give us guidance, give us wisdom, and give us understanding. Amen.

DECEMBER 28

IMPROVISATION

Donna Schaper

Then Jesus said to [the Pharisees], "I ask you, is it lawful to do good or to do harm on the Sabbath, to save life or to destroy it?" After looking around at all of them, he said to [the man with the withered hand], "Stretch out your hand." He did so, and his hand was restored. From Luke 6:9–11

IMPROVISATION IS WHEN YOU DON'T HAVE ENOUGH INFORMATION to do anything but just take the next step. Actors say the secret to improvisation is to go only as far as you have to and not a step or second more. They also argue that it is a great idea to make your partner look good when you speak. That keeps the story moving. Jazz musicians say the same thing. What did you play? "Oh, just something that the first chord told the second chord to say."

To theologically improvise requires keeping the conversation close and moving. It also involves a concrete choice of partners, among a sea of partners. The powerful will always present themselves as snarkily in charge. The withered will also always know the danger they are in. Theological improvisation involves looking straight towards the withered and ignoring the people who are playing games with the rules or the theology.

Improvisation is the art of the short-term. Improvisation is when you go with the withered who are in front of you—and decide to make them look good or feel good or at least not suffer any more or any longer. Good improvisation chooses whom it will listen to—and takes the next step.

PRAYER: Jesus, you knew how to take the next step and let the rest go by. Help us to do the same. Send us to the unlikely partners as our source of life. Make sure we know whom it is we listen to. Amen.

KEEP ON . . . KEEPIN' ON

Ron Buford

Those who go out weeping, bearing the seed for sowing, shall come home with shouts of joy, carrying their sheaves. From Psalm 126

LIFE SOMETIMES KNOCKS US DOWN. It happens to everyone. The key is to get back up and keep moving. The psalmist offers a simple formula for getting through tough times: First, remember ways God has brought you through past tough times. Second, ask God to do it again, and; third, show that you believe by moving forward before there is tangible or visible reason to do so—even while weeping, sow seeds for the future you envision, though the path may be uncertain and you may just not feel like it . . . yet.

You may be worried about a job, finances, a relationship, illness, fears about aging, trouble with kids, aging parents, an old hurt, or just "the blues." Whatever it is, God specializes in restoring life's greatest fortunes— love, joy, peace, and more—even before we feel it or see it coming. Leave the "how" to God as you focus on your hope. There will be a harvest. Go out; look for it. But it may come in a surprising new way or from surprising places. Be open. Don't miss it. Weep freely, but always with nagging, unrelenting hope in God.

PRAYER: Gracious God, I need your help right now. Please restore my life to better times. Forgive me for the way I tend to forget the ways you have been with me in the past. For the faith I lack as I say these words, please help my unbelief and send your Holy Spirit to pray for me when I doubt and forget. Guide me. Teach me. I'm getting up and out . . . today, thanking and praising you now. Amen.

Having a Bad Day

Anthony B. Robinson

And you still don't understand? From Mark 8:21–24 GNT

I'm sure Jesus was good and wonderful, but here I'm feeling for the disciples. He's sounding testy. They are sounding dull as donkeys.

First, he warned them, "Beware the yeast of the Pharisees." What in the world does that mean? Had the Pharisees gone into baking? They stared at each other desperately and said, "It's because we forgot the bread." Pretty much a total miss and they are on the defensive.

He didn't let up, but quizzed them as if this were one of those terrible vacation Bible school drills. "After the feeding of the five thousand how many baskets of leftovers were there?" "Twelve" they mutter. "And after I fed four thousand, how many then?" "Seven."

"And you still don't understand?" he demands. Well, no, not really.

This is feeling a lot like Algebra II. The bored teacher would explain a problem a second time and say, "Understand it now?" "I think so," I would lie, desperate not to sound as stupid as I felt.

Or when nothing is working and patience has become a well run dry between my wife and me. She's says, "there," I say "where?" She says "black," I say "white." Mars and Venus or just a cosmic black hole we've fallen into. There are days like that.

When anxiety or frustration set in they can strike us blind, deaf, and mute. What then? Take a break. Take a few deep breaths. Go for a walk. Figure that everyone has a bad day every now and then, even the disciples, even you. Even Jesus maybe. And then take it again tomorrow.

PRAYER: God, when I (or someone close to me) is having a bad day, help me to step back and trust that tomorrow will be better. Amen.

KNOW YOUR BIBLE

Quinn G. Caldwell

[Peter said], "But God raised him up, having freed him from death, because it was impossible for him to be held in its power. For David says concerning him, 'I saw the LORD always before me, for he is at my right hand so that I will not be shaken.'" From Acts 2:22–36

THE HOLY SPIRIT HAS JUST SWOOPED into that upper room in Jerusalem and shaken everybody up. They all look at one another and ask, "What does this mean?" Some have an answer ready: everybody's drunk. Peter stands up and sets them straight by quoting scripture.

If God busted into your house today and did something cool, would you know enough scripture to tell the people around you what it means? If God came into your life and worked a miracle of healing, or service, or generosity, or peace, would you know enough scripture to tell yourself what it means?

Part of the Christian life is being able to recognize God at work in the world, and to do that, you need to know the writings the ancestors left for you.

If your church doesn't have a Bible study to sign up for, offer to start one. There are plenty of good resources out there that don't require experts to lead them.

Whenever God enters the world, there is always someone right there ready with the prosaic "They're drunk" explanation. And most people will believe them—unless there's someone around who knows enough to stand up and tell them the truth.

PRAYER: God, make your scriptures to sink so deep into me that I cannot see the world except through them. Amen.

ABOUT THE AUTHORS

RON BUFORD, the former coordinator of the United Church of Christ's "God is Still Speaking" campaign, consults with UCC churches across the nation, and appears in the DVD-based progressive theology series *Living the Questions 2.0.*

QUINN G. CALDWELL is the pastor of Plymouth Congregational Church, United Church of Christ, in Syracuse, New York, and co-editor of *The Unofficial Handbook of the United Church of Christ.*

MARTIN B. COPENHAVER is senior pastor, Wellesley Congregational Church, United Church of Christ, Wellesley, Massachusetts. He is the author of *Living Faith while Holding Doubts* and co-author, with Lillian Daniel, of *This Odd and Wondrous Calling: The Public and Private Lives of Two Ministers.*

LILLIAN DANIEL is the senior minister of the First Congregational Church, United Church of Christ, Glen Ellyn, Illinois. She is the author of *When "Spiritual but Not Religious" Is Not Enough*, and co-author, with Martin B. Copenhaver, of *This Odd and Wondrous Calling: The Public and Private Lives of Two Ministers.*

WILLIAM C. GREEN is vice-president for Strategy and Development of the Moral Courage Project at the NYU Wagner Graduate School of Public Service. He is the author of *52 Ways to Ignite Your Congregation: Generous Giving.*

ANTHONY B. ROBINSON, a United Church of Christ minister, is a speaker, teacher, and writer. His newest book is *Called to Lead: Paul's Letters to Timothy for a New Day.*

KENNETH L. SAMUEL is pastor of Victory for the World Church, Stone Mountain, Georgia, and the author of *Solomon's Success: Four Essential Keys to Leadership.*

DONNA SCHAPER is senior minister of Judson Memorial Church, New York, New York, and the author most recently of *Sacred Chow: Some Holy Ways to Eat.*

CHRISTINA VILLA is the editorial director of the Stillspeaking Writers' Group and the director of Marketing-Communications for the United Church of Christ, Cleveland, Ohio.

Titles from the Stillspeaking Writers' Group
. . . hearing God where you live (and other
surprising places)

A BOOK OF (UN)COMMON PRAYERS
Extraordinary Prayers for Ordinary Occasions
64 pages /$6.95

If prayer is an expression of our ongoing relationship with God, then every time and circumstance is an occasion for prayer. That conviction gave rise to this little book. The occasions for prayer addressed here—such as When You Are Running Late or When You Cannot Pray or When I Am Tempted to Whine—may not have occurred to you before. If you keep this booklet close at hand, your own prayers will be more fully interwoven into your common daily life in a most uncommon way.

THE JESUS DIARIES
Who Jesus Is to Me
48 pages /$9.95

In this short book, nine writers from varying backgrounds and with different perspectives talk candidly about who Jesus is for them. Brief but compelling, these very personal essays reveal not only the writers themselves, but also a fascinating picture of some of the many ways we see and think about Jesus. Includes blank pages at the back for you to write about who Jesus is to you.

OMG! DEVOTIONALS FOR YOUNG PEOPLE
50 pages /$5.95

Here are devotionals for young people that are short on moralizing and long on empathizing with the lives of teenagers. Funny, thought-provoking, and always encouraging, the fifty brief, one-page reflections in this collection include topics such as "Confidence," "Reputation," "What Matters," "Other People," and even "The World."

Other titles from The Pilgrim Press written by the Stillspeaking Writers' Group Authors

LIVING FAITH WHILE HOLDING DOUBT (updated)
MARTIN B. COPENHAVER
128 pages/$15.00

From the introduction: "This book is not for those who are free from the grip of doubt. . . . Neither is this book for those who are utter disbelievers. . . . This book is addressed to those who find themselves between these two groups. They have neither luminous belief nor utter disbelief. They can affirm a belief in God, on occasion at least, yet still hold doubts and never quite get used to the uneasy mix of doubt and belief in their lives. Their belief is hesitant, uncertain, sporadic, often unsatisfying. They may yearn for belief, yet find it elusive. The words of the man who turned to Jesus echo in their own hearts, "I believe; help my unbelief" (Mark 9:24).

THE UNOFFICIAL HANDBOOK OF THE UNITED CHURCH OF CHRIST
QUINN G. CALDWELL AND CURTIS J. PRESTON
320 pages/$16.00

The Unofficial Handbook of the United Church of Christ is a lighthearted, humorous look at the United Church of Christ denomination. The co-authors—two young UCC ministers, Quinn Caldwell and Curtis Preston, who are lifelong "UCCers"—have written The Unofficial Handbook for all UCCers, but particularly for millennials: confirmation-aged youth and teens. All of the facts are reliable and all of the humor is totally "unofficial."

WORDS FOR THE JOURNEY
Letters to Our Teenagers about Life and Faith (revised and updated)
MARTIN B. COPENHAVER AND ANTHONY B. ROBINSON
176 pages/$18.00

An excellent supplemental confirmation resource, or meaningful confirmation or graduation gift, *Words for the Journey: Letters to Our Teenagers about Life and Faith*, first published in 2003, is an original collection of letters written by Martin Copenhaver and Anthony Robinson to their teenagers. They discuss a wide variety of topics—God, church, Bible, vocation, relationships, difficult matters, faith, doubt, prayer, sex, abortion, race, and homosexuality—and share what God and their faith means to them.

STEWARDSHIP FOR VITAL CONGREGATIONS
ANTHONY B. ROBINSON
112 pages/$12.00

Would you like to learn how your congregation could create a culture of giving and generosity? Lay leaders and clergy will appreciate and benefit from Anthony Robinson's *Stewardship for Vital Congregations*. Robinson provides practical tools to engage you in the spiritual practice of Christian stewardship. Theologically and biblically informed, it offers particular strategies and "how-to's" relating to money and giving. *Stewardship for Vital Congregations* includes questions for reflection, discussion, and action in each chapter.

TO BEGIN AT THE BEGINNING
An Introduction to the Christian Faith (revised and expanded)
320 pages/$18.00

Fresh, bright, and readable, *To Begin at the Beginning* is an enjoyable, enlightening journey into the basics of Christianity and an invitation and encouraging provocation to deeper study. This revised and expanded edition includes study questions at the end of each chapter that can be used individually or in group study. Copenhaver has written a clearly accessible guidebook to familiarize new Christians with the terrain of belief and even more, it opens up new vistas for long-time church-goers.

Related Titles from The Pilgrim Press

PRAYERS FROM CHAUTAUQUA
JOAN BROWN CAMPBELL
224 pages/$20.00

From the foreword by Sister Joan B. Chittister: "A person's prayer is the measure of the heart of a person. We can hear in prayer where the human heart finds its heights and at what lows it has crossed its gorges only to rise to another level of life—wiser, clearer-eyed, more understanding, more caring, and more abandoned to the ever loving

Will of God. This book is living proof of all of that. It is a collection of prayers that mirror both the aspirations of a great national vision but also the commitment of that nation to be a genuine interfaith community—to be touched by one another's hopes and fears, by one another's needs and gifts, by one another's spiritual insights and moral perspectives. Most of all, these prayers lead a people of diverse traditions to become, at the same time, one spiritual community grounded in reverence and respect for the vision of the other in ways that deepen and grow our own."

THE LIVING BOOK OF DAILY PRAYER
Morning and Evening Prayers
KIM MARTIN SADLER, EDITOR
384 pages/$23.00

The Living Book of Daily Prayer: Morning and Evening is the result of an overwhelming number of requests for another volume of *The Book of Daily Prayer: Morning and Evening*, last published in 2004. As with previous volumes, this new, living volume contains daily devotionals in inclusive language for every morning and evening of the year, used in conjunction with one's Bible, and is written by a diverse group of individuals in a style referred to as "praying the Scriptures."

To order these or any other books from The Pilgrim Press call or write to:

THE PILGRIM PRESS
700 PROSPECT AVENUE EAST
CLEVELAND, OHIO 44115-1100

PHONE ORDERS: 1-800-537-3394 ■ FAX ORDERS: 216-736-2206
Please include shipping charges of $7.00 for the first book and $1.00 for each additional book.
Or order from our web sites at www.thepilgrimpress.com and www.uccresources.com.
Prices subject to change without notice.